THOUGHT AND WORLD

THOUGHT AND WORLD

The Hidden Necessities

JAMES ROSS

University of Notre Dame Press
Notre Dame, Indiana

Copyright © 2008 by University of Notre Dame
Notre Dame, Indiana 46556
www.undpress.nd.edu
All Rights Reserved

Published in the United States of America

Library of Congress Cataloging-in-Publication Data

Ross, James F., 1931–
Thought and world : the hidden necessities / James Ross.
p. cm.
Includes bibliographical references and index.
ISBN-13: 978-0-268-04056-7 (cloth : alk. paper)
ISBN-10: 0-268-04056-7 (cloth : alk. paper)
ISBN-13: 978-0-268-04057-4 (pbk. : alk. paper)
ISBN-10: 0-268-04057-5 (pbk. : alk. paper)
1. Necessity (Philosophy) 2. Philosophy of nature. I. Title.
BD417.R67   2008
110—dc22

2008027216

∞ *The paper in this book meets the guidelines for permanence and durability of the Committee on Production Guidelines for Book Longevity of the Council on Library Resources.*

FOR KATHLEEN

Contents

Preface ix

Introduction: Structural Realism 1

CHAPTER 1
Necessities: Earned Truth and Made Truth 11

CHAPTER 2
Real Impossibility 23

CHAPTER 3
What Might Have Been 45

CHAPTER 4
Truth 67

CHAPTER 5
Perception and Abstraction 85

CHAPTER 6
Emergent Consciousness and Irreducible Understanding   115

CHAPTER 7
Real Natures: Software Everywhere   129

CHAPTER 8
Going Wrong with the Master of Falsity   149

Notes   173

Works Cited   207

Index   217

Preface

This book initiates and invites some new analytic thinking about meaning, truth, impossibility, natural necessity, and our intelligent perception of nature. The outcome is an account of thought and world that is discernibly classical in its antecedents and distinctly realist about the intelligible structures in nature and about our abstractive ability to discern them; it is realist as well as about common objects, social constructs, and midrange science. The topics also include perception and media for thought, knowledge of spatially and historically remote realities, the false, the naturally impossible, real kinds, and what might have been. They all knit together in their explanations.

The method is to support the new considerations with articulated reasons that pivot on examples and to develop their strategic interconnections without certain constraints that trace to the seventeenth century.

I begin from observations about the hidden necessities that overflow the words we use and the science of one's time, explaining how they require revisions of metaphysics to accommodate them. Next I examine how to understand natural impossibility and natural necessity without resorting to "possible worlds" ontologies. Then I explore how contrary-to-fact suppositions are, unless grounded in the real natures of existing things or in formal and conventional structures, deprived of earned truth values and indeed are referentially vacuous. That occasions considering true judgment in general, where I conclude, and explain, that what we know really is what is so, but not by formal (logical) identity, and that truth is explanatorily derivative from cognition, not the reverse. The challenge there is to explain what such real sameness is and how it can happen, especially given that neither the true nor the real is a univocal domain.

The ability of humans to discern, even to invent and to materialize active intelligible structures, software, revives an idea discarded at the dawn of modern quantitative science but needed now: namely, that there are active, repeatable, explanatory natural structures, like those of electromagnetic waves, ocean and sound waves, that are accessible as such to intelligent beings alone. It turns out that the ability to grasp and understand such structures, and generally to reason, is not reducibly physical because it has formal features that physical structures cannot have. So, although animal consciousness may, for all we know so far, turn out to be reductively or at least constructively or emergently physical, human understanding is not, even though it requires a base in animal cognition. Last, I consider, but only initially because the phenomena are so varied and the phenomenology is so complex, how one can think what is not so—not just state it, but think it. The hidden necessities of things prompted and grounded this rearrangement of matters that philosophers have usually treated as settled otherwise.

The scale and scope here is broad, as was C. I. Lewis's *Mind and the World Order* (1929), David Lewis's *On the Plurality of Worlds* (1986), and Robert Nozick's *Invariances* (2001), and the exposition is not aimed to dissolve contrary convictions that might block sympathy for what is proposed, but to step back from the tangles of very recent philosophy to evaluate another pattern, one that coheres with general experience and science, fits together as a whole, and exposes some bedrock positions that divide philosophers.

Because philosophies cannot independently establish their most fundamental principles (cf. Aristotle's noting that demonstrations cannot begin with demonstrations and Nozick's [2001, 3–11] similar observations)—even the preferable logic is disputed—philosophies have to be compared for satisfying intelligibility and depth, tight thought and their fit with, and utility for, the rest of what we know. Those are the targets here, along with simplicity and brevity too.

Very many recent writers influenced this effort. I thank them all, noting as many as I recall and apologizing to any I miss.

Introduction

Structural Realism

The seventeenth-century rejection of substantial forms in things[1] and the recasting of physics as quantitative terrestrial and celestial dynamics led to profound discoveries and technological applications still unfolding. But there were not good enough explanations of causation in nature, or of the relation of thought and the physical world. The notion of causation came to be one of invariant correlation, whether just by regularity in experience (Hume) or by a priori order for experience (Kant). Later refinements added the notion of counterfactuality to distinguish causation from merely orderly coincidence; but that was still not enough to explain the activity in nature.[2] Philosophers continue to seek explanations for causation and natural necessity and for a theoretical grounding for the sciences of nature.[3] The idea of embedded active structures, advanced here, goes partway toward resolving that by explaining efficient causation at one magnitude in nature by formal causation at a component one.

I propose to regard the active, intelligible structures of things and processes as software (embedded operating instructions), and to reconsider the features of human understanding by which we recognize and even make such things. That prompts the conceptual revisions and observations undertaken here.

Humans have found out how to make matter behave on its own according to intelligent principles that we invent, software (e.g., logical circuitry). That is like, but more than, the intelligent rearrangement of entirely material forces into a shovel, a wheel, or buttresses, or even into diodes, though in retrospect we can recognize that even such discoveries and inventions are materialized abstract structures as well; for instance, a lever/fulcrum/load-system (structure) is a (mathematizable) lawlike distribution of forces. Software design is an accomplishment beyond that because software, typically, is both constitutive and operative and is not strictly the same as the physical system(s) in which it is realized (for the physical system can often be the same and the software different, though not always). We make material things actively do what they cannot on their own, with input, content, operations, and results detectable as *what* they are by intelligent beings alone by means of physically embedded instructions for other physical processes. In some cases, the software cannot be deduced reliably from the inputs plus the outputs alone. You can perceive the structure in a mousetrap, but for an automatic landing system or a telephone system, you need access to the design.

Some things like electrical power distribution and computer-controlled automobile engines are distinctly physical but not within the organizational capacities of unintelligent nature. For them, we have invented little "laws of nature" by making intelligible structures operate through physical dynamics.[4] We have made "little minds in things"[5] where the successive physical events are not merely the physical consequence of earlier ones, but the operations to get the outcomes are intelligible only by way of the abstract structure (software).[6] Similarly, the physical movements of hundreds of students on a campus between classes, in what might look like no particular order, are in principle explicable at one level by principles of physics, but as human movements they are explicable only in terms of the purposes, beliefs, intentions, and social constructs (like classes and libraries) that, as such, are accessible to thought alone.

It was inaccessible and seemingly implausible at the beginning of modern science to think intelligible structures are intrinsically materialized and active. The mechanistic clockwork imagery of the seventeenth century supposed outside causation—whether springs, levers, and the like—all terminating in a divine agent. Mechanism was the industrial-age conception,[7] not systems engineering. It was fitting to think such causation wound down (or up) to a divine mover. But now we can materialize active intelligible structures, and have done so in complex ways, not merely by making very high-speed computers, as Blue Gene computes magnetic fields, or ones that can operate by simulation as Deep Blue played chess, but by embedment as electricity-grid programs and computerized systems distribute electrical power, and bank accounting programs process money. In general, software materialized distributes underlying energy but operates to do things not definable in terms of the energy system alone.

Nature acts at every order of magnitude as if following scripts. It is, I urge, a richer hypothesis to regard nature as software everywhere than to regard it as merely elegantly regular "occasions and probabilities of successions" without explanatory insides or encompassing intelligibility.[8] For one thing, the software of nature internests and interlocks, for instance, the way the systems in an animal are interdependent and layered and under master control, as are the circulatory, neural, sensory, and motor systems, and many subsystems like cell reproduction. My main hypotheses about real natures, knowledge, and truth depend on the intelligible order of nature as outlined below.

Throughout the following chapters there are arguments and observations for certain hinge claims. For instance, (i) that consistent conceivability ("silicon based life")[9] does not ensure real possibility, not even when supposedly mapped onto "imaginable worlds," and that imagination is an even less reliable guide to possibility ("time's slowing down"); (ii) that there are overflow necessities everywhere in nature; (iii) that there is no "one-size-fits-all" correct analysis for any central philosophical notion because (iv) every key expression—for example, "true," "necessary," "believe," "proposition," "judgment," "cause," "explain"—is context-sensitive and contrast-dependent (analogous),[10] adapting in meaning and in overflow signification to its varying linguistic environments; (v) that the de re overflow necessities (especially the hidden necessities) for any real kind from water to lead, and for even many less-regimented realities like conventional kinds (televisions), are overflow conditions of applicability (truth conditions) for our common names and predicates; (vi) that well-formed counterfactual statements often lack determinate truth value; and (vii) that intelligent apprehension and judgment cannot be reductively physical.

The general line of my reasoning goes like this. Nothing independently real is indeterminate in its non-indexed[11] de re necessities. Otherwise it would lack a sufficient condition for being at all (sufficiency being the co-presence of all the natural necessities). That only requires that anything that is de re necessary for anything is either de re necessary for *it*, or not. Yet *some of the necessities are hidden*, both overflowing the linguistic meanings of our words, and hidden in the yet, perhaps never, to be grasped complexities of nature.[12] For instance, "made of corundum" was not part of the ancient jewelers' meaning of "emerald" or "sapphire," and was hidden in the depths of nature for millennia; and probably few retail dealers even now know that corundum is aluminum oxide (Al_2O_3) or what that is. Yet it is a de re, indeed constitutive necessity for such stones. The circulation of the blood was probably a hidden necessity of mammalian life until 1612 when William Harvey established it. Such are the overflow de re necessities.

Because nature is constituted with such necessities everywhere, many things that appeared unqualifiedly obvious to philosophers, like "consistency implies possibility" and "consistent imaginability ensures real possibility," are false. Nor can they be saved by talk about possible worlds or even imaginable possible worlds, for reasons I will make clear.

Some recent efforts aim at finding delimited ranges for which such inferences are reliable (cf. Gendler and Hawthorne 2002), but that won't resolve the originating problems that concern the interpretation (the applied semantics) for modal logic. Further, reality enormously overflows truth no matter how comprehensively we state it (chapter 1). For instance, until a couple of centuries ago water was not known to be capable of explosive steam states (used in turbines), and, still later, further heated, of supercritical[13] states involving a breakdown of the chemical bonding of the molecules. Yet nothing could be water (the same liquid as the ancients knew) unless it satisfies those hidden necessities that overflow ordinary conceptions and knowledge, even now.[14]

That there are hidden necessities everywhere in nature makes one wonder how to explain or clarify that idea, since that sort of necessity is not merely a feature of propositions or statements. So, it is not explicable by reduction to the consistency of statements or even of thoughts. That also challenges any idea that physical reality is somehow constructed by our thought and experience, even though a great deal of our lived world consists of synthetic materials and social constructions that are also real. Thus, we have to look for differently grounded accounts of truth, impossibility, and natural necessity and of our intelligent perception of them. We also have to acknowledge the classical insight that to be is not the same for everything that can be said to exist.

Among the outcomes are these:

1. Natural necessities and impossibilities can be perspicuously distinguished from formal ones and from many sorts of fabricated ones, allowing us an improved understanding of contrary-to-fact conditionals, many of which have no earned truth values at all (chapters 1–3).

There are truths by inflation besides earned truths. Paradigms of truth by inflation are purely formal systems, like propositional calculus, with various imperfect forms ranging from law and chess to baseball—where being true of the denotata is explained by the forms of thinking that authorize the assertions and thereby constitute the objects (the denotata that verify or falsify the assertions). The reason 7 + 5 = 12 is that the thought system authorizes it and constitutes the objects (chapter 1). With truth by inflation, being (*ens rationis*) follows truth. The thinking, as form embedded in a practice, constitutes the objects: for example, "open-ended mutual funds redeem their shares" and "hanging powers of appointment must lapse to avoid taxation" (legal).

2. We cannot explain our ordinary success with applied science without clarifying the notions of "real natures" and "real structures," and distinguishing what nature does on its own from what we contribute to, project upon, or construct from reality by our classifications, measurements, and experiments.

3. There is no way the necessities of nature—the realities, not just our representations of them, say, "iron is magnetizable" or "water expands in freezing" or "objects contract in the direction in which they are accelerated"—can be known unless they can *become* the things known

while remaining the realities they are. That requires a revised account of understanding and of its relation to direct and abstractive perception.[15] Such an inquiry concerns the metaphysics of knowledge and natural necessity (chapters 4 and 5), not epistemology as an inquiry into the justification of belief, or psychology as study of organized cognitive systems.

4. Certain purportedly global analyses of truth and truthmaking need to be unraveled to disclose their limited explanatory scope, as in the case of J. Austin's and R. Chisholm's correspondence accounts. Instead, I reason that our cognitive base in animal cognition and our native and constant abstractive ability closes the reality–judgment gap, so that what I know *is* what is so by real sameness but not by formal identity (chapters 4 and 5), and derivatively, what I think is true when what I understand *is* something that is so. That will close what appeared to be a gap between the "space of reasons" and the natural world (cf. C. I. Lewis 1929; McDowell 1994).

5. The real natures of things—standing to their cases as active capacities are to their realizations,[16] as iron is to a kettle, say—are the locus for "laws of nature" and have reality only in their cases. The natures of particulars are the real basis of universals that as universal are structures-as-understood, though in particulars the natures, as structured matter, originate the behavioral regularities, for example, that iron flows at 2,400°F. (In traditional terms, the nature of a thing is its essence [its real "what"] considered as explanatory of its characteristic behavior: cf. Aquinas 1965, chap. 1.) Think of natures, for now, as materialized intelligible structures (of a lion, say, or of lead) that distribute natural forces into specific behavior. The commonness of natures is real enough, but it is a consequence of the multiplicity of cases and not explanatorily prior to individuals, as many philosophers, like Scotus, thought. Instead, it is form as such that is repeatable (chapter 7.4). There is structurally constant causation by real constitution—formal causation—the way the printed letters on this page constitute the shapes of the words, not just event-successive causation; in fact, the former is, in general, explanatorily prior to the latter.

6. We know prescientifically the "what" of lots of things—a horse, say, or bread—without knowing even the closely explanatory (once)

hidden, and now merely overflow necessities (like the genetic coding or the chemical composition or even sublimation);[17] and we also know in a scientifically articulate way "what" many things are, the way we know what Dacron or glass is. Besides, we can have an adequate prescientific conception of what something is (say, a leopard, fire, color, shape, wax, waves, or electricity) without having a correct scientific conception for it, even if one is available.[18] Prescientific and practically adequate grasp of real natures, which can be very sophisticated in the practice of crafts, is the foothold for descriptive and explanatory science, and is the original basis of our knowledge of what is potential and of what might have been (chapter 3). We have no knowledge of what might have been that involves empty names, empty kinds, natures without cases, or empty laws of nature or subsistent abstracta.[19]

7. There are dynamic structures throughout the cosmos (chapter 7), "software everywhere," that are the explanatory grounding for natural necessities and for earned counterfactual truth (chapter 3) and are understood by way of abstraction that discloses them (chapter 5). The laws of nature that we formulate have their ground in the natures of things, but as laws they exist only as expressed obtuse, smoothing, simplifying, and formalizing, abstractions (chapter 7),[20] either purely formal, or empirical like hydraulic piping principles in a civil engineering manual that are highly reliable approximations.

8. For humans, awareness that would otherwise be merely animal perception—the platform and medium for all human judgment—is always abstractive and judgmental. That cannot be reductively physical, though it requires a sensory medium that may be (chapter 6).[21] This is crucial to explaining how we can know the remote, abstract, and universal; it marks off this inquiry from other analytic accounts that explain such abstract and universal knowledge as knowledge of or about representations or expressions, rather than of the real things, say, iron itself.

9. Real sameness—as distinct from formal, or strict, identity—functions at several key points throughout this essay, particularly in the claim that what is known is really the same as what is so (explained in chapter 5.5), and in the claim that the structure of a thing is really the same as the thing, but not vice versa (chapter 7). Knowledge, and derivatively truth, is not a match-up, work-out, or hang-together relation

between thought and reality, or among thoughts or sentences and facts, or between propositions and states of affairs (chapter 4).[22] Right thinking is what makes truth. What is right thinking is different for different realities and for a wide range of inventions, constructions, and varied disciplines of thinking. Although there are applied localities in which coherence and pragmatic notions of truth function well (chapter 4), even there they are derivative, not explanatorily fundamental. I explain that just as in veridical perception the intentional *is* the real, so when I directly know something what I think *is* what is so.

Nothing animate except humans can have true beliefs, not only for the reason usually given—that they involve language that is unavailable to other animals—but more basically because true belief requires judgment, as does language, which in turn requires abstraction (the departicularization of physical things), which cannot be performed by a reductively physical system or process (chapter 6).[23] There is no physical process by which to separate the structure and nature of a thing from its particularity (cf. Aristotle, *De Anima* bk. III, for the original idea). But that is required for the understanding of things.

One key principle is that true judgment is explanatorily grounded in knowledge, not the reverse. Knowledge is not, explanatorily, refined true belief (say, justified or warranted); rather, true belief, even justified, that is not knowledge is an adaptive by-product of the system aimed at knowledge. For without knowing, there would be neither of the others. To be able to think what is true without knowing it is derivative by imperfection from being able to know things, just as to be able to think something that is false is derivative by privation from being able to think what is so (chapter 8).

10. Reflecting on the hidden necessities everywhere in nature occasions other realizations: (i) reality (real being) cannot be finally explained by causation because causation is explanatorily posterior to being; (ii) mere possibility cannot be prior to or explanatory of actual being or "extend" beyond it, for the same reason; (iii) the explanation for the being of the physical cosmos, if there is one, must lie beyond it or at least beyond its physicality; and (iv) it is naturally impossible for humans or other animals to have the experiences they have without their being embodied and in the midsized environment in which they

live (contrary to "brains in a vat" and evil demon suppositions); and (v) what is really impossible is defective or deficient in conception, because natural necessities are without genuine de re contraries, though verbal contraries can be formulated and even sincerely asserted (chapter 2).[24]

Once we acknowledge that there are de re necessities hidden in the complexity of nature that overflow our linguistic meanings but are part of the conditions of applicability of our words and judgments, and are part of the de re truth conditions, we find some new reasons to acknowledge the independent reality of the natures of things (aspirin and acids) and to affirm the real sameness of the known and the real.

Underlying the modest realism of all this, which includes synthetics, artifacts, and social constructs, is that there is software everywhere in nature, that is, materialized repeatable operative structures that are accessible as such to intelligent beings alone. This is disclosed by our ability to invent and design such structures and to materialize them (as programs and as lesser-invented structures, even as simple as a spoon or a gear). It repeals Descartes's exiling Aristotle's forms from science as without explanatory function. Instead, "hot iron has a mind of its own" is a metaphor well supported by metallurgical science. Various further hypotheses about abstraction, truth, and knowledge develop from our considering what cognitive and technical abilities we need in order to apprehend, invent, and materialize such structures as supercomputers and synthetics.

I aim to offer enough reasoning to open the field for these alternatives to current analytic views, and to exploit insights from a wider sweep of philosophical history, ancient and medieval, than is usually in sight. Maybe, given current philosophical restlessness, the unexploited resources and good ancestry of these hypotheses will earn them consideration.

CHAPTER 1

Necessities

Earned Truth and Made Truth

Necessities of Nature, Formal Truths, and the Blur in Between. — Necessities, as propositions and statements, divide broadly into what has to be so on account of the way things are independently of what humans ever think about (diamonds are graphite), and what has to be so because of some right way for humans to think (triangles are three sided; rooks travel on straight lines). The first are natural necessities and the second are formal, either logical or conceptual (and invented). There are also mixed necessities, with varying features of both the natural and the formal, depending on the extent of the rational constructions, as I will explain. The key point for now is that nonformal propositional necessities of nature (gold is malleable) typically depend for truth, inter alia, on the hidden, or at least overflow, de re necessities of real things.

Some Points of Contrast. — The necessities of nature, considered as propositions (things thought/understood), are notably unlike formal necessities. Contrast the physically interpreted "magnets attract iron," "$E = MC^2$," "$F = MA$," "copper corrodes," and "water conducts electricity" with the uninterpreted "$[(p \vee -p) > (p \supset p \vee -p)]$," "$A^2 + B^2 = C^2$," and with "not: $x^n + y^n = z^n$, where x, y, and z are non-zero integers and n is an integer greater than 2," as well as with "the bisector of the angle at the apex of an isosceles triangle perpendicularly bisects the base." The first group, though diverse in itself, depends for truth on particular physical natures like magnets or copper or matter in general; the second, which is also internally diverse, depends on formal or conceptual structures only.

The two groups are true and necessary in different ways because they have (i) different sorts of truthmaking,[1] (ii) different "compliant realities" (one spatiotemporal, the other not), (iii) vastly different "objects" (that is, distinct sorts of referents of common and proper names), (iv) opposed existential commitments, and (v) divergent conditions of certification. Further, (vi) truth is *earned* by necessities of nature, and made by *inflation* for formal truths. I explain those points below.

There Are Umbrella Notions. — "True" applies to "2 + 2 = 4" and "falling objects near the earth accelerate" under broad, protean, plastic notions[2] like "the truth is what to believe," "the truth is what is so," and "the truth is what is right to say and right to think." So, being "true" is analogous, that is, contextually sensitive and contextually adapted to particular conditions of discourse. Similarly, "necessary" applies under umbrella notions, like "what has to be," and "what couldn't fail to be," and "what is true no matter what" but has diverse explanations. "True" and "necessary" are among what Gilbert Ryle called "polymorphous concepts." The conditions for truth shape to fit differing ranges of discourse, about numbers, say, or opinions, or sensations, or colors, or times.[3] Some examples of things that "have to be so, and couldn't fail to be so," but not in the sense in which "2 + 2 = 4," are these: there "have to be" sixty-four squares on a checker board (even an imaginary one that is a regulation board); there "have to be" at least two parties in a civil action at law; open-ended mutual funds "have to" buy back their shares; humans "have to" be made out of chemicals; pigs "have to" have snouts. The notions of necessity are context sensitive and contrast dependent as follows.

1. Natural Necessities Are True of Physical Objects. Formal Necessities Are True of Ideal Objects

(1) Natural necessities[4] include (i) some observations available to common sense ("iron rusts," "cement cracks," "stars twinkle," "water

expands with freezing," "animals die"), (ii) some elementary science ("only mammals have hair," "only birds have feathers," "insects are cold blooded," "rusting is oxidation," and "heated air expands"), and (iii) mathematized scientific idealizations, like "E = MC²," "F = MA," and "A x V = W." Whole systems of mathematized abstractions like Newton's physics and Einstein's physics are like that.

Natural necessities are existentially embedded in things that might broadly speaking not have existed and are discovered through experience;[5] even the pure laws of mechanics apply strictly to idealizations and only derivatively to real objects like real accelerations, velocities, and forces, even though they were invented by abstraction from physical reality. The idealizations that show up in mathematized laws were fashioned to fit real things by approximation within empirical tolerances.[6] Such generalities, like "F = MA" are true *of* things they are not, strictly, *about*.[7] There was never a case of pure inertia—a thing moving under a single force forever. The proper objects of mathematized physical theory are all obtuse abstractions: abstractions constructed with formally neat and restricted features that have been substituted for the mixed and complex values of real things. Such formulations are intended to be both mathematically manipulable and to predict, within tolerances, observed values. Thus, to add a fifteen hundred watt toaster to a fifteen amp circuit with several lamps on it, we can calculate needed amps by dividing total watts by volts (using A x V = W), ignoring the age of the wires and ordinary variation in currents.

(2) In contrast, the objects of formal truths (say, of propositional calculus, arithmetic, set theory, modal logic, category theory, group theory, topology, and the rules of chess and games of cards) are never material objects. Pure formal objects are not obtuse abstractions (with made-up neat features replacing messy real ones) but are pure abstractions constructed for theoretical purposes. They are the denotata of pure theory. They are what the pure theory is about, the denotata of its variables and predicates. Of course, such inventions are usually prompted by abstraction from our experience. (Aristotle thought mathematics and geometry originated that way, as did J.S. Mill.) Formal truth does not depend on there being any particular material objects, even though productively whole formal systems like plane geometry and topology were in origin occasioned by reflection on experience.

Nor can formal truth be falsified or refuted by any physical condition. No arrangement of physical conditions is sufficient to make any such statement true either. Nor can the truth conditions for any such statement be stated as physical conditions because exact rectangles and pure doughnut shapes don't exist, though the formulas ("rectangles have equal diagonals") do apply physically within conventional measurements.

Individual physical objects exist contingently but formal objects "exist" necessarily though only as things understood, *entia rationis* (that's one context-bound differentiated meaning of "exist," intentionally). Humans happen to exist; it does not just happen that there is a product of 123 times 11. "Exists" is not univocal in natural languages.

W. V. O. Quine (1948, 1960) and Hartry Field (1980) wanted the ontological commitment of one's theories to be formulated in the canonical notation of first-order quantification, and to be regulated thereby, so that "exists" would be used univocally over one base domain, and any further ontological commitment would be reductively expressible in such fundamental commitments. That might be an aim for an ideally formulated natural science, but as an empirical matter it simply does not hold for English generally or any natural language. Formal objects, such as numbers, sets, and triangles, exist only analogically in comparison to physical things.[8] In English we generally express what philosophers mean by "exists" through the various uses of "There is a ...." As Aristotle thought, not everything—say, qualities, quantities, happenings, and living substances—can correctly be said to be ("There is a ....") in the *same* sense, for some are derivative in being from others, and derivative in various ways, too, as shadows from substances, for instance, and happenings from actions. "Is" and "exists" in their various senses are not reductively analyzable into some fundamental sense but adapt contextually.

Additionally, material things cannot be exact, that is, be entirely comprehended without overflow in conceptions or definitions.[9] Material things overflow our conceptions. Their overflowing features are not merely their individuality and accidents, but also many of their natural necessities. There is nothing more to a tetrahedron than its definition within the formal system provides. There is more to a sugar cube than is contained in our conception of it, even more than our best science contains or will, no matter how comprehensive that becomes, because the de re necessary conditions spread out into the inaccessible.

Finally, what is true of formal objects is true because the form of thinking constructs it,[10] whereas the necessities of nature—the ones not about our own thinking—depend on realities independent of our thinking. Truth, with formal necessities, is constituted by the form of thinking as form, like modus tollens, or solid geometry[11]—not by a particular act of a particular thinker.[12]

(3) With formal truths, if you think rightly according to certain rules, you get it right. That's because the thinking—its *form*, for example, addition or geometric proof—that justifies our asserting what we do (say, "25 + 25 = 50") makes our thinking true. *That is* truth by inflation. Not so with either necessities of nature or contingent truths. The thinking that justifies our affirming "iron rusts" is not what makes "iron rusts" true. That lies in nature. (Note also, I could read, repeat, report, remember, or imagine a formal truth, even a whole list of them, without doing the truthmaking thinking; but those would be merely derivative, secondary cases of my thoughts' being true.)

2. Necessities of Nature Earn Their Truth

Necessities of nature, both the statements and the judgments, earn their truth by expressing the real conditions of things (that iron oxidizes, that it is magnetizable), whereas formal truth arises by inflation, by belonging (with various logical constraints) to blocks of authorized judgments (most of which are merely potential), like plane geometry, or propositional calculus, arithmetic or set theory. There is no compelling need to say that logic, mathematics, or the like, are innate ideas, or are the innate structure of rational thought, or are about independently existing abstract, ideal objects, rather than to say that they are elegant expressions of human abstractive, inventive understanding.

Natural necessity, unlike formal necessity, does not ensure "certification by the designated objects under all consistent conditions,"[13] but only "certification actually and whenever there is a suitable subject, without decertification under any really possible conditions."[14] And even that is not a defining, but only a necessary and characteristic condition, because singular judgments of existence with proper names, for instance, "Socrates existed," satisfy it, but are not naturally necessary. Still, natural necessities, as propositions, have to earn their truth from what is so.

3. Many Kinds of Necessities Besides

There are other kinds of necessities including ones whose designata are not fully grounded physically as synthetics are,[15] but are not merely intentional objects either. Examples are bank deposits, workdays, official meetings, lawsuits, and the typical furniture of ordinary rooms, including the rooms themselves. Many are social constructs that are physically fully grounded, like the furniture and the rooms. Beyond that, there are innumerable and indispensable elements of complex societies in which things grounded in independent natures like physical movements (dance), voice sounds (opera), and utterances (poetry) are also phenomena under conventions (namely, dance, opera, poetry) or formal rules, for instance all the "events" of *Robert's Rules of Order* and plays in baseball, and all the events classified under the civil law. Independent physical realities are the components of socially constructed objects, like a chair or desk or a computer, or a crime. Such constructed objects are not reducible to the components because the "what" (e.g., chair leg or a robbery) is not explained by the component stick of wood or physical conflict, but only made of it.

Other features of things, though fully grounded physically, are also partly made up, like the rotational laterality of a building (how much it tends to turn on its center base in a wind velocity up to the 150-year maximal recorded wind in that locality), or its vertical stability (how much it tends to tip over like a cereal box in a 150-year maximal recorded wind). As defined, there were no such determinable properties before we had wind-velocity records and used them to define a physical quantity; but there was always a complete physical tendency of a building or a tree to tip in the wind, just not a metric for it.[16] But any precise and reliably manipulable description of that tendency involves constructed/conventional elements. The necessities about such things are a mix of formal features (the quantitative transformations) and natural ones (relative rigidity, earth tides, wind gusts, stability of steel, etc.) (chapter 7).

For instance, lamination is a real disposition of very long steel beams, more than two or three inches thick, "to slice into thin layers" like pastry because of "locked in stresses" (something real but defined by humans and not given in ordinary perception)—a disposition that caused the West Gate Bridge in Australia to collapse under wind forces when the beams just peeled apart (Salvadori 1980). Lamination had been one of the hidden necessities of molecular structure, unknown to materials science until it dramatically displayed itself.

The "space" between purely formal truths and simple necessities of nature is crammed with intermediates, sharing the features of the extremes in various arrangements depending on the natural or constructed or partly constructed status of the objects. Philosophers' theories have swept all these things into the same basket (often called "laws" and "regularities") and contrasted them as a group with statements ("a priori") that are meaning-inclusions or simple logical structures (called "logical necessities"). There aren't just two bins. Things are more complex than that in detail and, overall, divide differently, mainly into (i) thought constructions (some of which are fully based physically and others not—say, only partially or even not at all), (ii) real necessities, and (iii) various mixtures of the two (like baseball and civil law).

What ensures "coming out right under all relevant conditions" and "verification under all relevant conditions" differs for formal and natural necessities, and also for the intermediate cases. But at the one extreme "coming out right" has nothing to do with what happens, but only with how one is to do certain thinking. In intermediate cases, it has to do with both thinking and happening in varying proportions, for instance, whether a base runner is "safe" in a baseball game. And at the other extreme, like "mice are mammals," what we think, in order to be true, has to be what is so (chapter 5). That is why, disagreeing, we say, "That's not so" and "That's not how things are." Of course, when things are not as they are thought to be, the thinking is in some respect not done right, even though sometimes the particular defect is not accessible (chapter 8).

4. Necessities of Nature Exhaust the Relevant Content

Necessities of nature such as "humans can think" earn truth by expressing what is naturally so, and have necessity by being so "no matter what" (even though developmental necessities depend on what integrally *ought* to be as much as on what is, e.g., "humans are bipeds"). They are not made true by some conceptual or linguistic nesting, or by being the a priori structure of the mind. Instead, analytic and conceptual inclusions are results of purported cognition, not the explanation of it, and have no sure grip on truth (chapter 3.5). Nor are necessities of nature (e.g., $G = 6.7 \times 10^{-8 cm3/gm - sec2}$) so "no matter what" by having objects that exist "no matter what";[17] instead, they are so no matter what because their objects (and situations) are all the relevant possibility with content (the verbal contraries having no real content (chapter 2).

With formal truths, complete certification (that is, "that everything authorized to be said holds of its objects under every relevant condition") is enough for necessity because the designata have no traits that are not constructed by what is true, by authorized judgments.[18] Formal objects do not have "overflow" necessities hidden in the order of nature. What is authorized to be said (or thought) is fully verified by the designata and is what turns out to be so, and what turns out is all there is.[19]

For any physical thing, there are two sorts of de re necessities: (i) indexed necessities, such as the necessity of origin or production (like parentage), and of its stuff (material) without which that particular thing could not have existed (a statue of glass, a bug of proteins); and (ii) the non-indexed necessities of nature that overflow because not contained in the conception of the thing, though without them there could be no such thing: for example, rubies are made of translucent red corundum, emeralds of green beryl or translucent green corundum. Some of the overflow necessities are also cognitively hidden because not known to competent speakers even for millennia, or ever known by anyone at all, and so are merely incorporated into truth conditions by the reference to the objects.

5. Other Points of Contrast

(1) Transcendent Determinacy. — Empirical truths require dense realities. Real things overflow what we can say. It takes a lakefull of reality to make a drop of empirical truth. That's because (i) the compliant realities have "de re overflow" both of overflow necessities, some of which are hidden, and of accidents; and (ii) incompossible physical realities are equally compliant with the same statement. So, on a very cold day, when I might answer someone, "Yes, my car started, thanks," the reality might include my car's being in front of my house, or across the street, with its door open or closed; all are equally compliant, though mutually incompossible.

But formal objects have no necessities beyond what is contained conceptually or logically in the thought system, and formal objects have no intrinsic accidents at all. There are no incompossible formal realities that are equally compliant with a formal truth in the same system.[20] Formal objects cannot, then, be empirical, material things. They cannot unequivocally be individuals either. There is no formal principle of multiplicity for one-inch squares or for congruent equilateral triangles. As a result, first-order quantification over formal objects is equivocal with quantification over real individuals because the formal universal generalizations do not decompose into conjunctions of singular statements with genuinely proper names.[21]

(2) Conceptual Clusters. — Both kinds of necessities stand or fall in clusters, but in different sorts. Formal truths stand or fall in clumps because truthmaking for individual cases is from the truthmaker for all and for all together in a system, namely, a consistent and determinate form of thinking.[22] So a syntactical or semantic defect short-circuits a whole formal system at once.

Natural necessities cluster, too, because real kinds share general necessities of nature—like oxidation—that connects: "iron rusts," "aluminum pits," and "copper corrodes," for instance. But the connection is physical, not logical, and lies outside the statements.

(3) Transcending Conclusive Verification. — Empirical general truths transcend verification because there are always truth conditions that lie beyond practical checking. So there is a kind of induction, even for simple perception of singulars like "that's a zucchini." Ordinary

perceptual predicates, like "blue" and "weak," raise the same questions as induction in general (Duns Scotus noted that around 1300), and even raise an additional one about the justification of which predicate even to start observation with, as Nelson Goodman's (1955) "new riddle of induction" indicates. The idea that *which* predicate to project is merely a matter of entrenchment rests on a Humean denial of the idea of natural abstraction developed here (chapter 5); for nothing is processed in consciousness by humans as only a brute particular (cf. Sellars 1956 for the same idea).

(4) Webs of Belief. — Empirical statements are entangled, some logically, some by common necessities. So, they can be legitimated or banished as groups, with "core" truthbearers better insulated from being "picked off" by a clashing experience than "fringe" beliefs, just as Quine supposed. However, that has nothing sure to do with truth. Some people arrange their misguided, aggressive, and depressive beliefs so that nothing can pick them off: "Poverty is the fault of the poor" or "Morality is only a matter of agreement." The best insulated and most intransigent beliefs are sometimes thought confirmed by all experience with dissenters deemed stupid, gullible, or evil. Thus the webs of belief often have strands made strong and remote from evidence by prejudice, fear, and aggression. There are indeed webs of belief, but intransigence to evidence does not mark truth.

Sociologically, insulation of the centers of belief is varied, emotional, personal, socially conditioned, and peculiar to the subjects of discourse; so is what counts as being refuted or confirmed by experience. Bloodletting persisted in seventeenth-century medicine, handwashing was resisted by doctors in the nineteenth century, radical mastectomies and postmenopausal hormone therapy continued in the twentieth—all well beyond the arrival of discrediting evidence. Science and philosophy also display entrenched mistakes, repressive fashions, establishments, and enthusiasms; and bromides like the belief that conceivability implies real possibility, and the hoary, "what we are immediately aware of are our own ideas" and "the sensibly given is incorrigibly known," can last for centuries.

There is an analogue of Karl Jung's "islands of consciousness" too: that there are areas of one's reasoning isolated from one another because the principles of rational belief, of sufficient evidence, of relevant considerations, and of logical or inductive inference are discontinuous, even among well-adjusted adults. The most common and noticeable is the incongruity between one's judgments as to what others must or must not do, and what one thinks is permissible, even desirable, for one's self. Also, we often apply stricter scrutiny and higher standards of evidence to positions we don't like than we do to those we favor. Some corridors of belief can be shut off from the evidence allowed, even relied upon in others. In one's and one's community's webs of belief, not all the strands are reasonable or consistent or accessible from one another.

(5) Packed Virtuality. — Natural necessities (and all empirical truths) are pregnant with consequences not within the focus of one's thinking, but relevant, even necessary, for truth.[23] The consequences—sometimes called "pragmatic presuppositions," I also call them "material implications" (cf. Brandom 2000)—lie outside what the propositions contain syntactically and semantically and are usually unremarked in experience, unless missing. They are what we rely on and implicitly expect. When I say, "That table is strong enough for you to stand on," among the consequences not thought of are that the table will not change much within the time it takes for you to step up on it, nor will your weight or foot size change nor the laws of physics. Physical-object judgments are projective that way. They mean practically (not linguistically) what we rely on for their being so, for instance, what we notice when things go wrong, when we drop something or overcook something. The hidden necessities of nature are inaccessible presuppositions of what we say and do. When judgments go wrong, sometimes we do not even know what is missing (as when certain tropical bright plants turn out poisonous, though apples and tomatoes don't, or when certain liquids are found not to be mixable).

Practical thinking is more than the crisp judgments that bear truth or falsity (see Quine 1951). Every crisp thought needs an envelope of expectation and reliance[24] (cf. Polanyi 1966, on tacit knowing). The tacit background that contains hidden necessities as well as other presuppositions can go wrong. A whole family of crisp thoughts can drain away when the underlying convictions are punctured, as happens when people lose trust, fall out of love, feel betrayed, or just stop believing the market always goes up.

6. Outcome

"Necessary truth" is a plastic notion. Formal necessities and natural necessities, as propositions, differ in what is relevant to certification, in what is contained in thought, in the sorts of objects referred to, and in what counts as overflow conditions (i.e., truth conditions not contained in the meanings of their general terms). Natural necessities, like all empirical statements, are transcendently determinate (and indeterminate) in the ways I mentioned, whereas genuinely formal truths are not. Between the clear extremes of formal necessity and natural necessity of propositions there are varied intermediates mixing features of the one extreme with some of the other, mainly because the conceptions involved are in various degrees made up or dependent on certain experiences or social practices, as well as abstracted from real things. That includes many of the classifications of the sciences and crafts, as will appear. All the features mentioned separately here are meaning-relevant to "true" and "necessary."[25] That is, pairs of statements that differ in such features, though they may both be true and necessary in a broad sense, may need different particular accounts of truthmaking, necessity, and natural impossibility, to which I turn next.

CHAPTER 2

Real Impossibility

What would explain the impossible? Not inconsistency alone because some impossibilities are consistent (vampires, a phoenix). Not causation alone because caused impossibilities are only conditional on what causes them, for example, sounds someone can't hear, road signs someone can't read. What is really impossible lacks a determinate sufficient condition to be at all. Such impossibilities are deficient intentional objects, like a machine to make time go backward or airborne calories.

Propositional inconsistency cannot explain the really impossible. Propositions are thought dependent.[1] They might track such impossibilities but they can't explain them.[2] Instead, whatever is de re necessary has no real opposites. That is, there are no de re contrary situations with the same subjects and real sorts. The naturally impossible comes to nothing. That is what is to be shown.

1. Really Impossible = Impossible to Be Real

Apart from thought or imagination there exists nothing that is impossible.[3] Inconceivability—which is compatible with definability of the words and even with consistency—does not definitively mark impossibility; for the possible can be inconceivable as "dark energy" is to most people, as nylon was inconceivable till the twentieth century, and as the distance of the fixed stars was inconceivable to those using only Roman numerals. Where inconceivability is an epistemic relation, it is circumstance relative: the calculus was inconceivable in the eighth century. Where it is capacity relative it may not track reality: most people are unable to conceive of gravitational lenses or special relativity. Inconceivability is neither necessary nor sufficient for real impossibility.

Unimaginability is even less reliably a mark of the impossible. Imperceptible particles, the moment of maximum compactness, black holes, quarks, and hadrons are unimaginable for most people. For some, corundum is as unimaginable as parsecs, and quadrillions are indistinguishable from billions. Imaginability does not track possibility, just as unimaginability does not track impossibility.

Local conceptual inconsistency does not track real impossibility either: "a velocity mass cannot exceed" was inconsistent for Newton, as was "entirely relative physical space." "Parallel lines that cross" was inconsistent for Euclid; "subatomic particles" was inconsistent for Lucretius; "necessarily embodied human minds" was inconsistent for Descartes; "causation among physical objects" was inconsistent for Berkeley. One nest of concepts may exclude something that fits nicely into another.

Inconsistency of definition ensures impossibility of a thing qua defined. But if what is referred to is real or potentially real, inconsistency of definition or conception is just a mistake of thinking. One can conceive of a real thing inconsistently; many people think of themselves that way, either as mere matter (like meat-based radios) or as spirits with bodies. So inconsistency of thought does not ensure the impossibility of what is thought of, but only qua thought of. Generally, our conceptions are derived from nature, not prior and explanatory. So there has to be real impossibility, but without real "impossibles."

Impossibility has varied explanatory bases. Why there cannot be perfect Euclidean triangles is different from why there can't really be a theoretically pure gas, and different from why pigs can't have ceramic insides, and again different from why there can't be silicon-based life, and different still from why there can't be ammonia-based water. The impossibility of star-sized tomatoes differs in rationale from wood that thinks or rational finches, and again, from gold's being soon soluble in

Gatorade, or our occupying several places at once. Those all differ from things inconsistent in conception. But what they have in common is that each is a faulty intentional object because there is, in principle, no determinate sufficient condition[4] for such a thing to exist.

There is no impossibility with content apart from intentionality, though such impossibilities, for instance, a $1/8$-inch nut's fitting a $1/4$-inch bolt, are fully grounded in nature, that is, are accounted for by the way things are. For instance, before there were intelligent creatures, there was nothing definite that the actual things were not able to do, be, or become.[5] Not that things could do just anything or that the potentialities were not limited, but nothing articulated and made definite what the things could not do. The impossible is mind-dependent as content. Negation, in general, is an intentional penumbra of what is so.[6]

We can describe paths in water through which it is not possible to run your finger, but there are not impossible finger paths through water except as well-based conceptual constructs any more than there are in the water merely possible finger paths, except in weakly based conceptual contrast, say, to imaginable paths through which I cannot in theory draw my finger. It is tempting to reify impossibilities like the speeds airplanes can't attain and the ages humans can't reach, along with the fact that certain parts won't fit or certain motors will not start, as if they were realities on their own. But they are consequential realities that are conceptually derivative, conceptually projected, even when fully grounded in the features of existing things.

So, although some things are really impossible, there aren't any really impossible things or states of affairs.[7] Surface grammar doesn't track ontology. The content of the impossible as intentional derives from the actual because we get all our ideas from things. For example "star-sized tomatoes," "pigs with ceramic insides," "rational reptiles," "thinking electrons," "stones that see," "silicon-based life," and "vampires" are all conceptions whose components are abstracted from perceived things. In fact, unless we adopt an innate-ideas theory (like Plato and Descartes, or illumination like Augustine, or structures of thought like Kant), we have to side broadly with the Aristotelian–British empiricist tradition that all our ideas arise through sensible experience, though we do not have to side with either view about how that happens (chapter 5).

The reason inconsistent conception is sufficient for the impossibility of formal objects is that the existence of such abstract objects is a logical product of what is true of them (chapter 1). By contrast, you can have inconsistent beliefs about real things—say, that your cat is a demon—that in no way affect the being of the things. So, with respect to real things, conception, consistent or not, does not determine possibility.

2. Hidden Necessities

I sketched this in the introduction. Real kinds, specific kinds, whether natural or synthetic and whether basic or not, have non-indexed[8] de re necessities that are not part of the meanings of the common names or general predicates, but nevertheless are overflow conditions of applicability for those names and predicates, the way molecules are required for milk and proteins for bugs. The atomic and subatomic constitution of things was hidden from experience for most of history. Some such overflow conditions (not elements of the linguistic meanings, [chapter 1]) may exceed the science of one's time and, perhaps, be hidden even forever. We have discovered many such conditions through experience, crafts, and science, for instance, the micronecessities for familiar things like electric wire, magnetic fields, diamonds, gold, water, ocean waves, electricity, and chemical explosions.[9]

Items get to belong to the overflow conditions of applicability[10] for our words because talk in traction with action involves real things directly at hand (cf. chapter 3.5), things whose microstructure becomes incorporated by reference into the truth conditions of our statements, though not into the ordinary word meanings. Thus the atomic number, atomic weight, and other such traits of iron are not part of the meaning of "iron," though nothing can be iron without those traits. Expert gem traders could identify and deal in rubies without knowing they are made of (red) corundum (aluminum oxide). That was a de re necessity hidden beyond their experience. The foundation of dark matter and dark energy is similarly hidden from us so far.

Emeralds, long thought to be a single kind, are of beryl ($Be_3Al_2Si_6O_{18}$) and corundum (aluminum oxide, Al_2O_3).[11] Similarly, nephrite and jadeite were long thought to be the same (jade). So there are implicit errors about the overflow necessities of things. I call them implicit because the molecular composition was not known at all. Animal and plant taxonomies, based on morphology and the like, sometimes don't segment the biosphere at its seams either; genetic codes also may have to be used. So, more precise boundaries for common words may emerge after more is known about necessities presently hidden.

Of course, few of the real kinds are "*basic* natural kinds" where every item shares *all* of its non-indexed de re necessities (qua member) with every other, like the pure elements, humans, or perhaps electrons. Even that doesn't require their being the same "*all* the way down,"[12] that is, at every included order of magnitude, though there may be such kinds too. However, ordinary natural kinds—say, ones determined by common origin (e.g., from female mammary glands) and function (food, primarily)—like milk (cow, goat, yak, etc.) and common plant kinds (carrots and yams) differ in the non-indexed de re necessities among subkinds. But all the cases, even where the borderlines are indistinct relatively to our current divisions, have de re necessities and they are naturally determinate. Otherwise, there would be things that exist when some de re necessary condition for them is not satisfied. Of course, as with nominal and merely conventional kinds or mere aggregates like hillsides and river banks, sometimes there aren't definite overflow conditions and it is custom that determines the extension of terms.

Although it is not so that one member of every exclusive disjunction of predicates has to apply to everything of every real kind, every de re necessity for anything actual is either de re necessary for *it* (any arbitrary thing) or not, case by case. That's for the same reason.

As remarked earlier, we cannot conclude from a verbally consistent description alone that such phenomena as chronons (the smallest physical intervals of time) are really possible. For we cannot conclude that there are naturally determinate and nonrepugnant overflow conditions for such a thing to exist. We know that is so because the conception may be consistent while the sort to be composed ("thinking electrons") would have conflicting de re necessities, or the combination may be incoherently indeterminate ("hay that breathes"). The conflict may lie either in the overflow known necessities (like those for phlogiston, aether, and caloric) or in the hidden ones. So, mere speculation cannot be relied on for judgments of novel possibility.

Even less can we be sure that some other pattern of natural laws would allow material objects as we might imagine them, say silicon-based life, formaldehyde-drinking primates, time travel, or an intelligent extragalactic particle cloud (Hoyle 1957). For what can be a natural necessity has to cohere with everything else that is one. For someone to say about a putative impossibility, "not if the laws of nature were different," is a promise without collateral; we have no way of knowing that the laws of nature really could be arranged to fill out the overflow conditions to which we have no access. Such reasoning would be patently circular or rely on "consistent conceivability implies possibility," the very proposition already contested as false. Many examples philosophers imagine—like brain transplants and multiply embodied selves and brains in a vat—would have overflow conditions not within the scope of the imagining, and so have no reasonable claim to possibility.

Real necessity and impossibility are not logical relations because there are no logical relations in nature. There are basically two reasons for that. First, and most important, there can be no genuine (not merely simulated or approximated) logical relations among physical states. Second, the formal modal logics we have, like quantified S-4 and S-5, have no true interpretations (applied semantics, ontologies) (Ross 1989). And besides, extensional logic (first-order and higher-order quantification) does not express genuine predication (but only relative extension, see below).

First, there can't be logical relations among physical states because any physical relationship is formally underdetermined. W. V. O. Quine made a classic modern formulation of "underdetermination" reasoning (though it originated with Plato's pointing out that experienced objects have to fall short of the Ideas); Nelson Goodman extended the reasoning with his "grue" cases about how even to begin an enumerative induction; and Saul Kripke applied it in his "plus/quus" reasoning[13] to explain (in Wittgenstein's behalf) why rule following will not explain determinate meaning.

The same general reasoning (also used here in chapter 6) discloses that (i) no matter how precisely a physical process is characterized by inputs to outputs, it is always indeterminate among incompossible pure functions (that is, pure functions, e.g., conjunction, apply univocally to an infinity of determinate input-outputs and are complete in each single case);[14] (ii) logical relations are pure functions and thus not realizable by anything that could, in the same determinate state, realize an incompatible function—but, that is always the case with a physical process;[15] (iii) therefore, no physical process can be, or realize, a logical relation.

So, strictly, there is no such thing as entailment, conjunction, addition, or disjunction in the material world, only simulations (performances that are good enough) of idealizations of the materialized relations there are. That is not just a limit of knowing; it is a limit of physical being (cf. chapter 6). There is no feature of the physical events themselves that can so precisely mark off what is done. Therefore, real necessity cannot be reduced to logical necessity. Even negation is an intentional penumbra of positive diversity.[16] Negations in general are cognitive derivatives.

Second, the standard quantified modal systems have no true interpretation, no true ontology (see chapter 2.3). Some applied semantics for possible worlds are de re incoherent and some are just plain false, as is illustrated in the section that follows. If there is no true applied modal semantics, then, for a second reason, real possibility cannot be the same as logical possibility.[17] But if real possibility is wider in domain than that of natural possibility, so that some things naturally impossible are metaphysically possible, there has to be an explanation for that, something that provides such conditions of possibility.

Besides, the relation of predicate to argument (e.g., $\Box(x)$ (Hx $\supset$ Rx) (necessarily all humans are rational) as notated with first-order quantification does not *express* real predication (e.g., that every human *is* rational, that is, constitutively) but only extensional inclusion—that even "no matter what," as the necessity operator says, every human is one of the things that is (denoted by) "rational" or one of the things called "a rational thing," and so on. I won't dwell on that here. It's like Ockham's fourteenth-century deflation of the notion of predication into coincidence of names.

Metaphysically, "whatever is possible is necessarily possible" flouts the principle that possibilities involving contingent things have no content absent the existence of such things or of things capable of causing such things, and conflicts with the idea that such things and their properties exist contingently.[18] Further, there are no global possibilities with content, *instead* of everything that actually exists[19] (chapter 3). Those three considerations should be enough to indicate that real possibility is not reducible to logical (formal) possibility. We have to look elsewhere for the grounding of natural possibility and impossibility, and particularly for the grounding of any real, say, metaphysical, possibility that exceeds and conflicts with the necessities of nature. I propose that natural possibility and impossibility are grounded in the real natures of things and that metaphysical possibility that extends beyond natural possibility is rooted in the divine power but is inaccessible in content to reliable human speculation.[20]

Section 1 above reasoned that (i) inconsistency of description is neither necessary nor sufficient for de re impossibility, and (ii) one cannot detect real possibility from a consistent conception alone, or merely from a coherent imagining of a thing,[21] particularly because the conception of a physical thing or situation always includes less than all its de re necessary conditions. Now we add some further points.

Truth de re travels no farther than reference. Suppose someone says, "Perhaps there are silicon-based intelligent beings on some other planet." Not, if "silicon-based intelligence" is linguistically coherent but physically repugnant, as Escher figures are two-dimensionally coherent but physically impossible. The deficit of the supposition is de re. The deficit is in the overflow conditions: they are indeterminate. There is no truth value rooting without reference.[22] Having cases, actually or potentially, is indispensable to set the overflow conditions of what we think of. So, if a supposition is really possible, something actually existing must determine the overflow necessities.[23]

We can say, "Before there were humans, it was, nevertheless, true that humans are animals." But what "was before" is denominated (extrinsically, i.e., relationally characterized)[24] by reference to "what came to be," the real humans.[25] Likewise, how could it have been true no matter what that "humans can't breathe ammonia" when 5 billion years ago there was no such thing as being a human or even animate life at all? There *was* no such proposition or even such a determinate natural kind.

The supposed situation is constructed denominatively from what eventually came to be on account of the causes there were. Such a judgment is *vantaged*—that is, referentially anchored—in what really sometime[26] exists (later, in this case). And so, had "the later" not come to be, there would have been no proposition, no state of affairs, and no situation of "*its* not having been or not having been true." Similarly, had you and I never existed, there would have been no truth or fact that "you and I [by name] never existed." Empty general terms[27] made on the mold of natural kind or synthetic kind names, but arbitrarily combining properties, pick out nothing with determinate conditions for existing and so fail to name anything. Such purportedly referring terms are vacuous.[28] That includes "rabbucks," "rational galaxies," "backward time," and other fanciful inventions; they are referentially vacant.

There are no unanchored empty kinds, or what David Armstrong called "empty universals." That is because the kind[29] (as nature or essence) is the characteristic capacity of the cases, taken one by one, the way "human" is to Socrates. So, "no cases, no natures." The nature of a thing is the operative and constitutive capacity of the thing; it makes the thing to be that sort of thing, the way "Three Blind Mice" makes a particular singing or playing to be *that* song. Otherwise there would not be just the *one* thing that is both "that" thing (Socrates) and, say, "human." And furthermore, the sort, human, could not be genuinely repeated in other particulars (cf. chapter 7) like you and me.

To regard individuals as laminates of shareable properties, like an illusion on a stage made entirely by overlapping spotlights,[30] cannot account for the unity or the particularity of individuals or provide an explanatory relation between the properties and the individuals. The particular cannot be related by exemplification or instantiation to *all* of its constitutive features (properties); that would require bare particulars as the base, or treat individuals as the mere coincidence of the shareable properties. Something, not supplied by that conception, would be needed for the laminate to be one unified thing, and to be one distinct thing, rather than a mere coincidence.

The constitutive sort and the particular have to be really the same thing (chapter 7), not a multitude. Note that the relation "is really the same as"[31] (which has different truth conditions in different contexts) is not one of logical identity, but is a nontransitive and nonsymmetrical one, where, inter alia, at least one relatum cannot exist without the other, though sometimes the other can, and, where "*what* it is"(oak) is really the same (structuring it) as the thing, an oak. The general notion "really the same as" is further discussed at chapter 7.2.

3. What There Is. Being Cannot Be Exhausted by Logical Division into Kinds

To be is not a determinable (cf. Johnson 1927). Nor is "what there is." Being does not have species or sorts by addition of features; nor is being exhaustible by kinds, just as kinds are inexhaustible by mere individuation. Given enough material, time, and space, what would there be about the differences of human individuals that at some certain point no further different humans would be possible?[32] Which human one is cannot be explained by one's being human. In general, nothing could generate real ranges of kinds or of individuals of a real kind that would be replete (so full that no more can consistently be added). So, to suppose there is an extension of all possible humans is incoherent. Likewise, there is no replete domain of propositions, beings, or kinds of beings.

(1) "To be" is not the same as "to be an F" (where "F" is a kind name[33] or group of kind names). It is not a determinable, decomposable into kinds (like "primary color") or events, substances, or states of affairs. Nor is "to be" a *what* that can be discretely multiplied the way "is a human" is. Nor is "to be" the same as "to be physical" (though some philosophers think it is).[34] Others think there is no "to be" that is not completed by some sortal, say, "F"—that is, to be is to be some F or other. But unless there is an "F" that is really the *same as* (not in potentiality to) *some* thing's existing, there will be no final explanation for the existing of anything at all. That's because things of all other sorts, F's, do not exist on account of *what* they are.[35]

Consider this about modal semantics. Whenever anyone offers an ontology, an applied semantics, for a formal system (say, for a quantified modal logic), we should ask whether it is true: is that the real constitution of the world? Or is it just imaginary, devised as a domain of reference for some formal modal calculus? That would not be enough.

To justify a modal semantics requires reasoning that goes beyond whether the reading preserves the formal relations within the calculus. A calculus can have many interpretations. One needs independently to know that the domains of interpretation constitutively have the formal structure supposed by the interpreted logic. That's just what none of the applied semantics provides, even though David Lewis (1986), unlike the others, did design his ontology to have the formal structure of the modal logic and particularly to map contrary-to-fact conditionals, but did so without providing an independent reason for postulating an infinite domain of physical worlds standing as possibilities to one another, and each internally actual. The other writers just postulate domains of abstracta (properties, individual essences, relations, worlds, and so on) to fit the calculi without any independent reasoning at all.

On an orthodox view of divine creation, that nothing other than God has any reality apart from creation, there could be no such domains of realities, despite Plantinga's (1974) suppositions. Instead, one can regard the interpreted modal systems as merely instrumental for auditing our modal reasoning, just as we use first-order and higher-order quantification for other reasoning without any commitment that it is the structure of the world. Why suppose there really are other possible worlds and domains of real abstracta at all? Instrumentalism does fine (with a qualification below). Besides, I don't think many philosophers really believe there are such worlds and abstracta. Who has independently shown that any of the (diversely) ontologically interpreted modal systems (the "applied semantics" as Alvin Plantinga felicitously called them) *are* true? As I said elsewhere, the satanic notation whispered the ontology.[36]

Outcome. — We have no independently justified ontology for extensionally quantified modal logic. In fact, important axioms, for example from S-5, that whatever is necessary is necessarily necessary (e.g., $\Box(F = MA) \supset \Box\{\Box (F = MA)\}$), and "what is possible is necessarily possible," as theistically understood above, would be false de re. For real possibility ad extra is consequent on the divine creative ability, not antecedent to it (Ross 1986b, 1990a). With respect to created things, all possibility with content is the product of divine creative election, not something antecedent or independent. So, interpreted de re, it is neither true that every necessity is iteratively necessary nor true that every possibility is necessarily possible.

Further, to interpret "possible" as "consistent" and not take account of the overflow de re necessities not captured in the meanings is to ensure that the applied semantics is not true. Any form of the claim, "conceptual or descriptive consistency implies possibility," applied to things with hidden de re necessities is false. The very fact that it can happen that the formal system be consistent when the interpreted principles might be false shows that (i) the neat interpretation of the logic cannot ensure the de re truth of the applied semantics; so, (ii) an applied semantics needs a separate ontological foundation.[37]

Possibility with real content (e.g., lasers that make solids transparent [*Guardian*, February 20, 2006] or private sound without earphones [*New York Times*, March 5, 2006]) is either something actually existing or within the ability of a somehow actual cause, not prior to it.[38] The content of the "was always possible" in the statement "what is possible was always possible" is denominatively determined by what comes to be. The virtually unanimous belief to the contrary, even among materialists, is an illusion nourished on the straw of logical notation.

(2) "Being," actuality without qualification, is explanatorily prior to "possibility," not the reverse (section 2.6). But the modal ontologies seem to make possibility (possible worlds) explanatorily prior to real existence (unless they think the existence of the domain of worlds is self-subsistent). Their (i) doubling reality with necessarily existing immaterial abstract objects (whether properties, individual essences, propositions, or states of affairs, and worlds), or (ii) postulating that there are merely possible worlds, or (iii) regarding "being," "being physically material," "being possible," and "being, relatively, actual" as logically equivalent to one another but intentionally distinct, as did David Lewis (1986), are all implausible because (1) there is no explanation for the existence of such things (e.g., for the universal domain of "physical worlds" for Lewis, and the other possible worlds for the others), or (2) there is no explanation for why there should be ab-

stract objects at all, and, in particular, (3) there is no content to the "exemplification," "instantiation," or similar relations by which the abstracta are supposed to explain their physical cases (if any). By admirable craftsmanship the modal ontologists map an ontology for the formal systems without any independent reasoning that shows such things as they postulate exist at all.

Supposed possibilities whose overflow de re conditions are not determined by any actual things are merely verbal, de dicto,[39] like griffins, chronons, and hobbits—not real. Merely verbal possibilities are, in reality, impossible, like my becoming a spider. To call them logical or conceptual possibilities is misleading because, when the overflow conditions are vacant or would be conflicting, there is no possibility at all.

Is there a convincing reason for something that important? This may do: a material thing indeterminate as to the relevant general necessities of nature (e.g., physical, biological, chemical, etc.) in principle lacks a sufficient condition to be at all. For it cannot exist if the overflow necessities for it would conflict or would be unsatisfied. Thus, such an intentional object is really impossible (de re vacuous).[40] See chapter 2.6. One cannot merely construct an alternate world whose de re necessities are determinate "all the way down" because saying so will not make it so.

(3) There are no ranges of mere possibility. Some people imagine "everything else" as maximally consistent rearrangements of and substitutions for what actually exists. That idea is both too big and too small. Some "rearrangements" are not real possibilities, for instance: "There might have been formaldehyde-drinking primates." The idea is too small because, if there is a free divine creator, what lies within its absolute power is not captured within the creation it made (its ordained power).

Carnapian state descriptions may have in part prompted the applied semantics for quantified modal logic by suggesting a universal range of well-formed propositions (on the model of truth tables), like a list, each of which is determinately true or false, and every consistent permutation of which constitutes "some possible world" (each with a tier of well-formed assertions true in every world [necessities] and another, of the false in every world [impossibilities]), the remainder being the propositions true in some worlds and not in others (the various worlds). Interpreted, it's like a universal marquee, with some burned-out lights (the impossibilities), some always on (the necessities), and sometimes-on-bulb-patterns that spell out the particular worlds (like play titles, casts, and scripts).[41] Thus, one may talk of "all worlds," "some worlds," and so on, but the underlying supposition is a runaway Platonistic ontology of propositions or states of affairs. One has to ask oneself: "Do I really believe there *are* such things?"

4. What About Super-Addition?

A Brief Digression. — Could God have brought about any arbitrary combination of compatible predicates, as John Locke (1975) apparently thought, say, "stones that see," "life without water," or "extragalactic clouds that think" (cf. Hoyle 1957)? Locke's idea (cf. Wilson 1979) seems to involve the addition of a power to a nature already complete but lacking it—life to mere matter, sensation to living things, thought to sentience. It supposes a lack of active ability in a base power to which another active ability is added, perhaps resulting in another nature. But not all living things are passively capable of sensation: there is no way to add sensation to grass, yet the idea is verbally consistent (e.g., "The wondering grass hoped for rain."). Can God make high-voltage electric wire out of a spider web? Can silicon parts be arranged to feel? Can a keypad be made to love your touch? We may not know *why* the overflow de re necessities prevent such additions, but we know a consistent idea, even added to the supposition of unlimited divine power, is not sufficient to ensure real possibility.[42] The conceptions we have are anchored in the reality we know. The entirely otherwise is inaccessible.

Besides, the apparent logical addition of, say, "rational" to "animal" gives a misleading impression that a real condition "being rational" is conjoined to a prior real condition "being animal" as a mode or manner of it, when in fact being rational is a kind of being an animal, the way being yellow is a kind of being colored.[43] There is no addition at all. The lesson is that with respect to divine power, though one might be certain it is not confined to the order of nature and revelation (the ordained power), one cannot indicate items that belong to divine absolute power beyond the ordained power. For, as I said, such content would depend on untaken divine elections.

5. General Names and Consequent Natures: Various Sorts

Since one of the main claims here is that possibility and impossibility with determinate content are grounded in the natures of things, some rough and ready distinctions may be useful to indicate that "can" and "can't," "possible," and so on, have to adapt to context.

(1) Some common names are for infima species that further divide only into naturally separate individuals (dogs, barn swallows, and humans) and others are for stuffs with common constitutions like the chemical elements, the synthetics like aspirin, polyurethane, polyethylene, and polypropylene. The latter sorts divide into quantities or mixtures or compounds. Other common names are for natural sorts like soil, clay, grass, and skin that are resultants of more basic sorts. Some of the kinds don't have all their de re necessities in common (at perceptible magnitudes) but otherwise have general names like those that Kripke analyzed as rigid designators, say "skin" for human skin, snake skin, and bird skin (assuming that is a real kind).

(2) At the other extreme there are merely conventional names for grouped particulars—things without any particular traits in common beyond ones we impose by so-calling and so-treating the things, like junk, lots, refuse, things in my bag, sale goods, places, times, events, jobs, and spots.

(3) In between are names for kinds more general than infima species, kinds like animal, plant, mineral, food, mammal, rodent, lizard, and snake—kinds with real constitutions that are, however, resultants of particular species biologically or chemically or physically. Though real, they cannot exist only on their own; nothing is just a rat, a fish, or just a bird, but each requires something structurally further and prior. One reason, I suggest, is that the genus (to use an old-fashioned term) is naturally consequent upon the species and, though really in common

among the species (see discussions in chapters 5 and 7), it is so resultantly, and is not constitutive or explanatorily prior but is posterior, an outcome of structural similarities. To be a "salt" is a de re common and necessary chemical condition, but is a consequence, a physical outcome, of the particular constitution of each sort, for example, of sodium chloride versus sodium sulphate: they behave the same at a certain level of generality as a common outcome of their more particular constitutions.

(4) More dependent on human convenience, though well-based, but incompletely, in the real features of things are conventional kinds like city, nation, history, language, factory, tool, food, glue, paint, and family. The same is true for activity names like skiing, flying, racing, eating, rustling, hastening, editing, revising, inventing, and for disease and disorder names, for instance, about three hundred psychiatric disorders that are clinically distinguished. The contrasts among the items of such lexical fields are typically dependent on the other items in the lexical field and on the practical objectives of the classifiers (cf. Ross 1992).

The variety of common names for mixed natural and conventional features is so large and varied that some high points for contrast will have to do,[44] though all the refined arts, crafts, and technologies have vocabularies with all these sorts of names. Contrast the following:

(i) "a conception fully based in reality, but conventionally defined," for example, "rotational laterality" (building) and "displacement" (ship), and ones for particular things with common real constitutions like aspirin and sodium chloride, and for differing synthetics that have functionally equivalent constitutions, like ink, dyes, fabrics, and paints;

(ii) "a conception partly based in natural reality, partly in manmade reality, and conventionally defined": lawn mower blades, razors, sexually attractive, worth studying;

(iii) "a conception created by formal convention and constitutive of something real," for example, made by lawmaking or by a craft or practice: corporation, domiciles, graduate student, stock fund, banking, residential area (zoning), marketable goods, merchantability (law);

(iv) "a conception by convenience with incomplete and varying basis in man-made reality," like lodging, travel, shine, finish, shopping area, bargaining, agreeing; and
(v) "a conception for convenience or purpose, without an independent basis in reality" like in-and-out, table setting, new century, millennium.

Obviously that list is just tatters; but it indicates that notions of possibility, necessity, and impossibility employed throughout the range of such conceptions adapt contextually to their discourse neighborhoods. The notion "can't" is not the same in "You can't have wholesale outlets in residential neighborhoods" (zoning), "You can't have a rigid shape from just dry sand" (physics), "You can't have a live cat made of silicon" (common sense and biology), and "You can't have a good saw with uneven set" (woodworking). Further, one's modal inferences don't strictly follow the formal syntax of S-4 or S-5 as to iterated modalities. That is particularly obvious with natural possibility and impossibility because of the contingency of the natural order. Natural impossibility is, I think, mainly a matter of the absence of real alternatives to what is universally so, as will become clear.

6. Being Is Explanatorily Prior to Possibility

It is inconsistent to suppose there could be possibility but no actual being at all. Even the modal ontologists I criticized above seem to agree on that, though, except for Lewis, they don't offer explanations as to why. Usually one thinks that it is possible that there is a cause for whatever comes about, and nothing comes about without one. So, natural possibility and necessity is explanatorily derivative from actual being, not its container or frame. Existence is explanatorily prior to possibility, overall. The idea that the actual is a single subcase of the possible is a mere formal construction. The explanatory order is the reverse: the merely possible is an intentional projection from the actual and the potential.

The merely possible with content—say, evolutionary descendants of humans or fleas—must be or have been within the ability[45] of something that somehow exists or comes to be. Otherwise, such an outcome could not come about and, so, would not be really possible.[46] Not everything that is within the ability of what somehow exists also comes to be. So there is, *relatively* and denominatively, the merely possible; but that is a, perhaps well-grounded, thought projection from what exists, not some independent reality.

Some kind of active power/ability is needed to explain the possibility of some existent that is not also actual. Causal ability is the usual explanation. But that can't be the fundamental explanation because causation presupposes something existing. Though, in the abstract "to be supposes possibility" (logically), in reality "possibility supposes being" (existence is prior to potentiality). The first is so by implication; the second is by explanatory priority. So, there is something further to be considered about how possibility is ultimately grounded in actuality, but not right here (see chapter 3).

7. The Argument in Brief, So Far

Nothing real that exists individually or is a natural or synthetic real kind (whether phosphorous or paints) can be indeterminate (not merely disjunctive) in its non-indexed de re necessities of nature. For it would always lack a sufficient condition for being, for instance, being indeterminate among contradictories (say, winged or not, then tapered-winged or not, etc., at each joint without stop, as far as nature goes (cf. Kripke 1982). The exclusive disjunctions among real features have to terminate for the conditions to be sufficient. That is not, however, to deny there are also lots of resultant things in nature without distinct boundaries like gravel and cliffs, bays and forests; the things that are heaps, aggregates, composites, compounds, and the like eventually have components with definite natural traits.

By "de re necessary condition for," I mean a condition on the part of a thing, in nature, without which its name or description would referentially fail, even though such conditions may not be part of the meaning of a common name or even be known. Conditions for production and existence typically are overflow necessities, as for instance, what is needed to produce x-rays or humans. Were such an overflow condition in principle unmet, nothing real or potentially real would be picked out by the name. For instance, a phoenix, whose overflow necessities are not determinately settled by anything at all, cannot exist. Something required is always missing. That's enough for being de re impossible.

The Impossible: Defective Conceptions or Deficient Conceptions. — To say, "there is no real possibility that ergons exist" (ergons are the minimal units of energy throughout the cosmos, analogous to photons) is not the same as "it is impossible that there be atomless water." Ergons are impossible because reference is prevented (if energy is endlessly divisible). That's a deficient conception. The de re necessities are not determined.[47] "Atomless water," however, is impossible because its semantic content requires conflicting real necessities; that's a defective conception. Thus, the first case comes to "ergons are impossible because there aren't any naturally sufficient or even determinate conditions for such things," whereas, the second comes to "atomless water is impossible because of what atoms are and what water is."

In neither case is there any reality that is impossible. Rather, the concepts don't allow the statement (proposition) to present any reality to thought because the conceptions are deficient or defective, like "starsized tomatoes" and "phlogiston."

In answer to whether the opposites of natural necessities lack truth value, the reply is this: the propositional contradictories of de re necessities are typically false both de dicto and de re (e.g., "humans are not rational animals"); some propositional contraries, for example, "humans are pure spirits," are de dicto false because they conflict with a meaning relationship and de re vacuous because there is no such real situation and no determinate condition for such a situation. Some verbal contradictories of de re necessities are de dicto consistent (e.g., my not being composed of quarks) because that impossibility is not yet reflected lexically (see chapter 3.6). The contraries of natural necessities are de re impossible as either defective or deficient intentional objects, even where they are de dicto consistent.

Some notions that at one time lack determinate overflow conditions can be cured with an increase in knowledge and skill; thus, "There are humans living with the heart and lungs once another's," "There is a human walking on the moon," "There are flying machines," and "There are space ships," once de re vacuous as propositions (had they been formulated), later can express what is so.[48] From the time such capacities were known to be within the potentialities of things rather than just imagined, the possibilities were foreseen because the de re conditions (even those not foreseen) were determinate. Historians may disagree about which old speculations, like Leonardo's flying machines, say, conjectured real possibilities, and which were mere imaginings, like Icarus's flying or Buck Rogers's ray gun. But certain imaginings like "my brain's being transplanted into your body" and "that I have all my experience, absent the external world," are really impossibilities.[49] They are deficient conceptions.

Some impossibilities are discovered from a single experience. It takes no induction to see a dead bird can't fly. I had a childhood certainty, once, that an ordinary reel lawn mower turned over and pulled backward would cut tall dandelions because the blade and striking plate would be raised. On one try, conviction hemorrhaged into shame.

It is a myth that the necessities of nature are embedded in some logical-semantic scheme of abstracta so that real impossibility derives from some in-principle inconsistency (a semantic or formal contradiction). Unless there is some universal treasury of properties (neo-Platonic) or unless real possibility *depends* on what we can think of, there is no way that inconsistency could account for impossibility. Some philosophers, like David Bohm (1980), sometimes say natural necessities ($E = MC^2$, $G = AT^2$) are *really* logical necessities. I think they mean that the basic laws of nature are conditions for all material being (Descartes), perhaps even for being at all.

But what determines what really conflicts with what? Aristotle's account of nature, the cosmos, stops without an explanation of *why* the necessities of nature (which for him were the exceptionless and eternal order of things) are as they are. Some later thinkers said the order of nature follows from the emmanating divine nature and others from free divine election. Some conflated real impossibility with logical contradiction, saying the necessary is what has a self-contradictory denial. In any case, if the necessities of nature, the regularities whose verbal contraries are referentially vacuous, are in some way finally explained, whatever explains them does so *not* by acting from some feature of the physics of material beings—which is among what must be explained—and so must lie beyond matter (taken broadly), behind the blackboard of physics.[50]

Whatever the account, we don't need a domain of impossibles. For, though there are sometimes de dicto (intentional) contraries of natural necessities, there are no real ones (apart, perhaps, from some miracles).[51] The natural necessities have no contraries in nature with earned, as opposed to inherited, truth values. That's because when reference fails, truth value withers away. So the really impossible comes to nothing.

CHAPTER 3

What Might Have Been

1. The Various Counterfactuals

Suppositions, even convictions, about what might have been may lack earned truth value. That affects major issues.

This selective exploration of counterfactuals makes three points: (i) that there are true judgments with earned truth or falsity about what might have been, earned from what actually exists; (ii) that such earned truth typically depends on the real, active, and ready natures of existing things (e.g., the milk would have boiled in another minute); and (iii) that counterfactual conjectures, suppositions, by philosophers often have no truth value at all, or only de dicto transformational values, because the suppositions are not anchored in the natures of somehow existing things.

Suppositions (antecedents) with earned truth (and falsity) earn it from what is actually or potentially in being. Others have at most inherited truth values, truth or falsity de dicto by transformations from other propositions, for example, "If I hadn't been a human, I might have been a tiger and a lion as well." Some are not true or false at all because there is no fact of the matter at all, say, "If I'd been sixteen in 1066, I'd have joined the Norman Invasion." For some, a compliant reality is unascertainable, "If there had been silicon-based terrestrial life, there would still have been animals."

45

Incoherent ones, "If there were left-handed hay, guitars would be two-handed" and suppositions that contravene a constitutive convention—for instance, "If chess knights also traveled in straight lines, then queens would act as pawns"—also yield vacuity. When you can pick any truth value you want, none is either earned or inherited. The world of regret, of what might have been, had you married a Tibetan monk, or a milliner or a miner, trails off quickly into indeterminacy, though perhaps not as fast as a supposing you married a centipede. But the difference is a matter of few steps before what would really be required turns to mush.

In General. — Some counterfactual suppositions inherit values by way of logical and semantical transformations and by pragmatic conditions, for example, "If that step had cracked apart, a person would easily have fallen." Others earn them from the real natures of things: "If you mixed the milk and coffee, you couldn't separate them again" (true), and "If you were to back up the car for a mile, you could retread the tires" (false).

The one-size-fits-all analyses of counterfactual statements on the model of some well-defined implication or entailment fail to discriminate the true ones from the false, for instance, "If I'd bought the book, I'd have been pleased" from "If I'd bought the book, I'd have been displeased," as material implication (cf. Goodman 1955). Besides, people follow different rules for different cases with the same surface grammar. So, sometimes we count a counterfactual true because the antecedent is impossible: "If I were a single atom, you could still see me." Sometimes we count a statement true because of meaning inclusions: "If I were invisible, you couldn't see me." Sometimes we count a counterfactual as a material implication, and so, true: "If you were a test pilot, I'd be an astronaut."

Mapping such judgments onto possible-worlds ontologies doesn't help because of the implausibility of such ontologies (chapter 2) and because of their imperialistic revision of what we *mean* when they map "If I'd touched the hot lid, I'd have been burned" onto possible worlds, whether conceived as abstract entities (Plantinga, Stalnaker) or as computational rearrangements of the actual world (Lycan), or as parallel equally real "large objects" (D. Lewis), or as fictions (Rescher).[1] They stand in no explanatory relation to the actual world, where had I touched the hot lid, I would have been burned. Not one of those theories contains an *explanatory* relation between the actual world and some "other possible world." "Instantiation," "exemplification," and "counterparts" are not explanatory relations (chapter 2), they are just correlations of names. The possible-worlds paraphrasing of our counterfactual statements amounts to a revision of what we actually mean when we say something might or might not have been so.

(i) The Unanchored. — There are referentially unanchored "might have beens" that fall outside the potentialities of things, for example, "There might have been silicon-based rational life on earth" and "There might have been incarnated angels." Such suppositions either lack definite conditions to start with or trail off as soon as the natural kinds they involve first clash; that makes them impossibilities by defective or deficient conceptions (chapter 2).

Once you suppose something that clashes with a natural necessity (that there be unmeltable pure iron at midrange temperatures, say) or leave a natural necessity indeterminate (whether mackerel have hearing), you mush out of the lines of physical consequence. As a result you can't travel directly from what we know to what is merely supposed without relying on the false premise, "what is conceivable is possible," or worse, on "what is imaginable is possible." Supposing ingested lead is not poisonous leaves its chemical consequences indeterminate (and thus, not real). Suppositions, like "there might be personal teleportation by lasers," "there might be ergons colliding with chronons," and "there might be potable mercury" are de re impossible by vacuity (chapter 2).

(ii) The Embedded. — In general, the truth value of a counterfactual supposition depends on how the judgment is locked in and nested among other potential judgments and on whether its references succeed. Some suppositions involve meaning inclusions, like "If I were unemployed, I would be a jobless." Some rely on material implication, "If you are modest, I am a mouse." Some rely on craftbound conventions, like the musical "If I'd sharped the F, I'd have moved into G-major," and the legal "If he'd been foreign-born he wouldn't have been president." Some are embedded in mere fancy and ignorance, like "If I'd married her those beautiful children of hers would have been mine." And most presuppose some intermediate fabric of facts, like "If I'd taken that job all that office space would have been mine," and "If I'd remembered I'd have brought that book." Almost all presuppose, "All else would remain the same." The latter, if taken strictly, usually makes the suppositions impossible. And taken loosely, to mean mutatis mutandis, it makes the claim vacuous wherever such changed conditions are not determinate.

The most useful counterfactual suppositions are the ones tightly meshed in causal or other explanatory and craftbound schemes, like "If I had dropped that from a greater height, the force of impact would have been n-greater"(mechanics); "If I had ignited four times as much gasoline, the explosive force would have been n-times larger" (chemistry); "If I'd played that ace it would have topped his king" (a card game). Such schemes and presuppositions legitimize and determine the thought-out consequences the way a calculating system legitimizes outcomes.

Other useful counterfactuals belong to discourse based in crafts or social constructs like banking, law, social security, and public education systems, where the consequence relationships are determined by the systems, like hands of cards, so that if the supposition is system coherent, it is determinate. That is not to imply, of course, that such social systems have no gaps, inconsistencies, or, like the civil law, indeterminate situations where certain counterfactuals will be vacuous.

When we mix real kinds (natural and synthetic) and real traits (properties) out of the order of natural occurrence into loosely supposed ones—like galaxies of apples or silicon-based life, or possible worlds—we get intentional objects that are impossibilities by referential vacuity or defective conceptions (chapter 2). There are, in principle, no conditions under which what is thus supposed would be so.

(iii) No Names, No Truth. — On the whole, where naming fails, earned truth value is prevented.[2] As chapter 2 reasoned, earned truth travels no farther than reference. There can, of course, be incoherent thoughts, even incoherent thoughts about real things, but they don't have determinate truth or falsity, they just fail to pick out any definite situation. So, expressed counterfactual suppositions lacking referents for the general terms and for the names are de re empty. They are not about any things, but are only imaginings. That holds especially for the conjecture that there might have been things of entirely other sorts instead of anything that ever actually exists or that actual things are capable of. There is nothing to furnish such a cosmos with kinds.[3] I'll make that clearer, shortly.

(iv) Outcome. — The outcome of such reflections is that counterfactual judgments are not a class amenable to a "one-size-fits-all" analysis; for as many are without any truth value at all as are determinately true or false; and as many again have truth values by the formal or conventional systems they belong to. But the ones of most interest to science, and to this metaphysical discussion, are the ones dependent for truth and falsity upon the real, active, natures of things.[4] They earn their truth values from real things. For it is the natures of things that are the locus of natural necessity and of the intelligibility of nature. Real natures bottom out in repeatable, intelligible structures constitutive of things (chapter 7).

(v) Conceivability Does Not Imply Real Possibility (as argued in chapter 2). — Philosophers now mostly realize this (cf. Gendler and Hawthorne 2002), though it took unconscionably long for them to recognize that Thomas Reid (1764) had got the point right. Arguments often suppose we can conceive or imagine what has no cases, perhaps by stipulation, like Black's two identical spheres (1952), or Shoemaker's intervals of time without change (1969). That underlies claims of the form, "It is logically possible that, say, pain should occur without c-fiber firings," or the supposition that there might have been zombies[5] or witches. Causal connections are supposed by many to be only hypothetically necessary (given that causal laws—that are mere regularities only—are contingent), so anything could conceivably be caused by anything else. But that conflicts with the obvious. Shapes can't cause colors (outside a computer program). "But they might have?" No. The overflow necessities for real things prevent that. Consistent conceivability as far as it goes, for instance, of water with no critical temperature or of life without photosynthesis, won't ensure real possibility. Only existence, experience, and science can ensure that.[6]

Yet, some notable recent arguments rely on the premise that what is conceptually noncontradictory is possible: see, for example, Saul Kripke's (1972, chap. 3) argument that it is possible for something to feel pain that does not undergo c-fiber stimulation, that is, "for the pain to have had some other source" (cf. Passmore 1985, 62); Hilary Putnam, and others, arguing against central state materialism (see Smart 1959; Putnam 1975a), and others, too, supposing we know it is possible that something, say a robot, could have our mental states and not our brain states (even by generic kind), or David Chalmers's (1996) supposing there might be zombies with our same brain states without the mental states.[7]

Reasoning with imaginary cases that stays within the natural necessities can be inventively fertile. Thinking about what is really impossible can even yield insights about what is real. But as chapter 8 indicates, the imagination also lures one toward falsity. Because the de re necessities for a thing are not all components of *what* it is, they, like molecular bonding or atomic constitution, may overflow the known features lying hidden from the thinker, the way electron clouds overflowed what Ben Franklin could know about lightening. Suppositions that conflict, but not in their meanings, with such overflow conditions are impossible by defect, and ones that are indeterminate as to such features are impossible by vacuity (chapter 2). So a supposition can be impossible (e.g., that electricity is a fluid) without a person's or even a community's having access to that fact.

(vi) Real Natures. — One scientific objective is to attain descriptions of natural (and synthetic) things that from their microstructures under general laws can explain and predict their behavior, for example, of cells and superconductors. That resembles Aristotle's idea that sciences aim to understand the natures (essences) of material things, so that "*what they are*" is found to be explanatory of what they characteristically do. For example, the chemical structures of nylon and Dacron and rayon (plus the science of petroleum-based fibers and technology of fabric-making) explain the differing behavior of the materials. That includes both the regular observable behavior and the latent dispositions— for example, to stretch or to stain. For that sort of knowledge we need grounded counterfactual judgments.

2. Earned Propositional Truth Depends on Reference

Reference determines overflow signification (chapter 1). Because we have to use words networked in meaning and attached by calling[8] to things and kinds (how else would words have overflow conditions of applicability?), we cannot express a situation entirely unrelated to what there is. To say there might have been babies with wings, amphibious dolphins, or talking reptiles involves sorts that are familiar, but postulates what is really impossible. For the overflow necessities for the kinds we are conjoining will not so combine. That's because real natures carry (and their common names referentially incorporate) their nonincidental, causal oppositions as well as their capacities into any suppositional combination. That is analogous to the individuality a person carries into every counterfactual situation; so, there aren't any situations where you had different biological parents. (That's an example of de re necessity that is not a meaning inclusion.) When the imagined combinations of conditions clash with nature, the de re necessities trail off into vacuity (chapter 2). What is within the capacity, proximate or remote, of the actual is really possible; the rest is merely notional.

About other intentional objects—say, particles of diameter less than 10^{-23} m or animate life without water and photosynthesis, we don't know that real features would so combine. To say, "Well, it is not inconsistent and so, possible," is to get the cart before the horse. Failure to be inconsistent may only reflect incomplete conception like "life without water" or "sensation without perception." Franklin's conception of electricity as a kind of fluid was consistent as far as it went, just as was an earlier conception of heat as a fluid, but de re impossible. Likewise, no mouse can become a cat. The real explanation for all those cases lies in nature.

That's the way with uprooted common names and predicates. Tear out the reference and the earned truth values die, torn away from the overflow necessities, leaving only a verbal shell that might behave like a statement and may even be verbally true (by meaning inclusions) and express a coherent imagining, but fail de re to say anything definite, and thus, to say anything that is really possible. If there had never been roses there would be no true proposition, "There never were roses." Even an omnipotent being could not have caused *me* never to have been at all.[9]

One might say, using one sense of "possible" employed by Aristotle—namely, "within the ability of some agent"—that entirely other kinds are really possible by supposing there is an agent able but not compelled to make such things (a Creator or *Timaeus* craftsmen).[10] But we couldn't say what such other natural kinds are, given the untaken divine elections (or unformed intentions of cosmic craftsmen). We could sketch and conjecture from the capacities of known things, the way Leonardo conjectured a flying machine. Still, nothing about the actual kinds (as far as we can tell so far) requires that they be the only kinds.[11] Yet entirely other kinds could only happen on account of something that somehow exists, not something that might have but doesn't under any condition exist. So, we still conclude that the only possibilities with content, even those beyond the capacities of nature (if there are any), lie within the capacities of what actually exists.[12]

Constitutive versus Consequent Conditions. — (See also chapter 2.5.) The de re necessities for things are either constitutive (e.g., water is H_2O) or resultant (e.g., the conditions for cake, jewelry, or debt). The resultant constitutions are from natural kinds (wheat) or from synthetic kinds (zircon), or from social constructs (money) or combinations of them.[13] Such conditions are in part explicit in word meanings, partly presented in the sense meanings ("color" is presented in the sensation "blue"), and in part among the overflow conditions, like the molecular constitution of teeth (chapter 1).

Generic kinds (and class, phylum, kingdom, etc.) are not explanatorily prior to their individuals but consequent on similarities among individuals and species. Thus, "to be an animal" in the generic sense of "a thing capable of nutrition, growth, reproduction, locomotion, and sensation" is consequent, not a constituent of barn swallows, diamondbacks, and house cats. Those are constitutively animals but "being an animal" is not a constituent of them; it is a resultant of their constitutions. Moreover, though "being an animal" is fully based physically, it is not resultant as an effect, the way the plasticity of butter is. It is resultant structurally. Warm-blooded animals capable of vision differ neurologically from birds that can see; so the genetic constitution making them capable of vision is different, though vision is structurally consequent in both cases. In general, though being alive is a constitutive condition of every living thing, it is resultant from the specific organization of the things, of which there are, perhaps, millions of forms (cf. Ayala 1985).

The rotational laterality of a skyscraper is resultant from other material features, whereas the consciousness, the undifferentiated subjectivity of a mouse, achieved by natural molecular assembly is very probably emergent (not theoretically reducible to its physiology). By "emergent" here I do not mean "magical" or "unexplainable," but "with its explanation lying outside the organizational principles of its base components." Signals and messages may be related that way.[14] I need words to write the statements but the statements can't be reduced to the words. Thus, there would be emergence among orders of magnitude in nature when the organization at one order of magnitude is not theoretically reducible to the next included order of magnitude and has operations not definable within the included order, but the one does not appear in nature without the included order.

3. Intermediate Conclusion

So far, also relying on chapter 2, we can conclude (i) there is no one-size-fits-all analysis of the truth conditions for contrary to fact conditionals, and (ii) the counterfactuals of chief interest here are those with definite and nontrivial truth values fully anchored in the real natures of things. So, (iii) what merely might have been, as far as it is real and determinate, is accounted for by the abilities and dispositions of actual things and is otherwise empty, though there are also conventional, notional, definitional, and merely syntactical cases as well; (iv) there is no world of mere possibilia and a fortiori, no real domain of worlds; (v) metaphysics is not grounded in prior logic or in a domain of explanatorily prior and self-accounting logical possibilities. Explanation winds down to what exists and stops there.

4. De Re Necessities Are Neither Conventional, Conceptual, nor Linguistic

Here we collect four background facts from earlier remarks: (i) real necessities overflow linguistic meanings; (ii) real necessities are de facto prior to word meanings and human concepts in general; (iii) not all real necessities are known; and (iv) real necessities cannot all be expressed.

Next, we add and explain another fact: word meanings adjust to our beliefs, which in turn, adjust to natural necessity and to contingencies as well. That is probably obvious. Still, I note that it is not the verbal meaning of a common name that settles which are the necessities of nature for things; they overflow meanings and are, if discovered, known through experience and science. Words don't settle that iron is ductile or an element, but only what it or its property is called.[15] Besides, the discovered necessities can conflict with the verbal inclusions—for example, whales, despite the King James Version, are not great fish, nor are dolphins friendly fish (except as "swimming dwellers of the deep").

Meanings adjust to be useful in discourse, to include some of our *beliefs* about things ("water is H_2O," "coyotes are a sort of wolf," "deer are herbivorous"). Sometimes meanings include false beliefs as well, as when "dolphins are friendly fish" was believed, or "all swans are white," or "a constellation is a pattern of stars."[16] Truth conditions vary with the sort of discourse: *weightless*/astronaut in space; *weightless*/argument; *weightless*/excuse; *weightless*/jacket. That's characteristic of natural languages (Ross 1981). Conceptual inclusions, like meaning inclusions, merely record and transmit capsules of purported cognition, including the supposedly obvious and the supposedly necessary.

Natural necessity cannot be co-extensive with conceptual (or meaning) inclusions. For one thing, necessity overflows meaning in every area: manufacturing, engineering, technology, war, finance, environmental destruction, and, of course, the discoveries of science. Three ounces of dioxin, 2,3,7,8-TCDD, is lethal, and even traces are a carcinogen. Could lethal power be the result of our meanings and concepts? How about Boron trifluoride or chlordane?

The empiricist fashion from Hume to the logical positivists was to deny there are real natural necessities and to claim that the notion is incoherent and furthermore that there is no experience of necessity.[17] Who, in the age of plutonium poisoning, could seriously claim that? Kripke (1972), signaling a broad change among philosophers away from Hume and Kant on those matters,[18] was persuasive that there are necessities discoverable through experience, particularly identities (strictly, the *real sameness* of common substances and their atomic components) whose expression employs proper names and natural kind terms.

Though I think calling necessary sameness of constitution "identity," as if there were Leibnizian sameness, was a confusing mistake, the outcome, that real necessities of constitution are discovered a posteriori, is correct, indeed evident. Just consider the chemicals mentioned above and the vast quantities of atomic waste that will outlast the English language; their necessary constitutions were discovered through experience. Lethal regularity is not just happenstance and coincidence; it is iron necessity. Any proposal to map it as a coincidence among possible worlds is just to make a logical shadow, like finger shadows on a wall, projected by conceptual constructs, not an explanation.

Conceptualists, conventionalists, and irrealists can't explain how we happen on the previously unknown natural "identities" (constitutions) at the base of physical science (gold and its atomic parts, atoms and electrons); they can't explain why you cannot make milk by churning gasoline or make a cabbage think by connecting it to a battery. Pure conceptualism or nominalism or simple occasionalism defeats explanatory science.

5. What's the Point of Analyticity, Then?

The point of analyticity is cognitive convenience. The notion "analyticity" is confusingly equivocal and was dismissed by W. V. O. Quine, who was certainly right that there is no such source of certain, necessary, and a priori truth.[19] But there's still something to account for. Sometimes "analytic," "self-evident," and "necessary" are equated (mistakenly). Sometimes a statement is considered analytic if the concept of the subject is included in the concept of the predicate, or vice versa (human/animal), and sometimes, if the definition of one term includes or is included in that of the other (perceiving/sensing, square/equal-sided).[20] Whether there is such an inclusion is a matter of empirical fact, usually about usage, for example, whether "glove" includes "mitten." And, as Quine was aware, it is not rigid or stable.

The notion of "conceptual inclusion" comes up when we are talking about conceptual organization, say, of what is involved in our notion(s) of (triggering) cause (Mackie 1974), or of persons or the world.

Indeed, much of conceptual analysis is directed at making such conceptual relations explicit for clarity and exactness of thought. Some philosophers also try to determine from our supposed conceptual organization which conceptions and facts are presupposed, and opposed. The search for the fourth condition of "S knows that p" was such a case. Peter Strawson's (1959) "descriptive metaphysics" was, I think, supposed to disclose certain lineaments of the world from the organization of our conceptions (a Kantian theme) that, of course, supposed a certain phenomenalism about the real.[21] Conceptual exploration is undoubtedly useful for being explicit and to avoid confusion, though one must be aware that contrastive conceptions (e.g., a scientist's dividing choice-makers exclusively into "settlers" and "maximizers") may arrange or rearrange the domain of "evidence" rather than reveal how things are independently.

Analyticity, meaning inclusion, is a result of meaning arrangements that simplify transitions among convictions and conjectures.[22] Such arrangements of meaning can be invented and made efficacious too. So, in law, an open-ended mutual fund is one that redeems its shares; that is so by the legislative enactment that creates the entity and defines the word. The whole insider discourse about computers, including all the meaning inclusions, is invented for practical convenience. To adapt Nelson Goodman's (1968) remark about realism in art, analyticity makes for ease of access among convictions. It's a linguistic and cognitive convenience. And it is not a sure mark of truth.

"Meaning" for this purpose can be taken narrowly for linguistic meaning, as usage that varies with discourse, or as that, plus some of the known overflow conditions presupposed in common referential practice. So, sometimes "human" means "rational animal" and sometimes also means "male or female," "born as an infant," and "certain to die," or the like. Whether broadly or narrowly used, the word "human" signifies, but does not "mean," all the other unexpressed, overflow de re necessities like having blood pressure and adrenal glands, and the hidden de re necessities, say, the species-wide genetic assembly conditions we don't know yet.

Things like "triangles have three sides," "nothing is both true and false," and "parallel lines don't cross" were long considered analytic, that is, true on *account* of the meanings involved. Hume characterized what we would call "meaning inclusions" as "relations of ideas."[23] Such relations vary because one person's meaning inclusions don't always coincide with another's; "equilateral triangle" may include "with three interior angles each less than a right angle" for some people, but not for those whose conceptions are not as articulate. "Straight line" may mean "rectilinear" for one person and "shortest distance" for another. In part that's because one's familiarity with the lexicon is partial and variant. Still, adjusted for individual variation, there are Humean relations of ideas. But they don't have a sure grip on truth or the independence from experience that was usually supposed.

Inclusions (and oppositions) of meanings are bundles of (purported) cognition,[24] giving quick access from one thought to another. It is the semantic correlate of immediate syntactical transformation, and is subject to critical appraisal. So, of course, inclusion has no assured connection with truth. In its broader forms, such inclusion is pragmatic, somewhat the way Robert Brandom (2000) characterized "material inference," though that is more inclusive. That's a useful notion because linguistic competence includes expectations and practical reliances that are not explicitly represented in the vocabulary. So, to grasp that to walk one usually has to move one's knees and hips is not something directly reflected in word meaning the way "to walk is to move one's feet" is. But it is "materially" implied, or what some others called a "conversational implication" (cf. Grice 1967a; 1967b [implicature]; and Bach 1993 for related ideas).

Necessity, once known (or believed), can be condensed into a meaning inclusion—for example, "rust is ferrous oxide" and "water is H_2O." That's useful in the sciences, arts, and crafts, for instance, for conciseness and in teaching a person what to use to dissolve rust and why. Definitions are also used to classify materials; for example, "thermoplastics change from solid to liquid under repeated applications of heat."[25] So, we manufacture meaning inclusions where we need them.

Different Grounds of Analyticity. — Analytic statements are not all the same. "A saw is a tool you cut wood with," but not strictly, because there are ice saws, metal saws, stone saws, and the like. It is a truth by a paradigm case, like "cars run on gasoline." That is different from the legally definitive, "closed-end mutual funds do not buy back their own shares" or "broker-dealers make a market in securities, buying and selling for their own accounts." In Victorian society, "spinsters are unmarried females of a certain age" was a conventional social truth, whereas "castling is one of a pair of moves that interchange and move the king's and a rook's positions in chess,"[26] and "a straight is a hand of five cards in numerical order" are truths by rulemaking for games. Stipulation is a way of making de dicto truths, like "labeled exits are ways out." But "marsupials carry their young in a pouch," if taken to give the meaning of "marsupial," and "a pouch is the bag in which marsupials carry their young" are definitions that result from usage based on observation. Lots of dictionary entries are like that, though the truth of such entries just depends empirically on how the words are used. The same is true for the names of parts and their parts in complex assemblies, like an airplane, a computer, or a sewing machine (or something one buys to assemble).

Some cases that bear the name defined fail to satisfy the conditions expressed in the meaning. That is because of idealization in the conception. "Water is an odorless, tasteless, colorless, potable liquid." That's true of distilled water. But "water" applies to what comes out of city faucets, sometimes smelling and tasting of chlorine or worse. We don't say that isn't water. In fact, generally we use the name of the characteristic main ingredient for the impure or compounded cases, like water (in cisterns, sewers, and filthy ponds) and bread (for compounds with nuts and fruit, and even with different main ingredients, like rice or zucchini, rather than grains). So, "bread is made of flour" is true as a paradigm only (or, "flour" is broadened in meaning to include rice, etc.).

Notice, the belief elements of meaning—as Wilfred Sellars felicitously called them because meanings have factual presuppositions—are central in meaning inclusions, for instance, that mammals suckle their young, and animals with hearts have kidneys. Meaning inclusions make capsules of belief to facilitate thought relations. Meanings depend on beliefs about things, that "coyotes are a species of small wolves" or "deer are herbivorous." Of course, the definitions don't ensure truth de re. To say "warm-blooded animals regulate their own body temperatures" is not by itself an assurance that some animals can do that. Yet the belief elements of dictionary meanings show up in verbal inclusions, affinities, and oppositions to other words, in "relations of ideas." So, meaning inclusions don't stand on their own as an independent guide to truth.

A Distinction. — Because there are belief elements of meaning, analytic statements can be false either as to what is included in the meaning or concept (de dicto) or as to what is designated by the words (de re). So we have to distinguish "true by definition" from "false in supposition"; they can co-occur. Thus, "caloric is the fluid consumed to make heat and light" is true by definition and false in supposition. The opposite of "true by definition" is "mistaken in definition." For example, "being necessary is being true in all possible worlds" is both false in supposition and false (mistaken) in definition (I claim), unless merely stipulated to be equivalent to "true no matter what" (or to be a notion that applies to well-defined formal contexts). Even that would only provide truth by definition while still being false in supposition, if the proposition "there really are many possible worlds" is entailed.

Errors about nature do become parts of meanings: "An atom is the smallest unit of matter" claims *Webster's Dictionary for Everyday Use* (1988). I consider that false in definition and false in supposition, whereas the correct "An atom is the smallest [complete] particle of an element" is not what ordinary speakers usually mean. There was the ancient "An atom is an indivisible unit of matter" that was true by definition and false in supposition (Democritus and Lucretius). In the seventeenth and eighteenth centuries "being material" came to mean "having only the primary qualities" (Locke), and, for some, "being material" meant "being mechanical," that is, obeying mechanistic laws and perhaps having mechanical insides like a clock. Those turned out to be false in supposition, and, I take it, would now be false in definition (i.e., not what the word means) as well. Others took "being material" to mean "having the primary qualities of size, shape, position, etc." that we might consider historically correct in definition but false in supposition because of bosons and so forth. I take it that for the most part "false in definition" comes to "the word isn't properly used that way," though sometimes it means "that is a mistake about its meaning" (say, to treat "reticent" and "reluctant" as interchangeable).

The idea that matter is hard, solid, shaped, definite in unique places, and the like would by most people still be regarded as a conceptual inclusion, as true by definition, despite its being false in supposition for hadrons and leptons and maybe the "dark matter" of the universe. Perhaps that may turn out to be a meaning inclusion by paradigm case (mentioned above) and compatible with the strict exceptions. If one were to take it that "light is those frequencies of electromagnetic radiation which directly stimulate the organ of vision" as *Penguin English Dictionary* (1982, 442) defines it, one might take it that invisible light is contradictory and, so, impossible. Of course, contradiction does not guarantee impossibility, as that example shows. Instead, those dictionary writers probably took it to be a meaning inclusion for a typical usage, not defeated by the exceptions. So, they did not regard it as false in supposition.

Meaning inclusions bridge convictions into one another, simplifying reasoning. So, the person who knows, say, from dressage the precise differences among "walk," "trot," "canter," and "gallop" directly grasps much more from "She cantered up to the gate" than we who know only that canter is an equine motion different from gallop and trot. Her material inferences would be richer than ours.

Consider four patterns of meaning inclusions whose real cases may not have the features that are analytically contained: (i) idealizations ("water"; "a calorie"—"the amount of heat to raise one cubic centimeter of water one degree centigrade"; "heat is average kinetic motion of molecules"); (ii) paradigm descriptions ("a saw is what you cut wood with"; "cars go on gas"); (iii) meaning-incorporated false belief ("atoms are the smallest particles of matter"); and (iv) analogous definitions ("life is self movement"). There, of course, may be many more.

A Conclusion. — There is no direct connection between analyticity and truth. It is not just that synonymy is contingent, suspect, and indeterminate (Quine 1951). An inclusion may be false in supposition and even become false in definition. Conceptual analysis is not a method of science or of metaphysics, though skill at it marks clarity and accuracy of thought.[27]

Since, as Kripke, Hintikka, and others argued—and as was known from centuries before—necessities (e.g., identities, i.e., real sameness) can be discovered a posteriori, it should be clear that thought and meaning cannot explain natural necessity (unless one holds that the natures of things are somehow constituted by thought). The formal necessities (see chapter 1), by contrast, are in my opinion "free creations of the human mind," in Michael Dummett's (1991) neat phrase. (Poincaré, as well, held mathematics and other pure theoretical sciences to be free creations of thought.) Many other generalizations, like the principle of inertia and certain de re "identities" (water is H_2O, sulfuric acid is H_2SO_4), are grounded a posteriori by abstraction from observed natural regularities (chapter 5); the latter may be converted into meaning inclusions, into definitions; the former in their mathematized form are further abstracted into purely formal principles that are true of idealized objects and by approximation of physical things (chapter 1), for instance, pure Newtonian mechanics. The de re necessities have to be discovered.

The idea that the basic principles of nature are explained by their being exemplifications of abstracta, or otherwise by "obtaining in all, or in a suitable subset of all possible worlds," is no explanation at all because "exemplification," "instantiation," and the like are not real relations. The a posteriori abstraction route is the only one available (chapters 5–7) to explain our knowledge of them.

6. Linguistic Reluctance

Liberality about what gets incorporated into meanings is tempered by linguistic reluctance. Why don't most of the necessities we discover become elements of current meanings? Because we don't need them, that's why. They would clutter and inhibit thought, see "iron" below. For one thing, you couldn't tell by looking or hefting (and the like) whether a frying pan is iron under the scientific definition of "iron" in Van Nostrand's *Scientific Encyclopedia* (p. 903).[28]

Traits that don't function in talk that modulates action don't join into word meanings (no matter how necessary they are in nature), and ones that overcomplicate discourse are omitted too. This is not by some overt agreement, but by the way talk is molded in practice.[29] Discourse adapts to enable its uses. The refinements of unabridged dictionary meanings often aren't mapped into popular discourse.

Economy of communication weeds out the meaning elements of words. Laziness of mind tends to keep many notions vague, like "cool," "you know," "hot," "in." Few people think that glass is not a solid (but, rather, a very slow flowing liquid); so, the expression "solid glass" is not thought inconsistent, even though it does not mean the same as "solid ice" or "solid gold." How about "milk is organic" or "diamonds are just pressurized graphite" (cf. Asimov 1972, 278)? We do not incorporate de re necessities that are behaviorally nonfunctional into meanings, like rain suits into desert packs.

Besides, with things that are really the same, at least in constitution, you can know what one is and not know what the other is: "water is H_2O"; and "sapphires are translucent blue corundum." With real sameness, say, of constitution, conception is not transitive. In fact, in the terminology of chapter 5, where a conception is "the ready ability to discern a repeatable structure in things," conception of the one feature is not sufficient for conception of the other, even when the things are really the same, for example, surfaces and the bunched molecules.

Though we don't include nonmodifying necessities in verbal meanings—say, the atomic weight, 63.54, in "copper"—we sometimes do include accidental traits that have a behavior-modifying role in discourse, say, the color of tomatoes. "Motorcars use gasoline" is not necessary; it is not even strictly true, except as paradigm, because of steam, alcohol, gasohol, bottled gas, hydrogen, and electric engines. But it is or was analytic, de dicto true. And because it is a paradigm, it is not regarded as false in supposition. It is a useful typical belief. So is "bottles have tops."

Meaning inclusions, like conceptual inclusions, are thought-to-thought and thought-to-action connections.[30] So, where what is strictly false works well, it sometimes remains, as in rules of thumb: "water is a liquid"; "wood shingles are spaced 1/8 inch apart." We use proverbs that way too—"a miss is as good as a mile"—as well as such sayings as Murphy's law ("what can go wrong, will"); Damon's law ("every job has its traps"); and conventions ("a rising tide floats all boats"; "everything takes longer than expected").

7. More on Incorporating Overflow Necessities

Hilary Putnam (1975b) resolved his Twin Earth problem about whether "water" means the same thing for those on another planet whose tasteless, odorless, potable liquid is made of xyz instead of H_2O, by saying "water" does not mean the same thing as it does to earthlings. That is ambiguous. For, by his supposition, the sense meaning might be the same, as is the rose smell of genuine roses and of some perfume artifacts. Whether the linguistic meaning would be the same or not depends on whether the microstructure is partly incorporated into the linguistic meaning, as "H_2O" is for many earthlings nowadays (but was not for most of human history). If Twin discourse incorporated "xyz" into the meaning there, then the word "water" would be homonymous between earthlings and Twins as Putnam supposed. But if the Twins went only so far as "colorless, odorless, tasteless, potable liquid when distilled," a perception meaning, the linguistic meanings (lexical meanings) for earthlings and Twins might be the same, though the ranges of reference would be disjoint because of the microconditions and their water sciences would diverge.

That indicates that sense meaning (perception meaning) plus linguistic meaning is not by itself sufficient to determine reference, because the overflow conditions may be diverse or indeterminate. That's an important consequence, and one reinforcing what I take to be Putnam's correct idea that if one were a brain in a vat one could not *mistakenly* think what we do about the world, because one could not think (a lot of) what we do about the world at all.[31]

It is useful to distinguish the following modes of meaning: (i) *linguistic* meaning, what one knows when one knows the verbal contrasts, affinities, and dictionary meaning (at least competently for discourse); (ii) the *reference*, the attachment of a word in a particular use (or class of uses) to particular objects (correctly or incorrectly); (iii) the *extension*, or denotation, that is, the objects forming the range of things to which the word applies (in the same sense and with the same known overflow conditions); (iv) the *signification*, the conditions of applicability (including the whole overflow), that is, the conditions the objects in the domain have to satisfy in order for the word to apply to them (loosely, truth conditions for "a is F"); (v) the *overflow signification*, the part of the truth conditions that are not part of the linguistic meaning, and (vi) the *sense* meaning, the experiential-perceptual basis for a word, for example, for "magenta," "fuchsia," or for "ascites," or for "wanting chocolate."[32] Men often lack sense meaning for color words familiar to women like magenta, mauve, taupe, and so on.

When we use a natural kind word—say, "lead" or "tomato"—acquired in talk about its real cases, we by usage incorporate the de re necessities for such things (whether known or not) into the truth conditions for assertions about things of the kind or about the kind itself, that is, into what an object has to satisfy to bear the name. But only some of that signification—the lexical part—belongs to the linguistic meaning; the rest, say, "having certain electrostatic behavior" or "being made of organic molecules," belongs to the overflow signification, some of which may be mastered in material implications (say, how it looks or feels or weighs) and the remainder of which belongs to the overflow de re requirements for such things, like the plant's genetic sequence.

One can know zinc is a bluish-white metal, an element, and in trace amounts needed for the human diet without knowing, perhaps even misunderstanding, its atomic number, atomic weight, density or chemical properties, and its contrast to pewter, nickel, bronze, and brass. But nothing one is talking about will ever be zinc without satisfying those other conditions. Thus, if you mistakenly call pewter "zinc" the grounds of your mistake may lie beyond what is accessible for you to know.

Philosophical arguments based on suppositions not known to be really possible are unreliable. They have to be employed circumspectly. Possible-worlds mappings of counterfactuals are particularly awkward because they don't *explain* real contrary-to-fact situations and conflate deeply different sorts of conditionals as if they were the same. Further, such mappings treat as extensional over individuals truths like natural necessities that cannot be about merely possible individuals or classes, since there are none.

So, to suppose gold might have had a different atomic constitution is as vacuous as is supposing Julius Caesar had different parents. It's not that imagining can't be useful or inspiring; it's just swampy, not only by being incomplete, but by inviting false judgments (cf. chapter 8).

8. Conclusion

Many verbally consistent counterfactual suppositions are neither true nor false; they are de re vacuous. The counterfactuals with earned truth values are conceptually anchored in actual individuals or their potentials and in the real natures of things, for example, what lead would have done in vinegar. That aims my inquiry toward explaining how there can be such grounding common natures of things (chapter 7) and how such natures can come within human cognition (chapter 5), and then at the distinctive ability of humans for recognizing such structures (chapter 6).

We need four more things to round out this account of the consequences of the hidden necessities of things: (i) a sketch of theories of truth and their limitations in order to disclose that truth is a kind of rightness of thinking involving the real sameness of what we think and what is so (chapter 4); (ii) a sketch of the relationships of perception to understanding and of the way abstraction makes remote things and events into the content, not just the referents, of our current and habitual judgment (chapter 5); (iii) an explanation of why some aspects of thought are irreducibly nonphysical (chapter 6); and (iv) some reasons why there are intelligible, repeatable structures that are active in, and indeed constitutive of, the real things that are the subjects of the natural sciences and of our ordinary comprehension of the world (chapter 7). Let's turn to truth next.

CHAPTER 4

Truth

The trouble about truth comes in part from taking features of sentences to be features of thought, from imagining that something other than thinking causes truth,[1] and from expecting to find a single basic, even reductive analysis of "it is true that" and "it is false that."

Truth, globally, is right thinking, detectable as right to thought alone, as to what is or is not.[2] Thus, *what I think is true just when what I think really is what is so.* But there are lots of ways that can come about, for instance, by sight or by report; the most fundamental is our own perceptual knowing. The other ways are derivative, as will become clear.

"True" is a plastic notion, adapting in diverse contexts[3] and needing multiple analyses to articulate its diversities of meaning.[4] Though the expression "is true" has general all-purpose meanings—"is so" and "is what to think" and "is what to say," for example[5]—and though it applies denominatively to statements, sentences, reports, theories, and the like, its signification adapts in diverse practices like arithmetic, logic, sciences, law, and even in contrary-to-fact speculation, so that (i) a univocal analysis won't express the diverse, even divergent, context-bound meanings; and (ii) there isn't a "core" notion with only "accidental" differential features, as Crispin Wright (1992) proposed, though that is a very helpful idea. Rather, the meanings have different "overflow" conditions in differing practices. For instance, sometimes bifurcation is required for truth or falsity (in applied classical logic); sometimes there can be no truth-value gaps (cf. chapter 3); and sometimes one or another form of cognitive accessibility is required (e.g., constructive proof).

Further, cognitive accessibility requirements can be diverse—for instance, "warranted assertability" versus "constructive provability" versus "pragmatic verifiability"—and sometimes such conditions are part of what one explicitly means, and sometimes they are overflow conditions in the context or practice.

The textbook theories of truth (e.g., correspondence, coherence, pragmatic, redundancy, disquotational, etc.) aren't generalizable into a unified global theory, and, as usually expressed, fail to explain what they purport to. For instance, the correspondence theories[6] that are "same thing" theories don't explain how what is true is the same as what is so (see below).

Sometimes there are no independent standards for verification or comparison: "The Industrial Revolution was more destructive than Colonialism." What is the measure among movements of relative destructiveness? Is it determinate? Truth, there, may be a craft-based matter among historians, or perhaps a matter of interpretation of other data. Sometimes, in fact frequently, there can be truths and falsities even when we don't acknowledge any independent fact of the matter: "That's an exact fit" (clothes), where length and cut varies with fashion, and "fit" varies with culture and class.

Judgment flows and swirls, as sensible awareness does; our awake cognitive states are continuous. Judgment includes whatever is contained in one's habitual locked-on and flowing reality commitment. Philosophers tend to scab that over with sentences to match-up with pairings from reality that we call "facts" or "states of affairs." We need such sentential formulations to explain the formal structures of reliable reasoning. But the commitments of flowing intelligent consciousness don't often divide up into such neat units, except by obtuse abstraction. The continuous judgment of a pianist's cadenza or a reader's comprehension can only be crudely imagined as a rapid fire of verbalized sentences. It is instead intelligent commitment, recognition, and execution in action.

"Belief" among philosophers has, however, become associated with sentences, whereas judgment, the maker and bearer of truth or falsity, changes like images on a turning mirror, being many at once, continuous, and mixed among reality commitments (existential commitments), characterizations (attributions/conceptions), and identifications (that "x is the same as y," and "that's what Y *is*, a human"). Judgment in action is more like the flowing response of a video camera than the imperceptible stuttering of celluloid film. When we isolate commitments by reflection, we get something more like sentential still photographs. The stills are immensely useful, but they are not phenomenologically fundamental.

Real things, events, and their conditions are intentionalized, enveloped, by animal awareness and by human judgment (chapter 5). The independent, even physical, realities are coincidently intentional when perceived. Yet only intelligent awareness involves truth. So, I survey some accounts of truth here, looking for the explanatory elements and conclude that we need to move from abstraction (chapter 5) to judgment, aiming to disclose that when what I think is true, what I think really is what is so. Perhaps the most fundamental and convincing reason will be that otherwise we can't explain our knowledge of the remote, the universal, and the purely abstract, or satisfyingly explain false judgment either (chapter 8).

An Historical Comment. — The seventeenth-century's deterministic, mechanical, and corpuscular reconception of the physical world as a system of mathematizable quantitative changes endures and is indispensable even now. Descartes, as I mentioned, decided intrinsic "substantial forms" favored in late scholastic-Aristotelian thought had no explanatory function in the new quantitative science. That obviated "abstraction" of forms as a native, essential, operation of human intelligence and as source of abstract ideas (in favor of innate ideas). No major philosophers (except perhaps Husserl and Merleau-Ponty) have since seen a need to resuscitate the idea of explanatory forms in nature. But as this inquiry aims to display, we do need both the idea of physically constitutive intelligible structures (chapter 7) and the idea of constant, native abstraction (chapter 5) to explain the cognition that involves understanding.

Descartes thought abstract ideas were innate, not derived from particulars by abstractive separation of what is repeatable in the particulars, and his British successors eventually dropped both innateness and abstract ideas from their theories (cf. Berkeley's arguments that there are no abstract ideas). What then was meant by "idea" changed into vague or indifferent image originating with sensation (Berkeley), and then into Hume's "ideas are faint copies of impressions." That meant that truth needed a new explanation too; and it gradually emerged as fidelity of judgment to the world by replication of it in consciousness (representationalism) or constitution of it by thought (phenomenalism), and, eventually, was explained as brain states correlating with (or the same as) true sentences. Animal conscious perception—say, animal hearing or sight—though discarded by Descartes, was eventually reacknowledged, but was gradually merged with human perception (e.g., of tunes), as if the difference of humans from other animals were only the possession of language (as complex communication system), for example, the variations of Dretske, Dennett, and Fodor. "Perception" and "judgment" became fungible ("animal judgment," cf. Hurley and Nubbs [2006]). Nowadays "abstract idea" is primarily associated with general words, and conceptions are treated as meanings of general words.

As philosophy leaned into its twentieth-century linguistic turn, and sentential logic developed, the notion of truth peculiar to humans became associated with verbally expressed statements and eventually with features of the expressions themselves, the sentences, as inquiries into meaning and reference developed. So, now philosophers talk as if "truth" is a semantic notion, even primarily a feature of sentences apart from their actual use by speakers.[7] It is to such more recent conceptions that I look with disappointment for an explanation of truth (and falsity).

1. Adjusting Some Theories of Truth: Correspondence, Coherence, and Pragmatic Truth

In brief, here is what we find: a correspondence theory is initially attractive; yet a match of diverse things, like sentences and facts, will not explain truth. Sameness of judgment and reality, not a match-up, is required (but not identity) and has to be explained. "Coherence" and "pragmatic" theories serve limited domains as local accounts of truth, but such "hang-together" and "work-out" theories presuppose a prior notion of truth. The others, like the redundancy[8] and disquotational proposals, while useful, perhaps indispensable for some formal contexts (where "fact" is the explanatory consequence of "truth" [chapter 1]), don't otherwise explain truth. The outcome is that some further explanatory feature is required for a general account. Here are some details.

(1) Correspondence. — Correspondence of pairs with different components will not ensure or explain truth: not by sentence-parts corresponding with fact-parts, not by thought-parts corresponding with reality-parts. For, pick any match-up relation (any correlation) you like, say, picturing, or modeling, or replicating, and suppose it is satisfied. Why is that "truthmaking"? A further account is needed, particularly to avoid matching by mere happenstance, like a mistyping.

Part-by-part match-up accounts, like "scale models," "mechanical drawings," or "pictures" (Wittgenstein 1922), fail because (i) the supposed parallel decompositions (that Russell and Wittgenstein constructed for atomic propositions and facts) were merely speculative for natural languages, and (ii) the supposed match-up didn't *explain* truthmaking. Something was missing.

The logical atomists' program of double decomposition into ultimate parts of reality to match-up with ultimate parts of thought (or parts of sentences) pair by pair turned out to be only promissory, or a mere construct.[9] It was an idealization based on the predicate-logic notation of function and argument, and did not fit natural languages whose components have no particular connection with fundamental ontological units. For Russell (even in 1948) the true proposition was still, part by part (subject, relation, predicate), to correspond (match-up by naming) with a complete complex of compresence, a spatiotemporal coincidence of (universal) properties, like coincident spotlights on a stage, that is the thing or event. But the accounts of the "parts," and particularly the Platonism about properties and the idea that individuals are laminates of the properties coincident at space-time loci, were unconvincing—especially the inarticulate presuppositions about spatiotemporal individuation.[10] And even if the double decomposition into matching parts could be devised, something would have to *make* it truthmaking (see "two-name" accounts, below).

Wittgenstein addressed the latter issue with the proposal that the true atomic proposition is a picture of an atomic fact. We were supposed to see that "being a picture of" is "being true," the way a mechanical drawing displays a machine, or an accident sketch shows a scene. But "being a picture of" ensures no truth (cf. Goodman 1968) because picturing involves construal, and can depict what never happened at all. Eventually correspondence by replication dried up, to be succeeded by semantic—particularly sentential—correlations (e.g., Austin, Chisholm, and Davidson, below), like shoes that fit.

An Historical Comment. — The notion of a representational match-up had become attractive after "the immediate awareness principle" and "the way of ideas" were adopted (the seventeenth century). Elements of inner thought (particularly certain ideas of sense, the primary qualities) were thought to represent outer reality to inner awareness. So, when one rightly judges objects to be as they appear, the subjective experience (the ideas composing propositions) replicates public reality. The components of judgment and the data of awareness were thus taken to be productions of the mind, usually ideas or impressions. When philosophy underwent its twentieth-century linguistic turn, the key representations for use in the sciences were construed to be sentences that, when true, correlate with the world. That schema had been anticipated as early as 1325 by William of Ockham, who thought a "line-up" of the parts of judgment with the parts of reality was made when the subject term of a sentence denotes what is the same as, or is included among, what the predicate term denotes: "Socrates is mortal" is true just when "Socrates" names one of the things "mortal" names. That was his two-name theory of predication, the kind of extensional analysis that reappears in first-order logic. It was fairly typical for medieval logicians to regard common names as decomposing logically into individual names, and to regard predicates as (i) decomposing into ranges of particulars (Ockham), though (ii) some thought predicates name common natures (e.g., "human"), and others thought they name concepts, abstracta. Frege's nineteenth-century view was something like the latter. They were all versions of two-name theories, a notion that still persists.

New Correspondence. — Instead of the two-name schema, John Austin offered a correlation account that he called a "correspondence" theory.[11] He said, "[A] statement is said to be true when the historic state of affairs to which it is correlated by the demonstrative conventions (the one to which it "refers") is of a type which the sentence used in making it, is correlated by the descriptive conventions" (Austin 1950, 121–22).

So, an expressed statement is true just when the state of affairs it designates is one it is for descriptively: "John went home" is true when the situation "it refers to" (John went home) is one it is for describing. That's a sufficient condition (perhaps also supposing "and otherwise not"—thus, being necessary as well) but it is not an explanatory analysis. It is a correlation of the expression with a situation when what is said is so. It does not explore what makes the statement so. And it does not cover the vast majority of true judgments that are not sententially expressed, for instance, the constant word-recognition judgment when you are reading this, or the continuous stream of judgments in action when you do something requiring skill, like driving a car, tying a shoe, or dialing a phone. Such intelligent commitments are all either true or false, but almost none are statements. When you are talking to others, you are aware, defeasibly, that you've said what you mean; that exhibits itself when it isn't so and you take something back, qualify or amend it. Austin's account of truth of statements does not cover that, and further, presupposes truth of thought (judgment) that goes unexplained. So his is really not an account of truth, and won't cover the case where someone says, "That's nothing for you to get offensive over," by verbal slip, for "offended" and yet thinks what is so, when not successfully saying what is so. How about a billboard that says "You are speeding"; does it go on and off being true depending on which drivers pass it?

Roderick Chisholm's correspondence theory (1977, 138) has the same and more limitations. Stripped of its technicalities (see Kirkham 1995, 133, for a fuller statement), it comes to saying: "A particular sentence is true just in case the state of affairs that it expresses obtains." Suppose we have an accidental sentence and mere coincidence: three airport limo drivers are holding up signs that just happen to be in order "Jones," "Cheats," "Smith" as Jones and Smith come out while Jones is cheating Smith. Is the accidental sentence true?

I suppose Chisholm, like Austin, meant verbally expressed cognitive commitments, not just lists of sentences on a blackboard without context. Still, Chisholm's account, like Austin's, lacks an explanatory element, and additionally supposes a (Platonic) realm of expressible states of affairs, even impossible ones, that either obtain or not, without any explanation of what "obtaining" is, or how states of affairs, that exist no matter what, could be the same as or constitute any physical event.

Donald Davidson (1986) and Marcia Cavell (1993), and other late-twentieth-century philosophers, held that sentences are the bearers of truth or falsity, and that "truth" is a semantic notion, in fact, a sameness between what a sentence means and what is so, that can be illustrated with Tarski's disquotational model for formal discourse: "'p' is true, if and only if p." Thus, "there are no tigers here" is true just in case there are no tigers here. That is an inviting idea. Davidson thought it would ground a general account of sentence meaning in natural languages as the truth conditions for well-formed sentences. The "match-up" problem is avoided because no match is needed. But the cost is that we are told we assert, and believe, *sentences,* and we don't. Even to say that sentences are true or false (on a test, say) is denominative, attributive, not the intrinsic predication Davidson needs. For all truth can't be by extrinsic denomination any more than all intentionality can be merely attributive (as Daniel Dennett once proposed). We use sentences for assertion, that is, to express judgments; but judgments, both true and false, embrace a lot more than just what we assert, and nothing in the Davidson-Cavell account even begins to explain the truth of judgments.

The Davidson-Cavell proposal has other difficulties because (i) sentences are treated as if their meanings are independent of linguistic context and speaker use—that is, as if fixed objectively and combinatorily in the language as a function of all the others—and as if truth or falsity is not dependent on there being someone's belief, but belongs to sentences underivatively; (ii) the view implicitly supposes an infinite domain of facts and impossibilities to be item equivalent to an infinity of potential sentences; and (iii) the proposal supposes that natural language sentence tokens amount to assertions apart from anyone's definite judgment. But well-formed sentences don't: "The sun turns faces black." (Also see Kripke's [1982, 70 n.60] critical comment about Davidson's supposing the formal structure of natural languages is that of first-order quantification.)

Look at the general formula Richard Kirkham (1995, 132) proposed as a summary for both Chisholm and Austin, and a general pattern for correspondence theories: "(t) {t is true if [(Ex) (tRx) & (x obtains)]}." Here "t" could be a judgment, a statement, a proposition, even a sentence. "R" could be "asserts that," "says that," "expresses that." And "x" could be a positive, negative, conditional, modal, etc. state of affairs—but what is a state of affairs? The domain of states of affairs is ontologically problematic whether or not one is a Platonist. And "obtains" is shrouded in even more smoky mystery than "exemplifies" and "instantiates."

Chisholm, Davidson, and many others think a sentence is true just in case what it expresses (means) obtains. But that's too strong. It allows for sentences to be incidentally true (e.g., machine generated or written by mistake), and it is also too weak because far more judgments are true than are ever sententially expressed (note the shoe-tying and reading examples again). Besides, sentence meaning is context dependent. (That sentence shows that.) Truth, therefore, is not, underivatively and undenominatively, a relation between sentences and the world.

Davidson and many other philosophers thought what a sentence means is what is sufficient and necessary for it to be true ("meaning is truth conditions"). But given my repeated showing here, that practically anything we say has truth conditions that overflow anything the language determines (chapter 1), we cannot accept the consequence that sentences mean, rather than just require, things that are totally inaccessible to competent speakers, indeed, things for which there are no extant means of expression (as there was no way for millennia to express the molecular conditions for water or gold). That conflicts with, and I think falsifies, Davidson's view of meaning in a natural language and of linguistic competence. For ordinary linguistic competence doesn't extend as far as Davidson's theory needs, namely, to all the truth conditions for a claim like "water is lighter when frozen." Meaning would have to be restricted to truth conditions as far as the language determines them. But then satisfying the conditions of meaning would not be enough to determine truth.

Further, the more remote oppositions and affinities of meaning (linguistic meaning) for words in English are unknown to most of the speakers whose working competence embraces less than a tenth of the vocabulary of the language. That would mean on Davidson's theory of meaning that they usually don't fully grasp the meanings of their sentences because they don't know their contrastive truth conditions (which he thinks are determined by the entire language, though not by overflow conditions of the physical world). That situation is worsened by the automatic polysemy of natural languages (see Ross 1981) where the affinities and oppositions among words change with new verbal and pragmatic contexts, "He *missed* his/chance/turn/train/dog/appointment/e-message." There are concurrent new usages, meaning adaptations, by other speakers that are inaccessible to a given speaker at a given time. Davidson accommodates such phenomena, as he does metaphor, by thinking of them as diverse uses, rather than as diverse meanings of a common word. That, as one can see from simple examples, like *catch*/a ball, a cold, a mistake, a stitch, is just ad hoc; the meanings do differ.

The sentential accounts of truth would make sentences underivatively true or false. Thus, a machine that produces random well-formed English sentences is randomly producing truths and falsities. In fact a digital clock is always saying something (we do ask: "What does the clock say?" but we mean it denominatively). Most of us would think unused sentences dropped from a machine don't say anything at all; they are like suits on a rack, nobody's clothes yet. Now, there is no harm in regarding machine-made sentences as denominatively true or false, as they would be if someone used them, like saying a food on a shelf is filling, as it would be if consumed. But that's an analogous usage of "true" and "false" and not the one that needs explaining, since nothing will be true or false in that sense unless some judgments are intrinsically true or false, regardless of whether they are sententially expressed. The sententialist theories substitute a by-product, sentences, for the originating judgments. It's like taking a print to be the museum original. Nevertheless, I acknowledge that sometimes there can be no same-judgment without the words, say, "Life is a bowl of cherries."

A gauge that reads, or sounds out, "low fuel" would be telling you something derivatively from a genuine saying by a person. Readouts are a by-product of our judgmental and linguistic abilities, but not the genuine article, even though we would say, "It says 'empty'" and we might also say, "That's true." Sententialists take truth to be successful signing, like good road signs, correlated—even by design, a curve—with what they express. Signing and meaning are not the same. Correlation of sentence and fact is not enough for truth. The priority of understanding over linguistic expression is being smudged. No matter how tight the correlation of sign with situation, something more is needed for non-denominative empirical truth, namely, true judgment.

Correspondence theories lack an explanatory element. We cannot reduce the thinking that is true or false to the sentences by which it is expressed, despite the confidence of Sellars, Brandom, and McDowell that thought is language consequent and language embodied, though much of it is, of course. I would have thought it obvious that language develops as an outcome of knowledge among people who need to communicate with general notions, and is refined and ramified with use. So we are still left with the classical problem of explaining the truth of judgments. Such an inquiry looks at judgment as an *intelligent* activity, one that typically begins with direct perception, and includes the remote, the universal, and the speculative by further abstraction, as I explain (chapter 5).[12]

(2) Coherence: Constitutive and Relative. — Coherence has its uses in explaining truth, especially truth within thought constructs, but won't do as a comprehensive and independent account of truth. Let's distinguish comprehensive coherence from relative (local) coherence. Comprehensive coherence includes all one's judgments of a given domain, perhaps even all one's judgments without qualification. On such a conception, truth, like strength in a stick-built house, comes from mutual support, but, unlike the house, without relying on an outside foundation (Donald Davidson is a recent example of such a thinker). Some philosophers, conceptualists, think the "space of reasons" is like that. In contrast, relative (local) coherence supposes a background or foundation to begin with, like axioms or rules or, perhaps, the practice of some craft; or a domain of appearances. So it is a local notion primarily applying to formal and social constructs, games and the like.

Coherence whether comprehensive or local doesn't require bifurcation (truth or falsity for all well-formed statements) because it doesn't automatically require that any arbitrary well-formed assertion be either coherent or incoherent with the body of accepted propositions. Brand Blanshard (1941, 206), however, was a comprehensive idealist who seemed to hold bifurcation, and held that consistency among propositions is what truth is. C. J. Ducasse (1944, 325) objected that "no coherent set of propositions can be comprehensive of all propositions," and "for any coherent (consistent) group A, there is an equally coherent but logically opposed group B, and they can't both be true." But later coherentists like J. O. Young are not impressed with that objection because the relevant body of propositions is the ones one believes, not just any group; and some coherentists suppose, further, that one has sensory experiences that are a nontruth base for coherent experience but thereby limit the domain of relevant propositions. Davidson (1986) seemed to favor some version of that design. The details can be sidestepped for now, while we consider whether all such theories are presuppositionally regressive.

Even though coherence for such writers, running back to Hempel and the logical positivists, is usually more than mere formal and semantic consistency, requiring mutual confirmation, overall simplicity, neat explanatory order, and other conditions like predictive fruitfulness, and testability, for which there are not automatically relevant competitors (cf. Davidson 1986), such theories run into another sort of problem: they are presuppositionally regressive.

For coherence at each level depends on presupposed coherence from a further and prior standpoint, where the embracing coherence requires more than the included one, say, nesting in a wider framework of claims or with different sorts of coherence factors (for instance, reason giving ones). Such nesting is not merely a consequence of first-level truth, but is an explanatory a prerequisite for it. Thus, the explanation of truth neither "bottoms out" nor "tops out." There's just a regress.

J. O. Young (2001a, b), who recognizes a regress objection, thinks it is benign whereas I say it is an interminable chain of *pre*-requisites for any outcome at all. Every such coherence depends on a prior and distinctly based coherence, without end. That's different from our ordinary notions of "truth" where each first-order level generates a reflection, but as a logical consequence, not an explanatory prerequisite, the way "'p' is true" generates "It is true that 'p is true,'" and so on, as far as one likes. Whereas, to be coherent at level n (say, perceptually), the belief has to be coherent at level n + 1 as a precondition, and that requires coherence at diverse level n + n without end.

So, truth and coherence cannot in general be the same thing.[13] Human cognition, instead, is built up on a platform of animal cognition, with constant abstraction aimed developmentally by natural interests and refined by social development. While one can't step outside the fabric of all of one's convictions to assess whether the world is as one thinks it to be, supposing the world is not or might not be at all as one thinks it is leads to an explanatory dead end with no gain over supposing that things are on the whole as we think they are. (That's a realist's analogue of Davidson's idea that most of one's beliefs are true.) I suggest it as a methodological principle that in philosophy one ought to reason from what one thinks to be so, rather than from suppositions one merely entertains, at least until what one thinks displays inconsistencies or unpalatable consequences. That's the practice followed here.

Truth in Formal Thinking. — In formal thinking, consistency relative to a base makes every statement that is authorized by that form of thinking to be fully satisfied (verified, confirmed, and fulfilled) by everything of which it is authorized to be said. The formal system generates the objects by which it is satisfied. Axiomatized systems are a good example. The thinking, as practiced form, constructs/projects the compliant "realities" that the authorized statements express: so "'p' is true just in case p," and "$2 + 2 = 4$" just in case $2 + 2 = 4$. But the explanatory order is by constitution from truth to fact, not the reverse (chapter 1). You can show this by inventing a game that will have objects (tricks, positions, innings, hands, etc.) and rules that you define, and truths for internal events, for instance, which of arbitrary hands of cards is the better. The existence of the items—say a trick or a hand, or pieces or board positions—is a consequence of the structure you invent. And inconsistencies lurking in the thinking may cause surprising anomalies; but they are still internally generated. That, of course, is also my hypothesis about the objects of arithmetic, set theory, and the other formal sciences.

The formal thinking that makes the truths constitutes the compliant objects and situations—for example, natural numbers (abstracted from multitude), plane figures (abstracted from physical shapes), games, compositions, diatonic musical elements (notes, rests, meters, etc.)—abstracted from sounds and natural rhythms and intervals. We basically start with concepts either invented or abstracted and with initial truths by abstraction, simplification, or fiat—for instance, "every natural number has a successor by one (chapter 1) or "every chromatic scale-tone is separated from the next by one half-diatonic step" for a chromatic scale, and rules of transformation (that need not be explicit, but can be complex as are the rules of diatonic harmony). Note, for an object to be generated by a system it does not have to be actively thought of by anyone ever using the system; being an inevitable outcome of permitted transformations is enough. So, there are natural numbers and irregular polygons no one will ever think of. The explanation of there being more English sentences than anyone will ever make is more complex because the vocabulary alters by polysemy and accretion that depends on actual uses, besides all the merely potential transformations. I don't think "there exist (there are) x's" means the same in "there exist (are) numbers no one will ever think of" and "there exist (are) sentences no one will ever formulate"; for the former are determinate, while the latter are indeterminate potentialities.

Because we can't use the anemic notion of "implies" that we find in propositional logic for a general definition of consistency, and because a more robust notion, like "entailment," involves some thicker notion of truth as well (see Walker 1989, 39, 144–45, 192–93), some philosophers have argued that one could not even explain coherence (lack of logical conflict) as constituting truth for formal systems without a prior notion of truth.

Generally where the truths are about realities that exist independently of the system of thought, coherence as truth constituting will require an additional notion of truth that connects the system of assertion to the domain of independent realities. Otherwise, a coherence account has to treat the perceived, the experienced world and its hidden features, as constructive conceptualism does—the way I want to treat formal objects—as constructions of what is right to think.

(3) Pragmatism: Limited and Derivative Too. — Pragmatism, taken broadly—"what is true is what holds up in experience"—also has its uses. It has many versions, some quite sophisticated, that I generally group as "work-out" accounts. Pragmatism is the idea that the truth of a belief (or a theory) is its working out in experience, its serving our "interests in the way of believing" (William James) or, in its epistemic form, its being approved by some (perhaps ideal) community of appraisers (C. S. Peirce), or fulfilling the expectations of some designated group (e.g., eschatological pragmatism [John Hick]).

Pragmatic truth cannot be a global account of truth because of the same kind of regress that afflicts coherence. If the working-out is not constitutive of what is so, it has to bottom out in something else. That some belief does work out, or is approved by its appraisers or that some expectation is fulfilled, cannot always depend on a further approval or authentication: for truth would always be unexplained. We'd have the same sort of regress found in coherentism.

Peirce avoided such regress with "an idealized community of scientists" whose final agreement constitutes truth. But that led to a final surrender to idealism; as Mautner (1996, 414) put it, Peirce thought matter is "effete mind," and "ultimate reality is mental." So, Peirce was willing to accept that in the end ideal agreement constitutes truth, that is, constitutes reality. Pragmatism pushed consistently is a kind of idealism, a construction of reality (Zanstra 1962). That has been the temptation even of physicalist philosophers, like Nelson Goodman and Richard Rorty, and does seem the natural outcome of pragmatism taken globally by materialists: physicalist idealism—an anomaly.

Sometimes pragmatism is understood more locally: "to be satisfactory" is "to be so." That holds for various crafts, arts, and social practices, and for subjective appraisals. The truth of "she's the one for me" may be fulfillment of my expectation or surpassing it. The truth of "that's the latest fashion" is being considered so (by the relevant community). And "that's neat enough" may be no more than satisfying someone. Sometimes the truth is "what counts as so" by some interpersonal standard or by some arbiter, but is not an entirely independent reality. So people measure a beam: "exactly 12 feet," one reports (to the fractions of the craft, and not to just any unit of length, like 128ths.). Skilled judgment counts to read the measure too (cf. Hacking, 1983); not everyone's reading counts.

Where there isn't an independent measure, "not good enough" is the same as "not so." Piano tuning is an example because perfect overall intervals are excluded from equal temperament, and correct tuning needs adjustment in the middle octave to fit the instrument (the temperament octave), and of the octaves, successively, by slight "flattening" of the fifths and "sharpening" of the thirds (e.g., "E" a third above middle C [= 256 cps] is tuned up from 320 cps to 322.54 cps—all this assuming

A = 440 cps), continuing proportionately as one goes "out from the center" (the temperament octave). But such mathematical values are only approximate because even an oscilloscope cannot ensure good tuning. Whether the piano is well tuned is a matter of meeting a craftsman's or a performer's expectations relative to the instrument. I take it that Hilary Putnam (pretty much in accord with Nelson Goodman's last chapter of *Languages of Art* [1968]) thinks successful science is like that.

A belief is pragmatically true or false just when either a subjective or skilled, or otherwise regulated experience, as experience, is all that counts for its being so or not. And furthermore, pragmatists reason that we have no cognitive access to any reality beyond what we experience (consider, e.g., Putnam's internal realism about science).

The message from the hidden necessities, that are central here, is that reality *does* overflow experience. The nature of water did not change as expectations about its microstructure, its critical temperature (at which it acts explosively), and the sonoluminescence of droplets did. So the question as to how what I think can be what is so, when I know something, is still to be answered.

(4) No Advance Is Made by the Eliminative, Redundancy, and Disquotational Hypotheses Either. — The merits of these hypotheses are for formal contexts. The disquotational option, reductively to eliminate "true" as a predicate with content, not only lacks explanatory force outside formal contexts, it locates the problem as if it concerned the relationship of a linguistic item, a sentence that could be produced by machines, to the obtaining of what it conventionally means (as if ambiguity were no issue or overflow truth conditions do not affect truth). Besides, not all the sentential uses of "is true" in natural language can be disquotationally converted into the "object language." As W. V. O. Quine pointed out, "(p) is true" cannot always be reduced, even formally, by simply asserting p. An incompleteness proof like Gödel's has to characterize truths that cannot be stated. "Semantic ascent" is for talking about the world by talking about what we say about the world, as Quine remarked (1970, 11–12; cf. Kirkham 1995, 319). And we need that for various purposes, one being oblique discourse, for instance, "What he just said is true," and for concessions, "Maybe that's true but consider . . . ."

2. Sameness of What Is Thought and What Is So

Because the accounts mentioned either lack an explanatory element (as does correspondence theory), or have to ground out in a further account of truth (as do coherence and pragmatic theories), or function primarily for formal contexts (as do disquotation theory and formal coherence), we need to look for a further explanation for what I think to be what is so. We need an explanation that does not require that what is so be a consequence of or a construction from what it is right to think, but one that acknowledges the independence of most things it is right to think, though not always *as* thought of.

What I think is true just when what I think *is* (that is, is really the same thing as) something that is so. That can happen (i) when right thinking constitutes the things that are so (as in formal thinking and the efficacious thinking that brings about what is asserted, like legislative enactment and promising),[14] and (ii) when what is thought is really (the same as) what is so, as when we perceive something (where what I hear *is* the singing and the song, or what I see *is* the hitting and the assault). For that, one needs realities presented in two ways, both abstractly and concretely at once; a cat hears the singing (sounds) but not the song, as we do.

So, we have to inquire into abstractive perception (chapter 5) and into its foundation in things (chapter 7), and into whether judgment (chapter 6) is physically reducible, say, to neurophysiology.

Overall, the classic formulations—like "truth is rightness of understanding perceptible to the understanding alone" (Anselm) or "veritas est adequatio mentis et rei,"[15] and "truth is thinking what is really so, to be so"—capture the idea that truth is a kind of rightness of thinking, a kind of getting it right. The backbone through the diverse uses of "is true" is that there really is right judgment, detectable as right by (someone's) understanding alone, that is truth. How do we accomplish that?

CHAPTER 5

Perception and Abstraction

What is perceived is what is so, though not formally identical with it, just as the magnified text for a person wearing glasses is really the same as the unmagnified text on its own. They are not strictly identical, for the text can exist without being magnified while the text thus-being-magnified and read can't exist without the unmagnified text. Moreover, both the text as the particular marks and as an intelligible message are in exactly the same place and accessed by way of the same sensory processes. That should lead us, upon reflection to follow, to realize that what is known really is what is so.

First, I describe some aspects of human perception with its coincident abstraction (focused by conceptions) that grounds true (and false) judgment in reality.[1] Then I describe how that native activity, abstraction, makes spatiotemporally and causally and historically remote particulars and universal situations present in judgment—for example, that ice cracks, that the Milky Way is billions of stars, that Rome fell, and that lead is unmagnetizable. By contrast, a fundamental weakness of opposed views of knowledge, as will become clear, is that they cannot explain how those can be the *very* things we know.

Abstraction, which is a constant natural—indeed, native—condition of human awareness, has to be focused by conceptions (operative concepts) to present repeatable structures that are, otherwise, entirely saturated in individuals things, saturated the way the function $N \times N = N^2$ is saturated in $5 \times 5 = 25$ and also in $4 \times 4 = 16$ (really there, but accessible only to one who thinks a certain way).

Without constant conceptions focusing abstraction, we can't explain our nonperceptual knowledge of remote realities like "Caesar was assassinated,"[2] "the United States is usually at war," or "the French Revolution happened after the English one," and "zinc is a metal," because we can't otherwise explain how such situations are made what is known. Such knowing is not just knowledge *about* sentences or representations or reports (though sometimes it is). Rather, it is quite typically a grasp of realities. That requires the remote or universal situation to be intentionally present even when its presence is wraithlike, like a childhood excursion remembered, or wrapped in anachronistic or made-up images like one's knowledge of Marco Polo's travels. We need to explain that.

The abstractions involved, as we will see, cannot be merely images, sensations, or sentences at all, or be reduced to them. Abstraction is, instead, a constant activity of ours that transforms the particular. It is not a making up, but more like an x-ray. Sometimes I compare focused abstraction to fluoroscopy and sometimes to magnification, but not to mirroring or to sonograms that are intermediates. Abstraction is not representation, but departicularization. That requires a focus, like a lens adjustment, to determine *what* is disclosed. I am not proposing to explain reductively how we do that, but instead why we have to be able continuously to do that in order to do what we know we do, like read this very sentence.

1. About Perception

The perceived is directly presented; let's premise that. It is not by an intermediate and intervening experience of something subjective and made by us[3] that I see the print on the page, even though the enabling conception has to be acquired and the reality, the print, is a physically realized social construct. The same holds for all the senses. I see by the look of things, hear by the sound, but usually do not distinguish the look or sound from the things, or experience the look or sound intermediately. I don't have intervening experiences of impressions[4] even though the organ-cerebral systems respond distinctively to physical signals from diverse and distant sources.[5] Auditory, visual, olfactory, gustatory, tactile, and proprioceptive awareness is the medium in-which and with-which higher animals perceive. Conception with judgmental understanding makes otherwise animal cognition specifically human.[6]

The perceived is not a subjective appearance like a dream or like the "look" of a stick mistaken for a snake. The "look" can, of course, be attended to, even perceived instead, but is not perceived right when the stick is misperceived to be a snake. For the stick is misconstrued by being misconceived. The look and sound and smell of things can sometimes come apart from the presented thing and be perceived instead. Usually, optical and auditory illusions[7] are objective appearances, the way a stick looks in water, or a vase/face figure looks on a page. Our construals of them are not idiosyncratic. A book of illusions demonstrates that.[8] What we perceive, as we disambiguate figures in such a book of so-called visual illusions, is really there on the page. Varied conceptions focus abstraction for us to discern the thus-structured things.

The physical transmissions and brain states (call them "machine states" in comparison to the motherboard states of a computer) and our sensing are means by-which perception, based in animal cognition, happens. Sensation and desire is the medium in-which and with-which animal perception occurs. For humans there is a *what*, as well as the particular (*which* one) directly perceived, a *star* as well as *that*. Usually the background by which we perceive—for instance, light, color, or noise—is not perceptually focused as "what" or "which sort," but it can be.

There is sensation in multiple modes (Gibson 1966), yet what is perceived is other than sense as medium contains. Not only is sensation itself enhanced, supplemented ("edited," see below) by instinct, conditioning, memory, and imagination, perception is biologically developed, (e.g., one's sexual perception) and also learned, as "restored sight" indicates, and children learn to play tennis, young drivers learn to read the traffic, and people learn the refined discriminations of the arts, sports, and crafts. So we need to distinguish the automatic editing and abstracting of sensation from the post-editing and abstraction of the already perceived (our assigning meaning to a gesture, for example). The tyro driver sees the same flow of cars as the proficient; but what the latter sees is much more than the former does.

Perception is selective for humans by instinct, habit, or effort from among items in sensory input alignment.[9] For instance, clearly discernible common words that are part of a distant sign ("No Stopping") are usually read in being seen; but with a different interest, one might perceive the language, or the spelling, or the sizes or colors or their ready visibility instead. Those realities are all coincident with the surface visually presented. They are in input alignment. You can hear something I say, or my saying something, or my voice, or the timbre of voice, the pitch, or my excitement, as your interest/conception varies, just as you can configure a foreground/background visual ambiguity (face/vase) or perceive the diagonal arrangement of a calendar instead of the squares. That's because, in each of the cases, there is multiple reality in input alignment with the sensory signal and coincident with the perceptible "surface" (the sight, sound, smell, etc.). Outside a test laboratory, there are always more things perceptually presented than we perceive distinctly. As the examples illustrate, an understanding perceiver, enabled by the right conceptions and interests, can perceive various things in response to the same perceptible "surface." So there have to be conceptions to enable the various judgments.

But, is direct perceptual realism even possible? There seems to be a noticeable drift among recent theories in the direction of what used to be called "naïve realism" (Hurley 1998; Noe 2004). Still, some philosophers dismiss the idea because they can't see how it would be done (see Noe 2002 for a survey of some positions) or how to reduce it to something else. Yet there are lots of undisputed realities we can't explain reductively, most notably, how molecules can be assembled to make a conscious or even a living thing.[10] We are puzzled but not disbelieving.

If you postulate subjective intermediate objects (like a holographic heads-up display, an HHUD)[11] to intervene in awareness, like seeing through mirror images, you multiply the perplexity. For how are molecules arranged for us to be aware of such intermediates and then, *through* them, of objects? The problems just double rather than simplify. And they apply to all animals that see, hear, and so on. The story that we apprehend representations and infer to objects creates the "veil of perception" ground for skepticism and supposes a magical inference process to be the product of natural selection; and it requires that other animals do that inferring as well. Further it stumbles against Wilfred Sellars's (1956) "myth of Jones" speculation that the subjective may be a construction *from* the objective, and so not antecedent and explanatory of our object perception. For there is indeed *something* to Sellars's myth because so much of one's introspective awareness—for instance, the classification of one's feelings, emotions, motives, aims, and even judgments—is learned from our discoursing and interacting communities. (One understands oneself better through the experience of literature and art; so the subjective must be at least calibrated and organized from the interpersonal, even if not outright constructed.)

The supposed priority and inerrant accessibility of an intervening private world of appearances is misleading. So the more recent trend among philosophers, especially the phenomenologically literate, attends to how the direct presentation of distinct things is managed neurophysiologically, and how the presentation is modified at the conscious levels by instinct, learning, and invention,[12] not with the idea that something intervenes like an HHUD between us and the world, but that the manner, beyond species-specific animal cognition, of experiencing the objective world is learned and refined. With other primates that may be true too; but humans are marked off by their departicularizing conceptions, their continuous and native abstraction of the concrete, which enables judgments.

If sensations are reductively and eliminatively physical, how do animals perceive, rather than just differentially respond like especially sensitive thermostats? One difference is that sentient response is accompanied by subjective desire, pleasure, and aversion; and that's not mere conatus (inclination without awareness), but desiring awareness. The objects of desires and aversions, besides the activities of sensation, are things not present, not their mere appearances. (I think that's why Aristotle said where there is desire, there is imagination to focus it.) Somehow even the absent has to be made present.[13] Is the subjectivity of experience to be dismissed, as behaviorists did?[14] If not, subjectivity functions better as the medium of direct experience than as an intervener. Let's start with just the perception of present things and situations.

Does perceiving change things? Relatively, yes—the distant becomes present; but physically, usually not much, though taste and touch do change the things. Animal awareness envelops distinct and distant things, for instance, making the tree in sight be seen. That gives the perceived thing an additional, accidental manner of being, intentional being for the perceiving animal—what some used to call *inesse*,[15] and others, like Francis Suarez and, I think, Descartes called "objective being." It's having something (that is real) in mind.

A distant tree is potentially perceived wherever enough of its reflected light travels unscrambled from any place its suitable signal reaches a ready perceiver. But unlike a smell or taste, it is not itself present wherever the signal reaches. The distant thing, heard or seen or touched, becomes present to the animal by the animal's hearing it, seeing it, and so forth, but is present where it is, not where the animal is.

Presence to an animal is a denominative (relational) and accidental condition of things. It is caused by the perceivers the way your being observed is caused by someone's noticing you, say, changing your shirt in a public restroom. It is a resultant, accidental condition of your "having been noticed." It is relationally real, not merely conceptual or logical. It happens to the thing as well as to the perceiver. It's like someone's reading tiny print by squinting: it is the real print that is read. What is done to the thing is more than the mere backward logical necessitation that "makes" a decedent into a grandparent with the later birth of descendants.[16] But it is not enough for causation that affects the thing. That's why older writers called it "intentional" (or *inesse*) and medieval writers said it is a merely "rational" (mind dependent) change in the things perceived.

Perceptual presence of something to an animal is not replication, like a reflection in a mirror or an image on film. The sensory modality is a by-which and with-which for perceiving. You aren't usually aware of it together with being aware of the object, just as you can't be seeing the reflection qua reflection of a following car in your mirror[17] at the same instant you are thereby seeing the following car. Several people at diverse distances see or hear the very same thing, numerically the same thing, by way of the diversity of aspect presented, for instance, I see you from right profile and another sees you head on from further away, but both see you alighting from a car, say. Two people can hear a band, one up close and blaring and one from a distance and faintly. Those aren't just appearances like reflections in fun mirrors; those are presentations by way of real visual or auditory aspects of the things. What we both see is really the same but the visual aspects are not, though they, "in right profile" and "front on," are both real physical aspects of the thing seen. So too is a band's sounding loud close up and sounding faint at a distance. They are fully grounded physical aspects of the thing by which the thing is perceived.

Besides that, up to a point I can see whatever the signal (supplemented, see below) presents, for example, you, your face, your face shape, your being awake. But to do that, we have to be making the particular coincidently general.

Making the Perceived Present. — Animals, including humans, do something analogous to light's turning colors "on" (colors that are only potential without any light, colors are happenings). They make the potentially visible, or audible, actually so. We need to distinguish the relevant sense because the contrast of "potentially visible/actually visible" is contextually variant. The mountain in darkness is not visible; in sunlight it is; but when no one is in sight of it, it is not visible as it is to a person in sight of it; and, to the person in sight of it, it is not visible when he is looking down at the ground, but is when he looks up at it. The relevant sense is the first. The core of an uncut apple is only potentially white (or any color at all); but cut open in light, it is actually colored; it is reflecting light of particular frequencies. Sliced in the dark it is not actually white (except contrastively to other potential colors), but in daylight it is actually white and visible if anyone comes by. So, when there were no sentient beings, the lit-up colors of the earth were not actually visible in the second sense.[18] That's what perceivers do: they make the readily visible, audible, and so forth to be actually seen, heard, and so on. Of course, the potentialities, which are activities, like light reflection, in nature can exceed the response discrimination of any actual animal. So there may be colors no one can see just as there are sounds no human can hear. Indeed, there may be features of things that would be readily perceptible for animals that have not evolved yet, but will.

Perception lags behind the perceived because of the universal causation gap ($t = d/C+$, that is, the time lag is distance divided by the light constant, lengthened by the medium and the manner of the signal and response system). One could be vaporized before a kiss reaches the brain. Still, it is the real kiss, not its appearance, one perceives. What looks to be a grand and stationary land, sea, and skyscape (where we can just make out the silver glint of a giant airplane) is spread out with the foreground causally closer, the middle distance a fraction further, and the skytop maybe a fraction of a nanosecond further away from everything at sea level, with the visible sun eight minutes away.[19] So the whole all-at-once sunlit scene is strictly not simultaneous, but spread out like an orchestral sound that we call "all-together." The reflected and emitted light arrives "together" as the signals coincide in sight, the way the sound of an orchestra coincides in one's hearing, though the instruments are at various distances. Perception makes each item present to us, where it is.[20]

2. Conception and Commitment

There are, as I mentioned, general structures saturated in particular things, but undisclosed absent our rational perception, the way $F + F = 2F$ is present concretely in $2 + 2 = 4$ and in $3 + 3 = 6$. The abstract function $F + F = 2F$ is potentially apparent there to intelligent grasp, as is "even plus even equals even," as well. Some structures are discernible only to the practiced mind and eye, say, a Fibonacci sequence in a floor tile pattern or a fractal pattern in a shore line. The particular reality remains the same though one's conceptions make it accessible as variously structured.

Such structures are typically, though not always, active, for instance, a lintel distributes energy differently from a roof truss, though they as load-bearing beams are not active entirely on their own, that is, without the weight or other forces to distribute, as a simple lens distributes light.

Some rocks may touch one another in a stream, but that they arch or brace or overlap one another, or even touch, if they do, is entirely materialized and inaccessible for perception as such except by focused intelligence,[21] though it is physically there whether perceived or not. Animals hop along the overlapping rocks, but they cannot perceive overlapping as such; we can. The structure is absorbed in the particular the way a function is saturated in its values, or the pattern in the tiles.

Operative concepts are like night glasses; they make actually accessible what is there coincident in things but inaccessible otherwise.[22] Conceptions focus the constant native abstractive activity of humans so as to disclose repeatable structure in things (events or situations), for instance, for one to see a pattern of tiles as diamonds rather than rectangles.

Having the conception of a lever can be several things: an ability to recognize such a thing, the ability to employ such a thing, the ability to detect or predict its effects, and so on. You can "have the conception," "have the concept," to various degrees of discrimination, skill, and employment and with varying webbing among other concepts, for instance, having the concept of screwdriver with or without explicit inclusion of flat, square, and Phillips ones. So, "the conception of x" and "having the concept of x" are a family of related abilities all modifying one's natural abstractive ability to discern abstract structures saturated in particulars. Most importantly, general reasoning about particulars involves thought moving among conceptions, for instance estimating how long a lever is needed to pry up a certain stone and, even more generally, to grasp the principles of leverage, perhaps even to mathematize them.

Furthermore, to disclose the repeatable aspects of things, conceptions have to develop and form contrast-dependent networks from a baby's first conceptions guided by instincts and maternal care on though lifelong learning and discovery. Without the conceptions, aspects of things fall below our notice, say, whether someone is left-handed, or whether a baseball pitcher balked or whether a hand movement is a gesture or a signal. Without the conceptions, both as ready abilities and as the structures discerned, there can't be a relevant judgment.

Sometimes we project structure on things imaginatively, the way we might mistake a cut-off branch to be an owl, or a bird's song to be a ringing telephone. Such mistakes require abstraction. The abstraction, the configuring, as we will see below, is neither true nor false by itself; it is the commitment that is true or not. Conceptions enable but don't compel judgments. Imagination in humans is not just a sense capacity but is fantasy employed intelligently, and is used as a medium in-which for speculation, anticipation, reasoning, and reliance (chapter 8).

Lighting Up the World.[23] — Humans by nature fluoresce structures that are entirely solid with things, like radiated bones, thereby making the thus-structured particulars items of judgment: "that bird is alive"; "lying corrupts"; "she loves John." Conceptions, typically networked by habitual beliefs, enable one's noticing the graining of leaves, the fin-shapes of fish, and geological strata of cliffs. In fact disciplined and resourceful conception enables identification of innumerable such things. Having a conception in this sense is not just a matter of knowing the word; it is a matter of being able to discern the structure in particulars, whether it is cracks in machine parts, or layers of shale or schist. Even individuals, *she* and *Joan* as components of judgment are haloed with abstraction (as "person," "woman," or "friend"). There are no blunt particulars in judgment.[24]

Presence is particular and abstract at once. Whatever is the subject of a judgment, for instance, a shoe size, is abstractly present to judgment—even what is not real but, say, just imagined. It has and has to have particulars of presentation, say, by words, sounds, images, or feelings that are the media of our awareness. (Philosophers tend to regard the intentionality of what is not so as wholly like the presentation of what is so. But, no, the negative, the false, and the erroneous are derivative in mode of presentation. Cf. chapter 8.)

Let me recapitulate. Conceptions enable judgment. Abstraction, as I said, is a constant, native activity, along with one's constant reality commitment. Conception focuses abstraction. The foci, the conceptions, are acquired by maturation (partly from species-specific instinctual interests), and by nurture, teaching, socialization, experience, as well as by individual talent and invention. Conception and judgment are both constant and co-occur, but are different, the way my making orderly sounds enables, but isn't the same, as my saying words. For conceptions enable judgment, but only judgment is true or false.

One key sense in which we speak of a person's having a concept is having the ready ability to discern a repeatable structure of things,[25] for example, to discern pillars and beams, windows and halls as parts of a building, or to discover items of clothing or gestures. Related to that, is "concept" as "ability to organize behavior in *response* to a structure," for example, to park, to read, to type. The discerned structures qua discerned, also sometimes called "concepts," are themselves suitable to be subjects of thought, like "cleverness is not the same as intelligence." So anything we think with or of can be the subject of further judgment, including thinking itself—as that statement displays.

One's interests activate and motivate judgment. Without an interest, even mere curiosity, I may not notice that I see a whole field of dried cornstalks a thousand feet away. And, if I don't have the operative concept, the conception "cornstalks" (i.e., a recognition or action ability, an *empirical* concept), I may be unable to discern such a structure at all even if I am looking right at the cornfield, just as I can't tell a barley field from rye.[26] The whole may be perceived confusedly when I recognize a crop field and even know from someone's saying so that it is barley, but can't *see* that. That's the way with perception generally, and with discrimination of all sorts: refinement comes from experience and, often, coaching. Medical schools use hospital rounds, photos, and demonstrations to develop student's recognition, for instance, to tell by looking psoriasis from contact dermatitis, and by touch ascites from other abdominal distensions—to develop the sense meaning of the names (cf. C.I. Lewis 1946). You have to learn what you are looking at (hearing, smelling, tasting, or feeling).

Notice, knowing the verbal meaning of the word "barley" in contrast to "wheat" and "rye" as standing in close verbal contrast for crops and grains—call it, "SAT test knowledge"—is not, for this purpose, having the concept; nor is knowing wheat and barley are different food crops and grown in the mid-West or the rest of a dictionary entry. Those are concepts for other purposes, but not for perception. The concept, for this purpose, is part of a person's perceptual ability (like ability to recognize jeans versus pants, or music versus noise), and what the concept discloses is structure in things, usually as prescientifically understood.

Another example: most of us can't just by a glance distinguish a single-course (very old) fieldstone wall held up by its snaking loops, from a double-course wall with cross-stone tie-ins and large-stone repetitions, or a loose-stone from a tight-stone fieldstone wall unless it is pointed out, and, often then we don't see the difference. That sort of thing holds for every area of learned discrimination. People usually can't discriminate brick patterns, or poetic or musical forms either. Having the concept, in the sense that is key here, is being able to tell and respond to differences in things; and what is discriminated is the real, the intelligible pattern, say, of the brick and half-brick repetitions. The same holds for Garamond and Times New Roman typefaces. Having the concepts is the ability observationally to tell the one reality from another, though such telling can be mistaken, say, when you don't look carefully enough.

As Aristotle and Aquinas said, there is no truth or falsity in abstraction.[27] Construal doesn't carry truth or falsity, only commitment does. In fact, "correct" does not apply apart from judgment (except attributively from a supposed judgment). If we are disambiguating puzzle figures, conception and judgment may be co-occurrent, but the conception is still explanatorily prior. Aristotle seemed to think we come upon the essences (the real "what") of things by simple abstraction (often after experience with things); but more, we come that way upon any structure of interest or social importance to us. For the most part humans get the commonsense "what" of things right—and sometimes, as with "rational animal," it is the real, the constitutive, essence too. People come to know what corn is, and beets, and grapes, and horses, and cows, and so on, even though they do not have an articulate scientific description to offer, and even though there may be marginal cases about which they are or should be uncertain.

Without perception aimed at specific animal action, there would be no "internal" sense powers like imagination and memory because they would have no natural function; indeed there would be no genuine senses either. Mere detection-output systems, like thermostatic heat controls, have no need of sensation; they react right into single or scaled outputs and involve neither desire nor aversion. Chemical senses are just sophisticated detection devices; they don't sense anything. They can simulate sensation, sometimes very efficiently, but don't sense. Wherever there is sense there is desire and aversion and varied response modified by them and typically there are objects of desire or aversion not present, except by imagination or memory; and wherever sense is embraced by intelligence, there is the prospect of delight and of detestation. For humans, every mode of sensing is a mode of love.[28]

3. The Subject of Abstraction

What undergoes abstraction? That's complicated by the fact that there are not conscious interveners in perception, and yet some of the supplementation of sensation (from imagination and memory) and its unification of modalities (of sight, hearing, smell) is triggered by conception. We can initially phrase the question this way: is abstraction done to phantasms (unified sense presentations) or to things? When Aristotle and his commentators said abstraction is of the phantasm, I don't think they meant from an *intermediating* appearance attended to. I think they meant we abstract from the thing-thus-presented *by* "the common sense," sensus communis (the unified sensory awareness that is supplemented from memory, instinct, and imagination by habit—what we might now call the "phenomenal presentation" that is ordinarily coincident with the thing perceived). That is what I think to be correct. What we abstract from is more than the external senses alone detect because that sense response is significantly augmented, edited, and supplemented, as mentioned. It is not a look or sound, smell, feel, or taste that is perceived in *order* to perceive the thing (though we *can* do that on occasion, for instance, when learning wine tasting or learning to touch fabric). Rather, the thing is perceived by means of the unified and supplemented sensory response of sound, smell, feel, taste, and so on.

The phantasm, the unified sensory response about which Aristotle speaks is not an intervener but an enabler, a focal adjustment of polarized awareness. By "polarized awareness" I mean object awareness of what is not itself a part of one's subjectivity. I think we perceive by means of supplemented (and instinctive) sensory modalities (visual, auditory, olfactory, etc.) that are the signum formale quo, the enabling adjustment of awareness. If you imagine your expected lunch with your eyes open, you can "see" a ghostly sandwich, but that is not a picture of one. In direct perception the "ghostly" is absorbed in the vivid objects/events. But in correcting misperceptions one can sometimes just catch the ghostly misconstrual flitting away. Genuine, open-eyed imagination is something like a holograph, but denser. Imagine a route you would travel, and the noisy traffic passing, to a nearby store. That is not like mere pictures of objects. Even if you notice how a long hall looks *as if* it converges, you are still attending to how the real hall looks,[29] not to an intervening presentation. Abstraction is from things presented, the way we can attend to how the hall seems to converge. On the difference of phenomenal geometry from projective geometry of the physical space, see Hatfield 2008.

Our conceptions, as I said, operate like automated multiple focal adjustments of an elaborate lens (say for color correction, night-time distortion, and field of vision distortion). That makes our awareness both particular and abstract at once. There is the same double presence for the merely imagined, remembered, and mistaken as well. We edit presentations and suffuse them with emotive and cognitive fillers, both instinctual and learned. In reading for sense, sometimes whole words are added (a missing "is" or "with") or omitted (an extra "it" "it"). Some of us are poor proofreaders because we are biased to read for sense. Paul Kolers (1968) showed multilingual persons can't consistently identify the language in which a message was read or heard; for them the sensible presentation is just a means for perception not something intervening or perceived, and often, not even recallable.

Abstraction is constantly focused by conceptions to regulate expectation in action, for instance, how tightly we grip a coffee cup or a milk bottle to lift it, how far to turn a steering wheel to guide a car, how far to lean forward climbing a hill versus stairs.[30] You see something in the woods, take it to be a dead animal, and feel repelled. On a reluctant second glance, it is tangled leaves. Those are construing abstractions enabling judgments. Judgment is usually an all at once sequel to abstraction, almost instantaneous, though we may hesitate or check the entirely unexpected, or the anomalous.

4. About Perceptual Presence and Real Natures

(1) Default Reality Commitment. — This point is very important for both metaphysics and epistemology, and is usually not remarked: when awake, we have a locked-on, default, constant reality commitment—a defeasible judgmental state. We are constantly reality aware, but with continuously changing content as attention moves. The reality commitment is a continual judgmental state, perhaps even sometimes mistaken when we are dreaming or daydreaming. The locked-on reality commitment reveals itself when we doubt it, "this couldn't be

real, could it?" and "could I be dreaming?" and when we realize on awakening that we took what was dreamed to be real. We can of course deliberately imagine and remember things without that commitment. Exhaustion or high emotion or surprise, illness, lack of sleep or dislocation can make things seem unreal and even make us unsure momentarily or for a while whether "it is really real"; and various chemicals can make experience seem unreal (or extra sharp and vivid). The fact that the reality commitment can be disrupted or modulated indicates that it is the normal and constant condition of intelligent awareness. It is the ground of the traditional metaphysical claim that the first object of awareness is being, and that being is what is apprehended when anything at all is.

For us, to be—to live at all—is to be the sort of thing that continuously judges, with a constant but defeasible reality commitment. That is the default state of intelligent wakefulness. The Empiricists did not offer an account of our constant native, but defeasible, reality awareness, a feature that involves truth and falsity yet does not employ any sentential vehicle at all (cf. chapter 4), and nevertheless can be mistaken.

(2) Presence. — Perception goes backward physically, as mentioned earlier. It makes the spatiotemporally distant attentively present. Usually the lag is negligible, but sometimes it is significant. We can see Polaris now even though all the light we will ever see it by is "old light," years in transit. That's like the short radio lag in a reply from an astronaut. "Now" for us is, metaphorically, "then" for it; physically, it is "before" relatively to our perceptual "after." If someone drops an empty barrel, or cars crash on pavement two thousand feet away in plain sight, you can see it about two seconds before you hear it (on a calm day). You might even say to someone, "I saw it before I heard it." What you saw and what you heard are the same thing (the barrel's hitting the ground, the cars crashing), with the seeing before the hearing. Strictly as presented, the happenings differ, as do a sound and a sight, but as happenings they are each the same, "the drop" or "the smash." It just takes longer for the sound than for the sight to make the happening present to you. What we perceive is where and when it happens, though we might hear it (as event) later than we saw it.

Twice presented is not twice happening. So, for two drivers seeing a stoplight change, it is twice present, once for each. And for a whole concert audience the concert is variously and multiply present. Yet for each hearer, what is present is really (the same as, but not strictly identical with) what happened. That holds too for events that are historically remote and for universal and abstract realities known by many. (More on that later.)

(3) Quite Abstract Things Can Become Subjects of Direct Perception (especially causation [real production] and natural necessity [to breathe] and impossibility [to reassemble a broken egg]). — That has already been remarked but needs elaboration, especially because the post-Humean denial has been so intransigent on the point. Many things cannot be perceived without suitable conceptions. A new infant has no conception of object persistence through visual interruption (a ball's passing behind a chair), nor can a little child understand the same liquid in differently shaped glasses to be equal amounts (Piaget). Some things cannot be conceived before physical maturation, like the point of adult kissing, and, of course, many indeed cannot be conceived without education. Conceptions are refined and elaborated in the course of intelligent practices like canoeing, sailing, fishing, gardening, farming, mathematics, music, sports or history, science, and art. Refined conceptions enable refined judgment and refined feeling and they often obviate the need for slow deliberation and calculation.

Humans fasten perception on the features they need, use, or are fascinated with, typically first as modes of practical competence and gradually, or with special talents, as modes of reflection for art and science, personal interaction, and employment. Following are some physical-object examples of things that become perceivable with suitable training.

Folks commonly understand the flexibility of a willow branch and the elasticity of a rubber band as shape recovery, even without the words for it. They also prefer standing on wood floors instead of concrete. One can bend a board or oar up to a point and it recovers, though after that it cracks. Only a few grasp that all solids are somewhat elastic, recovering shape when compression is released, wood much more so than concrete. Having noticed such a feature, a curious and reflective person might then notice reversibility, as such, and guess at Hooke's law that the strain in a solid is proportional to the stress (up to its elastic limit, where it dents, cracks, etc.). So, with further abstract reflection, one may notice that in general the mechanical work expended bending an oar is recovered by removing the stress, like a spring (cf. Holden 1965). Under a further, quantitative abstraction, such phenomena can be mathematized—that is, formulated as orderly mathematical transformations. But it's all there in the particulars (chapter 7), right there from the start. Stair builders and diving board manufacturers rely on it.

Maxwell (1865, 89) showed there is an analogous recovery property, "dielectric polarization," in insulators (of which every solid, not supercooled, is one to an extent). In fact, elastic distortion, dielectric polarization, and heat capacity are all reversible, analogous properties (properties with the similar quantitative meta-properties), each of which can in cases produce the other (see below). Thus the structures qua abstracted are seen to be causally related. Those are all real structural features (chapter 7), active causally (that is, having specific energy distribution effects) exhibiting formal similarities and capable of causing effects in other forms of energy (like heat's expanding metal). They are structurally operative in things and ready for abstraction (chapter 7 considers this further).

People know a hot object heats its surroundings, like a flat iron or a radiator as it cools. But they may not think of it as *radiation,* as a general intelligible structure with its own lawlike features. So they may not know, as some do, that heat conduction, like electrical conduction, is a "transport property," a broader structural feature common to several sorts of properties. Such conceptions have to be acquired, usually in a community of special interests, but once possessed they disclose real features of particulars that are entirely coincident with the physical things, yet become perceivable. One should not confuse the conventional metrics we use to measure and employ such properties with the independent structural reality repeated in particulars, for example, in all the radiators in a house.

Everyone recognizes tin's or aluminum's denting without breaking, like a can's being crushed in the drinker's grip.[31] Automobile doors and fenders dent and crush too. "Denting" is both a common concept and a refined notion. So a scientist and layman, using the same word, may have overlapping but differing conceptions of the same phenomenon because conditions that overflow word meaning (say, passing the point of elastic recovery) may be explicit, even part of the meaning of the word for a scientist, while not even thought of by the layman.

You may notice that heating a solid expands it, for instance, notice a door's jamming on a hot day, but might not think of that as producing a mechanical effect with heat (like heating a rusted nut to loosen it from the bolt). To recognize a mechanical effect of heat as such is to abstract a structure saturated in the particular reality. That requires an operative conception to enable the recognition. The names "mechanical effect" and "thermal change" are invented; the phenomena are real and solid with the particulars.

Heating tourmaline (a gem stone) produces an electrical charge (the pyroelectric effect); it is a reversible electrical effect of a thermal change. Likewise, an electric current in some solids will produce a mechanical effect, for example, a slight bending that reverses if the charge is removed, like an electromagnet that, when charged, bends a piece of metal, and when the current is off lets it recover straight shape; for instance, some time locks and bombs go active when the current goes off (rather than on), closing a circuit.[32] Generally in solids, electrical causes can have mechanical and thermal effects; heat can have electrical and mechanical effects; and stress (mechanical bending or pressure) can have heat and electrical effects. Now add the chemical production of heat, electrical, thermal, and molecular effects, and we have a wide array of causally ordered real structures in nature (chapter 7) that, with training, are perceivable.

All those things are perceptible and quantifiable with appropriately trained abstractive judgment (concept-guided observation). In fact, the relations among the properties are natural necessities that we can represent with mathematized laws. If practical and explicit use in manufacturing is a further test of reality, then these structures are all real and entirely coincident with particulars. Their structural relations (chapter 7), grasped by abstraction and then mathematized, are made part of a general theory of solids, part of materials science. They are "universals" (in current, not classical, parlance) repeatably realized in particulars, ready for focused abstraction and trained perception. They can be as much present to comprehending perception as the particulars are, just as the heat of a lightbulb caused by electrical energy overcoming resistance in a filament is perceptible to the trained hand. The Empiricists, Hume in particular and his followers, were imprisoned in a narrow view of what knowing and particularly what perception is, and ended up unable to account even for our perception of the kinds of explanatory causality I illustrated above.

5. Can What I Know and What Is So Be the Same? An Important Step about Truth

How can something I know be the very same thing as what is really so, when what is so is particular, unrepeatable, and has endless overflow features and transcendent determinacy of detail (chapter 1), while something I know can be particular and general as well, stored and recalled, transported, and can be the same as what other persons know, though their knowing is numerically distinct from mine and from what is known? (Of course, a CD too can contain the very concerto Prokofiev wrote and its particular performance.) How do we explain the supposed sameness? (Cf. chapter 7.3.)

If the physically particular can have a resultant manner of being (intentional being) on account of the activity of percipient agents, then the solution lies there.

Things can be really the same that are not strictly identical. It is no more change in a building to be photographed than it is to be seen. But the photo does not make the building present to anyone; it only conveys how it looks, whereas seeing, hearing, and the like are *presence* making for the whole thing perceived, including all its hidden parts and natural necessities, not, however, presented.

Being perceived is, crudely, something like being desired or admired: the very thing (say, a sandwich you see, with all the parts we can't see) is desired, but it gets that feature from an animal's wanting it, and can be desired by several at once and detested by others as well. Yet it is the reality (the sandwich) not a simulacrum that is desired. It is, as I said, like eyeglass magnification, with the perceived thing magnified yet really the same as the unmagnified thing. People with different corrective glasses reading the same print, see the same thing, though the text is differently presented to each.

Perception, concrete for other animals and coincidently abstract as it is for humans, gives things presence, an incidental and transient mode of being, *esse intentionale,* that is perceiver-relative being. There's no reason that a thing that exists on its own can't also have transient perceiver-relative being for many people who perceive it. Things don't have *esse intentionale* on their own, and things aren't physically changed by it (except incidentally by our tasting or touching), but still what is intentionally present to someone may be the very thing that is real.

Philosophers nowadays talk as if intentionality is an agent's or a thought's condition of object directedness, towardness, aboutness—as if it were a kind of referring or pointing. But I am using the notion of *esse intentionale,* "intentional being," as inclusion in awareness, the *presence* of real objects events or situations perceived or known. Anscombe (1969) does so too, and Searle (1983) as well. *Esse intentionale* is presence, especially and primarily of the independently real by the awareness of someone (or some animal).

The vivid presence of the perceived—a snake, a bad cut, a fire, a threat—is what needs acknowledging; it is not to be implicitly denied by supposing the *thought* is what is present and *about* some object, say a vista or a sentence understood.[33] Some recent writers, Sean Kelly and Alva Noe, among others, seem to have recognized too what Husserl and Merleau-Ponty had grasped and emphasized: the inclusion of "the other" in awareness, the intentional *inesse* of the independently real.[34] That is what in percipient animals obviates a mind/world gap.

Medieval Aristotelians regarded the relationship of perceiver-to-thing as *real* because it involves physical change in the perceiver, but the reciprocal relation, that of thing-to-perceiver as "merely rational" because there need not be a physical or other real change in the items perceived. Though strictly true, that seems not quite vigorous enough because presence is more than merely a logical or conceptual outcome, a logical reciprocal[35] of the perceiver's changing the direction of its animal attention. For it seems that there is more reality in a tree's being noticed by you than there is to the tree's getting farther from a fleeing rabbit. Rather, perceptual awareness is an including activity of animals as a result of the perceiver's physical response to a constant signal (a smell, say, or sound) from the thing-to-be-perceived. Presence is a transient status of the thing known, just as being discovered would be your status if you are noticed doing something personally private.[36]

If what a cat sees when it sees a bird (epistemically) were not really the bird, then the supposition that it sees a bird would be negated, and something like an HHUD[37] substituted. That would be a display from which a bird is inferred, or from behind which a bird is watched—as if animals and humans lived in a world of inferences or behind a veil, like guards with monitors and remote controls, or pilots of supersonic fighters, while humans denominatively call it "seeing for themselves," the way doctors looking at sonograms can say they see a fracture.

It is true that a craftsman, surgeon, or artist lives in the point of his tool. But that is where attention presents the world in *esse intentionale*. When I see a familiar person I no more conclude there is a person (as I might from flitting shadows or distant specks) than I conclude that I exist when I wake up. The known gets *inesse*[38] from the knower. Intentional being is being *pour l'autre* (a twist on Sartre); it accrues to the known.[39] It is a relational condition that can come and go without physical change in the thing.

Now you might say *esse intentionale* just gives a name to something's being perceptually or otherwise cognitively present to humans or other animals, without giving any explanation of how an animal can bring that about. That's true, it does not explain it. In part that's because a reductive explanation even of sensation, much less of consciousness, does not exist. Still, direct (not merely inferential) awareness of objects has to be acknowledged and acknowledged to include much more than just the sensibly presented. You really do see your friends, not by seeing replicas. The complexity of the neural states and sensory modalities by which that happens is a matter for the sciences and for epistemology naturalized, just as the motherboard operations of my computer are for the engineers and don't reach my awareness, or need to. Greater detail about the steps from object to brain will however not, I venture, explain how conscious awareness can envelop other things. Animal perceptive consciousness will, I conjecture, have to be treated as naturally emergent.

Talk of an *intervening* conscious phenomenal component is unnecessary. We can attend to the "look" of things that alters if we attend to the relative portion of the visual space objects occupy (Noe 2004), just as we can attend to the presenting sound of a band from different positions. But that, the look or the sound, is itself perceived then, and has its own manner of presentation. None of that shows there is a constant *double conscious* presentation, the one subjective and phenomenal and the other direct, though mediated. The phenomenal is the *manner* and means of objective presentation of things perceived (imagined, remembered, and thought of), just as the refracted image on reading glasses is. Using the glasses, one sees by *means* of the refracted light, but sees only the print and statements one reads.

Opposed views, for instance, representational ones, have a difficulty of their own beyond our shared impasse at naturalistically explaining animal perception and subjectivity. That additional deficit is the lack of any account of our knowledge of the remote, universal, and abstract, except to say such knowledge is of something *else* (of the reliability of representations or sentences, or statements—as indeed it sometimes is). Sometimes an unpleasant encounter or a very passionate one reappears, but as known not to be then actual; it keeps coming back in full disturbing or enchanting vividness, for a while, like PTSD in that respect, but without a commitment to its *current* reality. It is a less vivid re-presence of what *was* present. To explain all that, we need the originating vivid, direct presence.

6. Media for Thought

There is always some "medium in-which" for any comprehending awareness, even though there isn't a medium by-which, as there is for our writing something, say, by pencil or by typing (see chapter 6). That is, we don't understand and reason ("think") by doing something *else* a certain way, though we have to be *using* something else as medium like words, images, or actions in doing it, but not as instrument *to* do it (like using a knife to cut bread). Thinking is not just another more complex way of imagining or seeing, recalling, and so forth. Similarly, our statements are not identical with our words; otherwise they could not be translated. Nevertheless, what we say can be really the same as what we say it with, even though not strictly identical with it.

Media for thinking include sensations, words, feelings, memories, images and gestures, marks, facial expressions, postures, inflections, and performances. I emphasize that because it is usually unremarked that our concentrated doings are media in-which thinking and expression, and thus judgment, is done, just as ballet and folk dance are media of artistic expression. The language, say, French or English, may even be part of the personality of what is understood, and even indispensable for its force (*L'amour est un passion inutile*), but it is not identically the thought—otherwise you could not share it with someone else. Bodily action is a constant and usual medium in-which thinking is done, say, for lacrosse, auto driving, orchestral playing, traffic policing, or dramatic conversation.[40] Facial expressions can speak for us, even in spite of us: the "tell" in card playing and the eye-slide, fixed stare, or chin lift in lying.

Our unreflective self-awareness and our enjoyment of understanding, our awareness of saying what we want and doing so, are usually unexpressed; they subsist abstractly apprehended in what we are doing and feeling.

7. Consequent Realities

We distinguish seeming from being when we find we've made a mistake, feel dizzy, match a color, or wonder if that's the phone ringing. The just-rising full moon that looms large and a tractor, tiny in a distant field, look the way they ought to look—though, in another sense, that is not how they really are, but how they really look. In general, midrange, stellar, and even molecular objects are resultants, at their orders of magnitude, all the way to the atoms and the quarks (10^{-16} m), if they are real.

Our perceptible world of trees, buildings, stars, and galaxies is a world of resultants from imperceptible constituents that, at the component orders of magnitude, lack the characteristic features of the perceptible resultants. The resultants are just as real as the components and their constituents. But which things, at which orders, are perceptible depends on the natural capacities of perceivers and, in the case of humans, on such capacities augmented with telescopes, microscopes, cameras, and the like, as well as on all the effects of training and skill and cleverness. At naturally perceptible dimensions a table is solid and continuous, at atomic dimensions it is mostly space. That is the story throughout the cosmos: reality at one magnitude is constituted of realities that at a component magnitude, say, atomic (10^{-9} m), are qualitatively quite different. In fact, we often have no certain reduction from the phenomena at one magnitude to the subcomponents.

Nelson Goodman (1978, 71–89) reminded us that features like figure constancy are supplied in perception not transmitted from objects. The same holds for the uninterrupted continuity of vision over the blind spot and the continuity of vision despite the stuttering firing of the optic nerves, and so on. I take that to indicate that evolved sense perception aimed at veridicality for our sorts of animals supplies features not in the signal, but neurophysiologically, and from learning, imagination, and memory. Recent restored-sight cases seem to suggest one has to learn to see the world as humans do (*Guardian,* August 27, 2003). No doubt, the neurophysiology and psychology of perception involve immensely complex "with-which" processes for perception, for making vision right side up, for example, and to have the geometry of our visual perception (cf. Hatfield 2008), and for coordinating the sensory and imaginative modes of our unified awareness. Still, it makes more sense, it is a best explanation, to say evolutionary development presents the world species specifically (e.g., for humans, bats, cats, etc.) as it *is,* rather than to say it presents successful species-specific *constructions,* since the fundamental problem for any reductively aimed theory would be to explain, by processes lacking that feature, how there is any *display* of the world to any animal at all.

It's a good hypothesis that the systematic illusions, like the arrow illusions, are not defects in our perceptual systems, but rather are indicative of its veridicality, to discriminate inside for outside corners of walls for instance.[41] Magic and trickery rely on veridicality, for the point to tricks like shell games and three-card monte is that they make what normally presents reality, fail to; and magicians typically make realities appear to present impossibilities (e.g., levitation or the damsel sawn in half). The very same ability that can be tricked in those ways is one we need with that limitation to distinguish certain features of reality as it is.

Perception is selective, yet not less direct for that and can be misleading. I once saw in a morning's ocean fog what looked to be an impossibly large ghostly sailboat about a hundred feet in the foggy air, in full color, an amazing sight that lasted perhaps ten minutes, time enough for a friend to see it too. The fog dissipated and the appearance stopped quite suddenly like a change in stage lighting, and I saw a real, ordinary sailboat that had been all along in full sunlight beyond the refracting narrow bank of fog. I had mistaken the boat in the sky to be a mere appearance. In fact, it was a real boat with its colors refracted and apparent size enlarged, and place altered by light and fog.

Brain states are no more like what is perceived than the light fluctuations of a city (seen at night from the air) are like what the people do that causes the light patterns. The neural states are motherboard states for perception, thought, and action, but they do not explain how awareness of distinct things happens, though we know they are necessary and naturally sufficient (in an otherwise integral animal) and that neural and chemical changes alter and impair experience. Still, the necessity for such states doesn't block the immediacy of the perception, any more than the molecular constitution of my glasses blocks my directly seeing things by their refracting the light.

8. Remote as Well as Proximate Things Can Be Present in Thought

History is mostly by report, and a good deal of ordinary general knowledge is too. But sometimes remote particulars (say, that humans had evolutionary predecessors) and universal realities (that iron is magnetizable) are abstractly presented as something directly understood de re (in contrast to statements known to be so, knowledge de dicto). Such realities must somehow be made present states of our comprehension.

We can only comprehend universals like "iron is ductile," and "unregulated markets converge toward monopoly" with conceptions that focus thought to present the general realities themselves. The contemporary empiricists and rationalists treat "knowing that" for such things, as "knowledge *of* the truth of replicas or representations" (of imaginings, or sentences, or assertions, etc.), or as knowledge *about* some sentence, representation, or the like, that *it* is true. They treat "knowing that" (iron is ductile) as knowledge de dicto (about statements), when it often is in fact knowledge de re (learned, say, from a molten pour in a Pittsburgh mill).

Everybody knows you can't live without breathing. What needs to be explained is how such a universal reality becomes something we are aware of.[42] That knowledge is not a relationship to sentences or other artifacts. To say so amounts to an imperialistic replacement of what we mean, because it says our knowledge of the reality is actually knowledge of something else, say, of sentences—a bait and switch. Rather, "being iron" and "being ductile" have to be abstractly present to me. Otherwise, I do not know iron is ductile. So far, we know only schematically how that is done (by abstractive modification of awareness), but that is enough for present purposes.

Sometimes history is grasped *through* report, not just known about. If you tell me you took the stairs instead of the elevator, I'll come to know it (ceteris paribus). That's through report. It is *by* report when I know about the report of some event, that it is true, say, that someone told the truth. We know "the United States invaded Iraq" and "the Roman Republic preceded the Roman Empire" through report. Sometimes we come to know something from a reliable intermediary like a chemistry or logic text. A good deal of remote knowledge is even more abstract than that because the mediating images are contrived, while the reality is a universal and abstract one (plutonium is poisonous).

Practice and repeated trust may convert mere report to knowledge *through* the reports. Verbally the same item can be de re for one person and de dicto for another. I know de re that water doesn't taste like gasoline; another may know it only by a report.[43]

Perception, memory, and imagination are constant for us; but so is awareness of what is not at hand, but is nevertheless so. Such judgment floats on a surface of local perception, memory, imagination, and feeling, but requires more—namely, abstractions that, combined with chains of reference (most of which we do not know anything about), present events and situations, like Everest's being the highest mountain, Athens' having been a Greek city-state, and Franklin's and Washington's having been signers of the Declaration of Independence. Such thoughts are anchored in consciousness by images, feelings, and words, but those anchors are just media. Still, the knowledge is not just that certain statements are true, but is of the things.

Moreover, the presenting images may be fabricated and attached to the particular by intention and convention. When I know Napoleon fought the Russians, what I know through report is a historical reality, but the images I have are probably from a book print or are conventional, the way I think of the Spartans as warlike with beards, short tunics, and swords. The reality whose physical particulars are inaccessible to me has to be a particular case of the abstractions of my commitment, however arbitrary the presenting imagery or words might be, in order to be what is known. That's the explanatory point. The same holds even for "There are houses several streets from here." The reality is presented by proxy (by linguistic abstractions with images), the way medieval kings understood pictured prospective brides. Distortion lurks in the images, so that if I rely on their details (e.g., imaging Spaniards as if they were nordic, to remember the Spaniards colonized Louisiana), my otherwise true conviction may become false in detail (blond swordsmen in furs), just as kings got more or less than they expected.[44]

For the remote and abstract to be made present for judgment, it has to be presented through fitting abstractions and convenient (though, perhaps, not fitting) images and a chain of referring. Unless you are willing to claim that I cannot think of, and about, perceiving in general, you have to acknowledge that there is some way *my perceiving* itself, not just names for it, or images for it, or statements or propositions about it, can be present to me to examine, even if I am misconstruing it badly. That can only happen through abstraction that makes it coincident with, indeed a modification of, my awareness. Otherwise, you'd have to say I cannot do what I (and you?) just plainly did.

Abstraction is not only a formative operation in our perception; it is the means by which remote and general realities, say, that there are gravitational, electromagnetic, and strong forces, can become what I know.

So the manner of a thing's presence in my knowing, say abstractly, does not have to be the manner of its concrete reality in nature. In that respect we differ from all the other animals we know of.[45]

9. Conclusion

Since knowing the remote (say, that there are more galaxies by far than there have ever been humans altogether) is in the most important cases not knowing *about* some statement that it is true, but instead *grasping* something (e.g., that light is gravitationally deflected), there must be a way the abstract, the remote, and the universal are present in thought.[46] For what you understand when you understand that is not merely *that* some statement is true. Rather, you understand something about light and gravitational fields (maybe imagining a beam of starlight bending around a large intervening object). The remote and universal are presented abstractly by their natures or repeatable structures, usually mediated in thought with conventional images. That is done by the same abilities operative in human perception of nearby things. The repeatable structures of things are the ground of such knowledge. They are the subject of inquiry in chapter 7.

There is no reductive explanation of how we abstract the forms and features of things to perceive things *as* "such and such," say, elephants. Abstraction is a natural condition of intelligent consciousness, even of very limited humans. It does not decompose into neural operations. Nor is there a reductive explanation of how a distant tree is made present even by any animal's perception of it, even nonabstractly. Neither is there any physical or an analytic reduction of sensation or of consciousness. Those processes and states are not made up of or constituted out of other activities, the way a chair is made of pieces or a program of subroutines. For if they were reducible to components, either the components would have the ability (abstraction, perception, consciousness, sensation) or they would lack it. In the first case, the mystery would remain in a new place; in the second, the reduction would have to amount to the ability we recognize (e.g., consciousness) or we would not count it as successful, and so the mystery would revive, about how that phenomenon comes from (apparently) wholly different ones. On any account, there will be a reductive gap somewhere.

Supervenience will not bridge it; for supervenience of any strength is at most a logical correlation not an explanatory relation as causation or constitution is.

So, let's look next at a particular case, the irreducibility of the ability to understand.

CHAPTER 6

Emergent Consciousness and Irreducible Understanding

I. Introduction

Though we can't explain how to assemble molecules to make a living thing, and a fortiori, how to make a conscious thing like a mouse, we are pretty confident that such life and consciousness are either resultant or emergent[1] from physical organization. Human understanding seems to be different.[2] The main difference is that humans can do things both as to form and universality that no merely physical thing can do.

Humans who are developed and integral have the native ability and constant proclivity ("abstraction," chapter 5) to discern, recognize, and rely on intelligible, repeatable, structures of things, many of which are active and explanatory (chapter 7). Such ability cannot be reductively physical. For the underdetermination of hypotheses by data and its particular case, the underdetermination of the physical relatively to pure functions,[3] disclose that no entirely physical thing can do operations that realize pure functions determinately; yet, any integral human does that constantly. This reasoning treats the underdetermination phenomena as more than merely cognitive limitations.

115

This chapter has three parts: the main argument from the pure functions of understanding;[4] the parallel argument concerning the definite content of judgment; and several subsidiary considerations about causation, universality, and time.

II. The Main Argument

The Difficulty

Animal cognition and desire from the appetite of a clam to the vision of vultures is thought to have neurobiological explanations that result from, and are perhaps theoretically reducible to, physical processes. But human understanding seems to be different in principle. It seems that one cannot explain certain truth-carrying thoughts[5] as reductively physical, even though they always have a physical medium in-which.[6] That's because they require features no physical thing or process can have at all.[7]

That difficulty cannot be merely dismissed. For the underlying considerations are among the jewels of analytic philosophy: the underdetermination of hypotheses by data and the indeterminacy of the physical.[8] Further, to deny that our judgments are of definite logical forms—namely, pure functions[9]—conflicts with our accounts of validity and of logical transformations, and leaves us unable to explain what we do when we do mathematics, logic, or any other formal thinking or even simple conjunction.

In a word: our thinking, in a single case, can be of a definite abstract form (e.g., $N \times N = N^2$), and not indeterminate among incompossible equally most particular[10] forms (see chapter 6.II.2). No physical process can be that definite in its form in a single case. Adding physical instances even to infinity will not exclude incompossible equally most particular forms (cf. Saul Kripke's "plus/quus" examples). So, no physical process can exclude incompossible functions from being equally well (or badly) satisfied (see chapter 6.II.3). Thus, no physical process can *be* the whole[11] of such thinking. The same holds for functions among physical states (see chapter 6.II.5). The rest of the chapter unfolds that reasoning.

2. Can Judgments Really Be of Such Definite Pure Forms?

They have to be; otherwise they will fail to have the defining features of conjunction, disjunction, modus ponens, addition, and so on, upon which validity, consistency, and the like depend. The single case of thinking has to be of an abstract "form" (a pure function) that is not indeterminate among incompossible ones. For instance, if I square a number—not just happen in the course of adding to write down a sum that is the square, or inattentively do something by rote or machine, or merely follow some routine—but if I actually square the number, itself times itself, I think in the form $N \times N = N^2$.[12]

Reasoning by modus ponens ("If p then q; p; therefore q") requires that no incompossible form also be the equally particular form of what I have done. For to reason in a way that is truth preserving for all cases of that form, I cannot also be reasoning in a way that, under an equally particular description, for some of the same cases is not truth preserving. What is done, then, cannot be indeterminate among equally particular structures some of which are not truth preserving.[13]

Valid reasoning cannot merely approximate the ideal form, but must be *of* the form. Otherwise it will as much fail to be truth preserving for all relevant cases, as it succeeds, and the whole point of validity will be lost. That forewarns us that the evasion, "We do not *really* conjoin, add, or do modus ponens, but only simulate them" will not be correct. Still, I consider it below.

"Being truth preserving for all relevant cases" is a feature of the single case of validity. The whole function (e.g., modus ponens) is realized in the single case. It is not like "being punctual" that is realized over a pattern of occasions. The form of the reasoning that occurs in the particular case is "truth preserving." Otherwise it would not be "impossible by virtue of the form to proceed from truth to falsity" in *that* reasoning. So, the form of the actual "encompasses" (logically contains) all relevant cases whatever. (Wittgenstein [1953, 189–95], talking about the "use" of an expression, objected to calling that "in a *queer* way" being "all present at once," because it is so, in a straightforward way; cf. Kripke 1982, 70 n.58. So too for these cases.)

Squaring, Conjoining, Adding. — The pure function has to be wholly realized in the single case, and cannot consist merely in the array of "inputs and outputs." One reason, of course, is that diverse functions can have the same array of inputs and outputs, which, like a times table, is just a logical shadow, not what the function is.[14] Multiplication is equivalent to repeated self-additions.

Does anyone doubt that to be squaring, say, "4 times 4 is 16," I have to be doing something, "itself times itself," that is the same for all the cases, something for which any relevant case can be substituted without change in what I am doing, but only in *which* thing is done? Squaring is a definite form of thought ($N \times N = N^2$), the same for all relevant cases whether or not we are able to process the digits or talk long enough to give the answer. If my thinking is indeterminate among incompossible forms, it is not of the form $N \times N = N^2$.

Consider "conjoining," an even simpler function. Conjoining is the functional arrangement of an n-tuple of assertions (or convictions) into a single one that is determinately true just in case every one of the n-tuple of components is, and false otherwise. It is a manner of *understanding*, not just a grammatical form or a logical transaction. It is something we *do*, like thinking "I had the appetizer and the entrée." This is not about how many states we can be in. It is about the ability exercised in a single case, a definite thought form distinct from every other. It is all there, all at once.

Adding—genuinely adding, not estimating or routine following—is a sum-giving thought form for any suitable array of numbers.[15] If I add two "elevens," I am doing what would have given "forty-four" had I been adding two "twenty-twos" (and not making mistakes), and so on, for every other combination of suitable numbers. Most of us can't square 739 by mere comprehension, we have to "multiply it out," follow an algorithm, a routine. That's a processing problem, like my doing modus ponens in Latin. The adding I am talking about, like conjoining above, is a form of understanding. So too is modus ponens.

Definite forms of thought in a single case are dispositive for every relevant case, actual, potential, and counterfactual. The function is the *form* of thinking by which inputs yield outputs.

3. The Indeterminacy of the Physical

No matter what a machine does or for how long, what it is doing remains formally indeterminate. That's supported by W. V. O. Quine's underdetermination claims, Nelson Goodman's "grue" reflections (1955, 63–86), and the "plus-quus" considerations of Kripke (1982, 9 and passim). That suggests an argument as follows.

Whatever the outputs of physical process may be, there will always be a pair of incompatible predicates, each as empirically adequate as the other, to name a function from the input to the output. There is nothing about the outcomes or the materialization of a physical process to block it from being a case of incompossible pure functions, *if* it could be a case, rather than mere approximation, of any pure function at all. That's because the differentiating point, the point where the behavioral outputs would diverge to display difference of processes, can lie beyond the life of the machine or even the world. If the function were $x * y = (x + y, \text{if } y < 10^{40} \text{ years}; = x + y + 1, \text{otherwise})$, the differentiating output, distinguishing * from + would lie beyond the conjectured life of the universe.

Just as rectangular doors can approximate Euclidean rectangularity, so physical change can simulate, but not realize, pure functions. In simplest terms, that is because physical phenomena are never under a single quantitative relationship. There are no physical features by which an adding machine, whether it is an old mechanical gear machine or a handheld calculator or a computer, can exclude its satisfying a function incompatible with addition, say, "quaddition" (Kripke's [1982, 9] definition of a function to show the indeterminacy of the single case: "quus," symbolized by the plus sign in a circle, "is defined by: $x \oplus y = x + y$, if $x, y < 57, = 5$ otherwise,"), modified so that the differentiating outputs (not what constitutes the difference, but what manifests it) lie beyond the lifetime of the machine. The consequence is that a physical process is really indeterminate among incompatible pure functions.[16] That's not just an epistemic claim; it is a physical necessity.[17] So, the process does not realize any of them.

Adding is not a sequence of inputs to outputs, it is summing; whereas, if the process were "quadding," all its outputs from the beginning would be quadditions, not sums, whether or not they differed in quantity from additions (before a differentiating point shows up to display outputs that diverge from sums). For any outputs to be sums, the machine has to add. But the indeterminacy among incompossible functions is to be found in each single case, and, therefore, in every case. Thus, the machine never adds (except analogically); it *simulates* addition. That's the same sort of reasoning that Plato used to argue that spatiotemporal things can only imitate, imperfectly copy, the ideal Forms.

If the machine is not really adding in the single case, no matter how many actual outputs seem "right," there might eventually be non-sums. Kripke concluded that in such a case it is indeterminate which function the machine satisfies and, thus, "there is no fact of the matter" as to whether it adds or not (cf. 1982, 21: he thinks that can motivate the "sceptical paradox" that he attributes to Wittgenstein).[18] I conclude, however, that it is definitely *not* adding. If it is indeterminate—physically and logically, not just epistemically—which function is realized among incompossible functions, then none of them is. Machines cannot do what we can do.

A machine simulates adding, calculating, recalling, and so on. What it does gets the name of what we do because it reliably, even more reliably, gets the outputs we do when we add and can get those outcomes for cases we cannot efficiently process. The machine adds the way robots walk and use tools. The names are analogous, but not merely equivocal or metaphorical. The machine attains enough reliability, stability, and economy to achieve realism without *that* reality. A flight simulator has enough realism for flight training; you are really trained, but you are not really flying.[19] The same holds for Big Blue and chess.

We have no doubt that the operations of a mechanical adding machine and of a personal computer are entirely physical. Addition cannot be type identical with either of those physical processes because then it could not be done by the other sort of machine. Suppose that addition is identical with a common function among those processes, then the processes would have to realize that function to the exclusion of every incompossible function. But they cannot do that, as the examples above show. So, the machines cannot really (and univocally with us) add. They cannot do what we do. That is the heart of the matter.

What happened to nature? Don't natural processes, say the behavior of a freely falling body, realize pure functions like $d = \frac{1}{2}gt$? Doesn't an object in empty space decrease in length in the direction it is traveling by an amount equal to $\sqrt{1 - v^2/c^2}$? The functions are approximated, not performed. There are two reasons for that. The first is that the laws are idealizations.[20] The second is that even if an object falling to the earth "in a vacuum" were to fit d = ½ gt exactly, it would also fit some incompossible function, given the underdetermination arguments, and thus would, strictly and exclusively, satisfy neither.

Now, to accept the overall argument, one does not need to deny that there are definite, repeatable, natural structures like benzene rings, crystals, molecules, and force fields throughout the universe. The criteria for "physically definite structure" differ from those for pure functions.[21] The real structures of things require the material and its environment, say, electrons, atoms, molecules, and magnetic and gravitational fields (chapter 7), and so are not expected to match the idealizations exactly (Niiniluoto 1999, 139).

4. Retreat from People

To avoid the argument, someone may say, "Humans do not really add, either; we just simulate addition. Pure addition is just as much an idealization for us as is $E = mc^2$. We can define pure functions but cannot *perform* them." Now, that defense is expensive. It denies outright that we do the very things we were sure all along that we do. It's like saying we can't read these very words. Of course, we don't, strictly, multiply or add every time we loosely say we do (by rote); but we do it sometimes by comprehension. That is more certain than any argument to the contrary.

In any case, we can certainly *define* the ideal functions like adding and conjoining. But a formal definition is itself a pure function, for example, "if p then q, and p; then q" is modus ponens. That is not indeterminate among incompossibles. So, there is a pragmatic contradiction in denying that we can think in pure functions. To define such a function *is* to think in a form that is not indeterminate among incompossible forms. And to deny explicitly[22] that we can do a specified operation, whether add, conjoin, state the congruence of triangles, or define particular functions, like conjunction, is to do what is being denied. Such an epidemic of theoretical doubt as to what we can do, without any effect on one's own practical certainty, must involve a mistake.

A simulation, as far as it goes, can always be a case of something else; so if that were all we could do, it would never be determinate what we are doing at all. We couldn't really do logic or mathematics or any other formal thinking; we couldn't even castle in chess, but could only simulate it, without there being any explanation for what "it" is, since thinking so as to define it would be to perform a pure function. The relation of simulation to a mathematical or logical operation will, itself, not be definable without the prior notion of pure functions.[23]

5. Functional States

Kripke (1982, 36–37 n.24) remarked that "any concrete physical object can be viewed as an imperfect realization of many machine programs." But he seemed content with an epistemic conclusion, in Wittgenstein's behalf, when he said, "taking a human organism as a concrete object, what is to tell us WHICH program he should be regarded as instantiating? In particular, does he compute 'plus' or 'quus'?" We should, I think, conclude that if a person is only a "concrete physical object" then nothing determines, at a certain level of formal refinement, which program he "instantiates" when he thinks, because he instantiates none. Whereas people do add, define, and so forth, and are thus not just concrete physical objects.

6. Thinking, as Process, Always Has Other Cases

The main outcome is that some thought processes are determinate among incompossible functions the way no physical process can be. That holds for series of processes and physically determined functions among processes as well. Consequently, such thought is never strictly identical with any physical process or function; yet thought, as I remark elsewhere, always needs a sensory medium, like speech, images, feelings, or action. The thought can be really the same as a judgment expressed with images, words, or actions without being identical with it (see chapter 8).

That all thought is determinate that way is harder to make convincing because it rests on one's recognizing that whatever thinking we do, whether simple assertion, or hoping or wanting or intending (over the whole family of things each of those can be, according to its particular content on a particular occasion) is in *form* such that, in order to do that, we have to do what would be the same activity for indefinitely many other cases (sorted by content) that do not happen. Further, someone else might have thought, or said, or believed, or felt the same, in a way definite among incompossibles, though not in a way numerically identical with your or my thought, or even with a directly similar brain state or feeling.

Thinking always has "other cases" as to form—I can think the same thing again, or remember it, for instance—though the form may not be separately articulable by us the way mathematical and logical forms are. For a lot of thought is no more precisely specifiable than the expressions and actions we use for it. Yet asserting, in any one of its senses, cannot be "halfway" between opposed forms; it would not be asserting then. And so on, for every form of thinking as process.[24] That's true even when the thinking is inextricable from the expression of it ("life is a mess") and when it is shapeless, like most uses of "it's ironic that," that nevertheless contrast with "it's obvious that" and "it's startling that."

III. The Parallel Reasoning as to Content

Can the reasoning above be applied to content as well as to form? Not so neatly, but still, I think, substantially yes because (i) thought content has to be repeatable and shareable in ways the physical cannot be, for instance, shared by another person; (ii) thoughts lack the transcendent determinacy of the physical (chapter 1). Yet a thought and its medium (images, gestures, feeling, or action) can be really[25] the same thing, the way an assertion can be the same thing as its utterance. But the same thought can exist in numerically diverse media, either as something remembered or as something someone else thinks too. That is real sameness of thought and expression, but not exclusive sameness, nor is it transitive or symmetrical.

The contrast among thoughts is definite, even among vague thoughts, in ways the contrast among physical states cannot exactly mirror; so they cannot be identical. For instance, the judgment $2 + 7 = 9$ cannot be identical with a physical state or process that is theoretically indeterminate as to its structure, as all physical states are (see arguments earlier).

IV. Other Considerations

(1) *As to Causation and Constitution.* — Whatever is caused is qua effect as indefinite as is the cause. A wavering hand with chalk draws a wavering chalkline unless something, an edge, intervenes. Since a physical state is indeterminate among incompatible pure functions, then whatever the physical state causes will have the same, or more, indeterminacy of formal content. As a result, no physical state or process can be the same as, or be the (complete) cause of any definite thought, like "if p then q, p; therefore q."

The reverse does not hold, however: determinacy can be lost from cause to effect. The physical states that thought causes can and do lack the determinacy of the thought states and are compatible both as to form and content with mutually incompatible thoughts, for instance, the sentence "Everyone trips sometimes." The same gesture can mean something else. With music, the sounds may be compatible with competing scores made by transcription; and distinct and divergent sounds (e.g., tuned to A-440 in one case and A-444 in the other) can be compliant with the same score. Thus, even if there is causation of physical states by thought, as there undoubtedly is, the physical states are indeterminate in ways their causes or constitutive thoughts are not. (They are also indeterminate in physical ways not shared by the thought.)

On the other hand, if there is causation of thought from physical states—and there certainly can be such chemical causes—the causation cannot be complete because the thought states are definite in ways the physical states are not. But the effect can't have what the cause lacks (except by an intervention). So we can conclude that not only do the physical states not reductively constitute the thoughts, they do not wholly cause them either. Some other activity and explanation is required (thought). (See the comments regarding "subsistence" below.)

When you walk up a familiar hill, each step is willing, perceptive, and proprioceptive, but usually with no attention to the component actions like lifting your knees and moving your hips. In fact, walking is usually a kind of action thinking that goes on in parallel with remembering, imagining, conversing, ruminating, and so on. None of this is identity of thought and the physical. But it is real sameness, where the thinking subsists in and forms the action. When the natural sameness of thinking and physical enactment is disrupted, thought falls into transactional causation of movement: you have to intend the movements by conscious willing, as an injured person might move a limb.[26]

This is not a repeat of Descartes's argument in *Meditation VI* from the contrasting properties of *res extensa* (divisibility and primary qualities) and *res cogitans* (indivisibility and no primary qualities) to their real distinction and possible, by divine power, separate existence. For I am not, as he was, arguing that thoughts might exist without their bodily medium in-which.[27] I am instead arguing that each has features the other cannot have (determinate, repeatable content for judgments versus transcendent, unrepeatable determinacy for the bodily states), and thus that the bodily state cannot wholly constitute or cause the judgment (content) because the effect cannot be more determinate, in the relevant respects, than its cause or constituents.[28] Thus, thought is not theoretically reducible to physical states.

(2) As to Universality. — Another line of reasoning applies both to form and to content of judgment. This idea traces to Aristotle's argument in book 3 of *De Anima*, from the universality of the ability to understand. The idea, in germ, is that being able to understand something is in principle being able to understand anything at all except for impediments of circumstance.[29] It is like the ability to write words in one's language. That's because the ability required to do one (say, add 3 + 3) is the ability sufficient to do *any*, accidental features being ignored. The

ability to discern forms and manipulate them in judgment in a single case is the ability sufficient, barring accidentals of presentation and training, for any case. Once a child genuinely attains judgmental ability, it is doing the same thing it will do as the most learned and comprehending adult.

(3) Another important argument is that abstraction is a constant and native (like breathing) departicularization of what is physically individual, by the separation of intelligible structure coincident with it from the material particularization. That cannot be done physically since the separated structure is repeatable (e.g., "positive charges repel") and is not just the same as any particular result which is all a physical process can achieve.

(4) Humans can do more than computers (Penrose 1989), even more than Blue Gene (IBM 2006) doing a quadrillion floating point operations per second. Humans can quickly settle "which is the most cost-effective path for a salesman to follow among eight destinations," something not algorithmically practicable; in fact, as the number of destinations rises to a hundred, computational times and memory resources to do it with computers "would exceed the known future life of the universe" (Hopcroft and Ullman 1974, 98–103). That comment is only suggestive because the process humans follow is not computational, nor is that the only sort of machine there can be. But considering that subject ties in with my next point to yield something important.

Cryptography, closely connected with NP-incompleteness, undercuts the idea that all features of the message can be explained by features of the signal (the machine states)—as Descartes had noted, looking at the ink marks he used in writing. But, in Descartes's reflections, the additional organization or meaning was supplied by an intelligent outside cause, the mind.

That hypothesis distracted attention from the fact that a physical signal can contain a message that cannot be explained by the principles that explain the assembly of the signal. That is, the organizational principles of the message may belong to a system for which the signal system is only a carrier, a medium, not by itself able to make the message (perhaps the way a radio signal is related to the symphony it carries or that my scribbles are related to my thoughts). The sensory and imagery states as well as the underlying neurophysiology (brain states) are related that way to the intelligent cognitive states of humans.[30]

In a word, there can be an intrinsic organization (the message), which by way of notational conventions explains the assembly of the physical signal, that cannot itself be explained the other way around, the way a message transmitted by fireworks can't be decomposed into the physics of the explosions. So it should be no surprise that the content of judgments cannot be explained by the physical states, even the sentences, we use to make them, any more than the meanings of what we write can be explained by the physical shapes we use to write with.

(5) As to Subsistence. — "The mind is in a sense potentially whatever is thinkable," as Aristotle said. For the mind, as capacity, becomes its thoughts, as act of the ability to think, the way my driving a car is the actuality of my ability to drive. And the actuality of thought, of course, is what no physical process or material function can be, as reasoned above. Yet the manner of a thing's being has to be suitable for, and explanatory of, the thing's natural activity, otherwise we'd have something from nothing—Aristotle's idea again and one Avicenna and Aquinas and others employed vigorously. If the activity cannot be reductively any physical process, then the being of the agent can't be reducibly physical either. As Aquinas put it (*Summa Theologica*, Ia, q. 76, a.1c): "it [understanding] has an operation and a power in which corporeal matter has no share whatever."[31]

I now turn to the explanatory structures of things.

CHAPTER 7

Real Natures

Software Everywhere

1. Introduction

The intelligible repeatable structures of things and processes are real. They are constitutive of particulars. There is such software everywhere in nature. We can discern, formulate, and use the structures; indeed, a good part of science and technology does that. And we can make them. We make plastics, medicines, fabrics, metals, and everything from cosmetics to automobiles. More importantly, we make even more abstract things, the programs (the embedded instructions of other processes), and materialize them in computers and as entire information and communication systems. Some structures are theoretically reducible to component substructures, but some are not. The ones important here are the constitutive structures, like waves, force fields, and operating systems.

Particularly significant are the structures whose outcomes lie beyond the assembly capacities of inanimate nature and have inputs, operations, and outcomes that are accessible as such to intelligent beings alone, like electronic communication. For instance, the information entered into a tax calculator and derived as outputs, the tax owed, is not reducible to electrical energy though it subsists in it. Moreover, such processing structures are aimed at abstractly, as such, by inventors. Even inventing the wheel was aimed at "something that rolls on an axis,"[1] and the scissors at a "cutting blade against a sheering edge in a hand tool." Our information-age inventions are far more abstract than that.

The intelligible structures are like "little minds in things" determining what things are capable of and do, something Descartes quite reasonably dismissed at the infancy of the new mathematized sciences of quantitative change (the new physics).[2]

A Historical Comment. — Descartes decided *res extensa* moves by a created and conserved deposit of motion in accord with the divine laws of nature. His was a ballet world of divine choreography from an initial quantity of motion, like billiard balls moving after an initial "break" along lawlike paths but with collision being no more than mutual orderly backing off at determinate angles and moving on. Malebranche modified that idea with constant divine intervention and gave it the name "occasionalism." Both described physical causation as quantitative transitions, without appealing to real transactions in nature that the scholastic Aristotelians like Aquinas, Duns Scotus, and Francis Suarez had taken to be real, but had not made particular and accessible enough for the purposes of the new science.

Those earlier philosophers had thought nature *does* things and that productive (efficient) causation is genuinely transactional, transformational, not just occasional. But how such transactions happen was not uniformly or convincingly explained. Some had thought substantial forms originate activity (like agents, or packets of activity—something Descartes found not to explain anything), and others had thought natural forms locally modify cosmic motion, like channels for rivers and gears for clocks. Some thought living things transmit a form in generating offspring (perhaps the specific form of the male parent individuated anew by the maternal matter to form the offspring), and others thought substances modify the spatiotemporal arrangement of proximate matter, channeling the cosmic motion (from the First Mover by way of the stars and sun, as Aristotle thought), until new forms *emerge* from the readied material, even in animal generation (except for human souls that many said are directly created by God). By Descartes's time such earlier accounts had run dry for physics, while the study of nature as systems of celestial and terrestrial quantitative change had began to display extensive explanatory and predictive resources. But the puzzle about causation just changed its appearance, it did not go away.

Berkeley adopted instrumentalism about corpuscular science and denied there is any transactional causing in nature, that is, among physical things (which are ideas). Hume regarded natural causation as regular succession in experience between prior "at-time/place" states/events/impressions and succeeding "at-time/place" states/events/impressions. "Regular succession in experience" became the Empiricist notion of natural causation, and eventually was supplemented with the condition, "regularity holding counterfactually as well," to distinguish causation from the merely coincidental or statistical regularity. That "at-at" conception of nature (cf. Salmon 1984, 1990) still dominates, with counterfactuality variously treated, for instance, (i) as hyper-regularity across suitably similar possible worlds (e.g., D. Lewis 1973, who basically expanded Humean causation into transworld counterpart regularity of behavior within suitably similar possible worlds to account for counterfactuality), or (ii) as the synthetic a priori constitutive order of experience (Kant and some later Idealists).[3] (Probabilistic later readings of such regularities dispense with the mechanism and rigidity of early modern physics, but are otherwise occasionalist accounts.)

On all such accounts, causes do not *do* anything beyond happening in unchanging quantitative patterns called "causal," and forces are the constant and universal lawlike *patterns* of quantitative change at relevant magnitudes. Necessity and impossibility are not in nature, but in the abstracta. For instance, gravitation is treated as the warping (mathematically and behaviorally) of space-time, and mass and energy are treated as quantities determining (that is, mathematically) the geometry of space-time (cf. Greene 2004, 69–71, for illustrations). Of course, the phenomena themselves are fields, particles, and so on, regarded as quantities. It is as if the cosmos were regarded as a display in which various quantities occur in spatiotemporal relationships and the laws are the exceptionless abstract regularities among those quantities, without any further insides.

2. Transactional Causation

We know that if I lift my hand to scratch my face, I am doing that; it is not just happening. It is not just the appearance of information from an earlier event in a later one. A theory of causation that leaves *doing* out is just describing a logical shadow of the real. Yet we can't reduce the doings of nature to something other than structured energy. There does not seem to be energy without some form whether waves, fields, atoms, molecules, crystals, stars, galaxies, or, especially, living things. So that may be a start. We don't know yet whether there may be some fundamental energy form of which all other energy forms are chords, overtones, and harmonics, as it were.

It helps to distinguish formal causation (constitutive, operative structure, for instance) from transactional causing (productive or efficient causation), which is, overall, resultant throughout the cosmos. Wesley Salmon (1984) describes transactional causing as transmitting a mark to distinguish it from merely coincidental regular succession, like a succession of shrinking shadows on a wall (as a ball bounces away); but still he explicitly stays within the broad Humean model of "at-at" causation (Salmon 1984; 1990).

In contrast, the outcome of transactional causing as understood by ordinary perceivers is that something does something, something else is made to be or to happen, like a spark's igniting a fire, one's getting a shock from a hot wire, or water's perking up a plant; there is an energy transmittal and transformation. It is not just that information belonging to the "cause" appears in the "effect." Nor is it just the illusion of doing, like something a magician can display when startling us. Transactional causation distributes energy, like one's rocking a chair, whereas formal causation is the organization of energy distribution, like the rocking chair's design, say, the length and slope of the rockers that explains the pattern of the rocking energy.[4]

Generally, formal (structural) causation and an energy base at some included magnitude explains transactional causation at an including (higher) magnitude. Of course, the fact that formal causation explains transactional causation depends on some (relatively) fundamental energy (say, light or superstrings) that is trans*formed* in the physical phenomena. It may turn out, as with Aristotle's *materia prima*, that there is no unstructured energy even though every intelligible structure supposes prior structured energy. Or it may instead turn out that there are some fundamental energy forms that *are* what they do, without a base they structure, but only with interactions with one another (like chords, harmonics, and overtones).

3. Tunes, Waves, and Puzzles: Real Structures

It isn't as if something ghostly and immaterial is added to the material world to organize it. Rather, matter (at least the known matter–antimatter domain) is better regarded mathematically as complexly structured energy. In ordinary physical things, material is arranged so that, given an energy base capable of such arrangements, the organization explains the outcomes, the way sticks make a fence, pieces make a puzzle, or a certain computing architecture makes petraflop capacity.[5] The form or structure is really the same as its materialization but is not identical with it because the material can have other structures or none (see chapter 7.4).

(1) Tunes (melodies) are, with qualifications, a good example of active constitutive structures.[6] The page here displays several. They are structures that can be transposed to other keys, played on many instruments and sung, preserved, and transmitted in scores and digital media and radio waves. They are active distributive structures for compliant sounds; in fact, they have distinctive intellectual and emotive characteristics.

Johann Sebastian Bach, Musette

Jean-Philippe Rameau, La Tambourin

Johannes Brahms, Waltz in A-flat

The melody has no reality apart from some singing, playing, notation, memory, recording, radio transmission, and so on, or the composer's inventively imagining it. Yet it is not identical with any of those because it can be repeated and multiplied. It is a countable complete thing with its own musical characteristics, energy, drive, and resolution that it imparts to the correct performances. A melody cannot exist without materialization, though in some material (long radio waves) it is only preserved, not operative. That's also true of Word and Excel uninstalled. They are not physical individuals because they can be repeated. Nor are they Platonic universals because they can't exist without materialization, and they are not just intentional objects either (see chapter 7.5) because they can be materialized, that is, made to structure some sounds, say. A melody is an abstract particular, not identical with any materialization, but really the same thing—the same in being—as any adequate one. So when we say, "That's 'Twinkle, Twinkle Little Star,'" we mean that literally; it is the very thing the beginning violin player sounds out, and the very thing for which Mozart wrote variations. It can be in many places at the same time and realized in some soundings more perfectly than others, and is accessible as that melody only to comprehending beings.

Although abstract particulars[7] are forms, forms generally are not abstract particulars because abstract particulars can be materialized in generically diverse matter (e.g., print, sound, electronic waves), whereas constitutive forms, not merely accidental ones, can be realized only in narrow ranges of material[8] that are as much part of the thing as its structure; for example, animals require specific sorts of flesh and bones to be alive, all over with one life. Merely accidental forms can of course have varied sorts of material (e.g., doors can be made of wood, bamboo, steel, etc.).

(2) Waves are paradigms of constitutive forms. They are active, explanatory, and mathematizable.[9] They are thus, as such, accessible to intelligent beings alone. Some waves *are* forms of energy (say, electromagnetic waves and gravity waves) and some modify and distribute energy (say, sound and ocean waves).

Water waves move through the liquid, exchanging their particles as they go,[10] perhaps leaving one's floating hat behind. The wave organizes its particles into a hill of water. The hills pass through the water (mostly). The same is true for sound waves: the compression moves outward but the air stays (mostly) where it is. Yet sound waves can break, crush, and heat things, and at superhigh frequency can make water droplets glow (sonoluminescence). Electromagnetic waves and light have spatial distribution too, and can be moved around, as you can carry a magnet or point a light. Some waves, like light and electromagnetism, are constitutive as well as instrumental; others, like ocean waves, have a medium (water) and result from the behavior of liquid, wind, temperature, and the like, but still are mathematizable, lawlike, and real.

Efficient causation that is not voluntary is on the whole—I conjecture but do not attempt to show—schematically reducible to formal causation, to the structural programming of an energy base, as already mentioned. Sound waves, light waves, and magnetic waves *do* things that are not mere correlations of happenings; they distribute, or *are*, general forces. This reasoning is, of course, not sufficient by itself to displace a merely occasionalist notion of causation; but since scientific interpretations of nature that are not doggedly idealist or phenomenalist admit the reality of energy (light, magnetic, gravitational, strong force, etc.), and since we can't explain the success of technology without supposing there are actual structures explanatory of things and processes, those considerations together weigh strongly that real action in the cosmos is structurally modulated energy, and that there really is transmission as well as natural necessity (chapter 2) in things. Just as the rhythmic structures, iambic pentameter and dactylic hexameter, contrastively distribute linguistic energy, and 4/4 march and 3/4 waltz rhythms diversely distribute musical energy, so the physical structures of automobiles, airplanes, and explosives diversely and actively modify and distribute physical energy.

Such structures are accessible to human knowing, some by ordinary direct perception (ocean waves), some by theoretical science and experiment (light waves and electromagnetic and gravitational waves), and some especially by direct human making and intelligent perception (making a tune, or making MS-DOS and communication systems, and inventing dactylic hexameter and 5/4 time). Such structures are the real *why* of various phenomena, the way a moving magnet drags filings on a piece of paper. You can do things with them and can make changes with them, and, as Ian Hacking (1983) suggested, things you can do something differently with are real.

(3) Physical puzzles may be convincing examples of real, indeed constitutive, intelligible structures (though they are less dramatic than programming). They are human inventions physically materialized and account for what puzzle lovers understand and employ: like the Towers of Hanoi (that many students have tried), the more complex Chinese rings, or a six-by-six-row Rubik's Cube (one was built by a Greek inventor). One collector classified physical puzzles into ten basic structures, such as disentanglement puzzles (Chinese rings), interlocking solid puzzles (three-dimensional jigsaws), and take-apart puzzles (with subgroups like trick locks and secret compartments).[11] The structures, for instance, interlocking shapes that have to be moved in a certain order, are constitutive of the physical puzzles. The structures are not the immediate parts, but the arrangement of parts. And the puzzle can't be understood apart from one's grasping the structure. Yet the structure is repeatable—three-by-three-row Rubik's Cubes are sold everywhere. Thus, such intelligible structures are constitutive and real.[12]

The same holds for cellular construction generally, for instance, living cells in an organism, arches of medieval cathedrals, windows in renaissance buildings, bays of skyscrapers, spans in bridges, or the studs in a stick-built house. They modify and distribute energy. They organize material into patterns of hard-as-iron behavior. Cellular construction is of course obvious in classical music, thirty-two-bar popular songs, and in jazz improvisation, too. Structural repetition, contrast, and variation are especially pleasing to understand and pleasing to the senses, rhythmically as well, and they are everywhere throughout nature. Cellular, structural, organization is at the heart of architecture, building, manufacturing, invention, and art—even of literature and poetry too.

4. Real Sameness

At a number of points I say that things are really the same even though they are not strictly identical, sometimes not even with the "sortally relative identity" Peter Geach (1963; 1967; and 1973) discussed. For instance, the structure and material are really the same as the thing, and each is the same as the thing, yet the structure and the material are really distinct from one another. Again, what I see and the thing seen are really the same, but my seeing and the thing seen are really distinct, and so on.

I am talking about items the same in being, in reality. Some items that are "really the same thing" are also really distinct from one another (though not different things), say, as a structure (*Danaus Plexippus*) and the material structured—the genetic organization of that species of butterfly (versus the particular molecules of one single butterfly, where the structure/material distinction recurs as well). The notion of real sameness versus real distinction was common and diversely analyzed among late Aristotelians. It was familiar to Descartes, Leibniz, and Locke, and was also the contrastive pair: "real distinction" and "rational distinction."[13] We need the ideas again, now.

There are two related notions: "x and y are really the same F" and "x and y are really the same thing." The second is the one in focus here. The tree nearby and the tree you see are really the same thing, and what I know when I know that Mars is a planet is the same thing as what is so whether or not I know it, that Mars is a planet (chapter 5). The structure of a thing and the thing are really the same, and the material of a thing and the thing are really the same, but the structure is really distinct from the material, for the latter can change when the former does not.

Wrecking the structure or the material wrecks the chair, but destruction of the structure (by cutting the rockers off) need not be full destruction of the material (the wood), though destruction of the whole material (wood) destroys the structure of the whole chair (rocker). In some living things the entire material can be gradually changed when both the form and the individual remain the same, for instance, as we grow and age. So, "is really the same thing as" is neither transitive nor symmetrical. Also, it can happen that the whole thing may undergo merely accidental or merely extrinsic changes that affect neither the structure nor the material, like the rocker's being moved or painted.

Something I know (that you exist) and something you know (that you exist) may each be the same as what is so (that you exist), yet your knowing is not mine (they are different existents) and even your sort of knowing it (because of its viewpointedness) is not the same sort of knowing as my knowing it. More generally, a structure shareable by many is not strictly identical with its single cases but is really the same as each and, except as something understood, has no other reality as such.

It is not as if there is some reality that is spread out over many, but rather some factor in each that is repeated in others. In general, that is because *structure does not carry individuation with it.* To be a house cat is not to be any particular house cat, but there is no house cat unless there is some particular house cat.

Any nondenominative difference defeats identity, whereas the opposite of real sameness is more complex because things that are really the same can also be really distinct from one another, a song and a singing of it. Real distinction can either be among different things (copies of a book), or distinction of pairs only one of which can exist without the other (the perception and the thing perceived), or distinction of constitutive, correlative factors of one existent, like its structure and material, or distinction of pairs related as a capacity and its correlative actuality (like my ability to, and my actually pointing at someone).

Identity, whether in the sense of "every property of the one designated relatum is also a property of the other, necessarily" or in the sense of "everything true of the one designated relatum is true of the other, necessarily" is a logical relation, a mind-dependent one, both because there is no designating/referring without thought and because strictly there are no logical relations, pure functions, independently in nature (see arguments in chapters 2.2 and 6). But real sameness, say, of electromagnetic energy and of a given magnet's active field, is not identity or even mind dependent.

A natural structure/form is not individual on its own. It is individuated in the thing it structures, by its internal unity and difference from every other actual unit existent. It is the intelligible organization of a thing or process, a program, like the programs of living things that metamorphose. The structure in a pair of monarchs (*Danaus Plexippus*), though repeated, is really the same-F, thus "really the same," but not really the same *thing* because the butterflies are different. ("Same-F" is not prior to and explanatory of the cases; it is consequent; see comments on individuation at chapter 7.6.)

The notion "is really the same thing as" has context-variant senses with overlapping threads. One thread is that real sameness (say, of a word and its inscription, or of a statement and some expression of it, or of cognition and reality cognized, or of a thing and its constitutive structure) is not logical or Leibnizian identity but sameness of reality, sameness of being or existence. Those two cases, of thing and its constitutive structure and of cognition and thing cognized, are central to the larger metaphysical alignment pursued in this book. For the real sameness of things and what animals perceive, and of the things and their intelligently abstracted structures, as means of human perceptual understanding, obviates what was supposed to be the mind-world gap addressed notably by C.I. Lewis (1929), Wilfred Sellars (1956;1963), and John McDowell (1994), among many other philosophers influenced by the problematic encountered by Descartes and freshly addressed by Kant.

5. Real Natures

Real natures are materialized intelligible structures that account for the characteristic behavior and propensities of things like baking soda, bicarbonate, and lead. We discover the natures of things from what things do, by observation and experiment, refined with explanatory science that distinguishes the constitutive structures from the mere resultants and the incidentals. Science encyclopedias are rich with such descriptions.

6. Common Natures: What Is Common to Many?

An intelligible structure does the same thing with any suitable material. That's because it is not individuated by itself. That is a central consideration. Structures do not individuate themselves. With that simple consideration many puzzles about natural realism unravel.

Some philosophers balk at the idea that structure materially individuated and discernible by humans, though repeatable, in no case really exists otherwise. But the alternatives are even more unappetizing because they involve postulating a domain of existing abstracta (properties or kinds) as Plato did, or of innate ideas as Descartes did, or of properties and individual essences (as even some physicalist modal ontologists do), or involve our (phenomenalistically) treating the similarity and generality in nature as always and only constructed by or for human cognition (as it sometimes actually is).

In sum, the nature of a thing—its characteristic propensities on account of what it is, say, gold or a mosquito—is complete in each particular lump or bug. Its being *common* is consequent on the repetition of the structure (the form) individually, like playing a tune over; for the structure is singular in each thing or process. Community is real; it's just consequent on the repetition of a structure that is indifferent to its individuation. In that respect material structure is like a statement or a song; it is indifferent to individuation but can't exist without it.

If some burning paper falls on your hand, you can plunge it into water and extinguish the fire, even lessen the burning of the hand if quick enough. If some ignited napalm falls on your hand you cannot extinguish it with water, and the burn is far worse even if it occurs over the same time. The fact that napalm is gasoline thickened to flow jellied, either by soap thickeners or by polystyrene or by similar polymers, and can therefore have varying chemical constitutions, does not cancel its being a common nature different from ignitable paper. Characteristic propensities, like being nonextinguishable by water, causing searing burning, and consuming what cannot be ignited, may be resultant from somewhat differing chemical compositions (structure and components). So a common nature does not ensure a common more particular constitution. The same thing holds for other real kinds, notably for synthetics like concrete, steel, plastics, medicines, paints, and other finishes.[14]

Emergent natures—a controversial matter as to whether there are any—would be resultant from prerequisite organization, but conceptually irreducible to the prerequisite base and would satisfy further conditions. (Codes and messages might be like that, cf. chapter 6.IV.4.)

That, however, would not be supervenience. For one thing, the relation of base to emergent is not a merely logical one, whereas supervenience is usually described as necessary (transworld) two-way item-by-item reciprocal changes in base and in supervening phenomena, or as a one-way logically necessary correlation of changes item-by-item (Kim 1990) from supervenient to subvenient phenomena (or vice versa). But those are not the only options. The emergence relation may be of system to system, and not of item to item, or as component to component. And it may be of natural necessity (cf. chapter 2), not of logical necessity.

That might be the relationship of life to chemical phenomena, for all we know yet. Or it might be the relation of conscious states to brain states. It would be like a system of messages emergent from a complex enough system of signals, (i) where no item or group of the messages is reducible to, or one-to-one explicable by, any item or group of the signals, yet (ii) where there can't be messages without the signals (carriers or media), and (iii) where the particular pattern of signals would not occur without *some* messages, and (iv) where the distinction among messages depends on, but isn't reducible to, the contrastive capacities among the signals, and (v) further, where nothing about the structure of the signals is sufficiently explanatory of the messages.

A random carrier signal could be related to keyed messages that way in cryptography. That might also be how light patterns in the buildings of a cityscape at night might stand to individuals' reasons for turning lights on and off, where the pattern is explicable from their reasons (plus other data), but the reasons are inaccessible from the light pattern and other physical data alone. Presumably, the emergent system, in order to be emergent, would not have any cause in nature beyond the system from which it emerges.[15]

For the most part, we perceive things by way of their consequent perceptible natures, not the physically basic and molecularly or atomically constitutive ones.[16] Nevertheless, consequent natures—say, milk, meat, sunlight, and oak, acids, iron, and cheese, and anything else with characteristic behavior on account of what it is—are just as real as the constitutive components we cannot perceive unaided,[17] even those features that are species specific as to which animals can perceive them, like colors or smells or sounds. The music is as real as the sounds, though the cat can hear the sounds but not the music in the sounds. The resultants at next-magnitude are not mere phenomena of the component magnitudes, mere appearances made by us, the way some think colors are related to light.[18] That would imply that midrange perceptible things are mind dependent, like well-grounded phenomena (cf. Leibniz), or mere phenomena (Berkeley, Hume, or Kant). Phenomenalism seems particularly awkward for certain modern physicalists (e.g., A. J. Ayer, J. J. C. Smart) who want to say reality is only the ultimate objects of physics and yet that the physical is only phenomenal. Besides, physicalist phenomenalists do not have a good response to why no physical-object statement is analytically reducible to a finite set of distinct phenomenal truth conditions (a problem C. I. Lewis [1946] had recognized with the idea that the physical is the permanent possibilities of sensation).

7. Analogous Realities

There are intelligible structures that are analogously the same. For instance, the dielectric polarization in electrical insulators is a reversible electrical property analogous to mechanical elasticity, and to thermal gain and loss. More broadly, mechanical changes cause thermal changes and electrical changes cause and are caused by thermal and mechanical changes, all according to general quantitative formulas, as explained above. So there is physical causation among analogous (structurally similar) realities that are not reducible to one another. There is causation among structures as well as among things structured.

Realities are analogous that have different definitions and different material bases but exhibit common structural properties that are causally related to one another—for instance, such principles as are formulated in a general theory of solids. The structural similarity is well based, real, and explanatory. For instance, you could have a battery circuit where, when the temperature falls enough (heat change), the battery chemistry slows (chemical change) causing the charge to fall (electrical change) so that a magnet turns off (electrical change), a lock opens (mechanical change), and the thieves take the jewels.

8. What About Indeterminacy and the Borders of Natural and Synthetic Kinds?

The scientists in a discipline use the abstract formulations that fit efficiently with the rest of their theory, while staying within the tolerances of observation and rich prediction,[19] the way car wheels can be understood as circles for one purpose and as slightly flattened continually flexing doughnuts for another. That is basically the position of Nancy Cartwright (1983) and Geoffrey Joseph (1980), and, further refined, of more recent writers cited by Niiniluoto (1999, 132–44); it is mine as well. Intelligible structures are real, but our formulations and our empirical descriptions involve simplifying and formalizing abstraction (chapter 1, "obtuse abstraction") and can be improved or replaced.

We can find or make cases that fall on the borders or near the borders of natural and synthetic kinds. Sometimes prior knowledge wasn't refined enough to discriminate the real sorts (e.g., to tell nephrite from jadeite) or observation was too crude; sometimes what seem to be the same constitutions have differing behavior, and sometimes the same behavior at one dimension comes from different component constitutions (agent orange), and so on. Some anti-Realists reason that if natural and synthetic kinds are indefinite at the edges that way, and if the structures or forms of things measured carefully are not the same as the ideal forms, then we don't really know the forms or natures of the individuals. So, they tell us, we might as well conclude that there are no real forms or natures or natural kinds at all but only projections and constructs.

That's like saying "the angle of incidence equals the angle of rebound" is not really so or explanatory for basketball because the effects of breeze, backboard material, height of a player's jump, and a ball's inflation will make the measured outcomes deviate from the abstractly predicted ones. But we know the angle of incidence principle is both explanatory, and useful, especially for the players. Similarly, it is useful to know that a combustion engine has four stages—"suck, squeeze, light, and blow"—that have particular physical systems ("intake, compression, ignition, exhaust"), each with widely varying particulars from early "hit-and-miss" engines right on down to the computerized modern engines, each of which has its own individuating marks (deviating within tolerances from theoretical values). The common general principles are explanatory and are abstracted from the real structures of the things, even when our descriptions of such structures are provisional. This is not to say we can't be quite wrong in what we think the explanatory structure to be. It can happen. But the self-correcting empirical activity of science can be expected to refine and replace, on the whole, what we get wrong.

We are not in a Goodman-like theoretical perplexity about what predicates to start projection with, because human thought does not often proceed by simple enumerative induction, but rather begins with a conception that organizes perception (chapter 5) and usually with some prior theory or speculation. Without relevant experience and conceptions, one might be unable to locate the melody in a passage from Richard Strauss, or be unable to identify cells microscopically, or recognize hydrate of methane. That's no different from an outsider's not knowing when the windup begins and ends for a baseball pitch and, thus, being unable to see a balk. A lobsterman said, "When the fisherman sees the water, he sees the bottom"; perceptual abilities differ, even when the senses are equally acute. Discrimination as to what things really are has to be learned and be refined by experience, teaching, talent, and communities of expertise (e.g., science, law, art, crafts, and technologies).

Some of the puzzles taken to be fundamental about our knowledge of the world are projections from the impoverished notions of knowledge and experience inherited from the empiricist and rationalist traditions. When we realign the pieces, as I am proposing here, the problems change too.[20]

9. The Status of the Laws and Induction

Laws as scientifically formulated for theory, though they are strictly about idealized objects, fit the installed software of nature, the constitutive structures of things and processes (chapter 1). They are true of formal objects, but true about and for the real natures of things by tolerances experience has found suitable to the subject area. Revised observations can compel revised laws. So, Bernoulli's principle formulates the velocity change of restricted flowing liquid apart from the individualizing traits of particular cases. The behavior is independently real and consequent on the structure of confined liquids; in fact that's what guides us to defects in a particular system, a carburetor, say.

But, how are things *governed* by laws? They are not. My suggestion is not that laws hold among properties (universals) (see, e.g., Armstrong 1983; Dretske 1977; Tooley 1977); rather it is more like Carroll's (1994) and other "primitivists" and dispositionalists (cf. Mumford 1998; 2004), though I think of laws as man-made expressions (like $E = MC^2$ and $F = MA$) of mathematizable relationships of and among the intelligible structures of physical things (including force fields, light waves, elementary particles, etc.).

There are also principles sometimes called "laws" that are nonexplanatory empirical generalizations like some principles of hydraulics, engineering, and economics, as well some merely quantitative though useful laws like the Rule of 72. Those are not in view here. I am concerned only with explanatory generalizations directly grounded in the operative structures of things. The reality is where the energy and structure is; the formulation is in the textbook.[21]

Relationships of natural structures could, in principle, be differently conceptualized and expressed in different laws, perhaps without loss of the intelligibility of nature or of the explanatory or technological success of science, just as Newtonian physics can be expressed as (a special case of) relativistic physics (Joseph 1980), and crude theories of hydraulics can be improved by later ones.[22]

No one is likely to deny that there are natural laws, even natural necessities like "as the velocity of an object with mass approaches that of light, the mass approaches infinity," or "$F = MA$" applied to automobile crashes. Some may think such a law has ideal existence like a Platonic archetype and "governs" particulars or properties by some (vacuous?) relation like exemplification or instantiation, or that it obtains (what is that?) because of the divine will or immutability (Descartes).[23] Others think a law of physics is only an instrument for the prediction of experience (Berkeley, Duhem, Mach), or a mere generalization of experience (Hume), or even that it is a synthetic a priori condition for the phenomena of nature (Kant). Those options don't account for order and activity in nature that is independent of and indeed required for evolutionary local latecomers like humans even to appear (though one determined phenomenalist physicist opined that if there had been no humans, there would have been no Big Bang).

It seems far closer to actual experience and scientific practice to say the laws of physics need no basis beyond the intelligible structures active in nature anymore than the installed software of a word processor needs any reality apart from the electronic states of transistors, capacitors, resistors, and so forth, arranged to materialize the logical structure. We do not need two or more layers of reality. The explanatory organization is intrinsic to the programmed computer and active as modulator of its electrical energy.

10. Same Constitution and Replicability

You can't multiply things of the same sort without numerically differing components or relative locations (two electromagnetic fields, say) or some other individuating factor. Structure is not individuated on its own; that's why it is repeatable. Physical structure needs individuating material conditions, just as does the repetition of a statement or a tune. (Perhaps the most fundamental structures in nature *are* what they do [energy processes] and are not individuated at all, but have consequents of their interactions that are.)

Still, there aren't any universals in the independent world either, only the foundation for them in repeatable structure (each time individuated). *A* and *B* may be really the same structurally—each doing what the other does on account of what it is; yet the structure of each is really the same as that particular thing, and the particulars are really different things from one another. Still, we also say the structure of the one is really the same as the structure of the other; we mean that under abstraction, as made universal and predictable, the structures do not differ and that the things as far as thus structured do not differ.

Universals, as conceptions, are acquired habitual focuses for our abstractive ability (like automated settings for a microscope that would adjust focus if a certain weight or numbered slide lands on the tray).

We acquire concepts in the several ways already mentioned. We employ them by acquired readiness (habit) unconsciously calibrated by utility to us. There is nothing real and separable to be found in many things. When we say lead is ductile, we mean inter alia that a suitable amount of it, heated enough, will flow into a mold. It is the real thing, lead, a common nature presented by fluorescing abstraction, which is focused in our judgmental awareness, not a mere representation or surrogate or mere name.

The general shape of this account is natural realism.[24] There are constitutive structures saturated in the particularity of things that make unities (e.g., elementary particles, magnetic fields, plants, animals) and enable their characteristic behavior. The structures (i) explain the operative similarity of numerically distinct things, (ii) ground the intelligibility of material things, and (iii), as abstracted, become universals and subjects of further, and even formal, thinking, like topology. These hypotheses gain plausibility from their superior utility to explain the practice and revision of science and technology, and especially clearly, when we devise and materialize computer, aircraft, financial, communications, automation, and many other programmed systems.

Real structure is entirely coincident with particulars. It is abstraction that gives *inesse*, existence-in-awareness, to what can independently exist only individuated (chapter 5). This account only holds together if we recognize, in our own experience, abstraction as a native, constant human ability that grounds empirical knowledge, one that was exiled from cognitive theory by mere assumptions after the seventeenth century.

11. Conclusion

Whether it is the way butter melts or an overheated spoon curls and shrivels, or a spring pulls, or a crystal assembles in a liquid, or a woodchuck lives and breeds—in all instances matter is programmed, structurally organized. It follows scripts that are intrinsic and constitutive. Understanding, describing, utilizing, and explaining such structures is scientific activity. That's so with subatomic things (the ones that are real) as well as iron, aluminum, magnets, and stars. Since there are no outside scripts for nature, no Platonic archetypes, and since the order of nature is not a consequence of human thought, there must be intrinsic and intelligible structures that are the constant energy-modulating (formal) causes of both physical behavior and continued existence. Efficient causation in nature is often at one magnitude, what is structurally (formally) modulated energy at a component magnitude (with ranges of incidental, even random, outcomes, and a subrange of the animal and human voluntary).[25] If the machine program gets corrupted, a word processor ceases to exist. So too with things in nature generally. If corruption makes the material incapable of the structure, the thing ceases to be.

The organization of material things by structures suitable for physical repetition and for abstraction is the foundation of our cognition of the distant, remote, and universal (chapter 5). When we conclude "mass determines space and space determines motion" we are thinking of, and talking about, real mass and cosmic space as such, not the ideas or mere sentences. When we realize iron is magnetizable, what we know is the potentiality of whatever is iron, say, the core of the earth, not some statement or replica.

That sort of reasoning prompted my explaining natural impossibility (chapter 2) as a kind of intentional vacuity (analogous to a nonconforming placement of a chess piece that is no move at all in the game, though clearly imaginable by us), and my arguing that humans directly perceive realities both particularly and abstractly together on a foundation of animal cognition, and by those same abilities can be presently aware of remote and abstract realities (chapter 5).

So, what of our mistakes? We look at that next.

CHAPTER 8

Going Wrong with the Master of Falsity

The false is in the way of judgment what misses at being so. Something is wrong with the thinking. The false is as plastic as truth (cf. chapter 4) and has special problems of its own, particularly about the content of false judgment. The rest, like a false statement or false sentences, is explanatorily derivative. Even judgment is not all two-handed; some can only be true. And to make a false statement you don't have to make a false judgment.

Human intelligent awareness is continuous and mostly undifferentiated into items; it is more like the scene through a moving window with some reflections and distortions on the glass, or the continuous sound of traffic, than it is like a true-false list (cf. chapter 8.2.7). The vista can have impositions and distortions because so much of one's flowing awareness is supplemented, filled-out with anticipations and reliances, remembering, imagining, and habitual construal. Flowing awareness is not neatly segmented the way our statements and sentences might suggest, and it is self-enveloping and thus may be distorted in next reflection as well. One's current awareness is of many sorts of things, processes, and happenings all together, and it has depth, dimension, and heft from one's reliant expectation, motor and associative readiness, experience, understanding, and feeling—all contributing elements that can go wrong.

When a screwdriver jumps the slot because we turned it too hard, there may have been false expectation (or simple ignorance or carelessness), but perhaps nothing that, except by obtuse abstraction, was a false statement. We just expected more "give," and the tool popped up. The expected give was judgment in action and expectation.

Given our sensory and cognitive limitations, false commitment is a likely by-product of intelligent perceptive awareness, and its likelihood increases with the generality and variety of our thoughts. Moreover, throughout the many varieties and sorts of false judgment, there is an operating master of falsity,[1] the imagination, and a natural motivator of commitment, willing reliance aimed at reward.

Ours is continuous view-pointed, reality-committed, and intersecting awareness of what may be particular, remote, or universal. A constant part of our awareness is readiness for what is not so, both the not-yet and the not-at-all, including awareness of what is not in sight, taste, reach, and so on, that nevertheless frames and gives depth to our awareness of what *is* so. To see a chair is to see something you don't expect to fly or dissolve or collapse under your weight. It is imagination, that constant condition for and part of veridical experience, and medium for memory that enables falsity.

The subject of the false is scrubby terrain without the well-worn paths there are in many parts of philosophy. For instance, Aristotle, Aquinas,[2] and Descartes (*Meditation IV*)[3] treat the matter briefly and mainly as if it is a feature of propositions—a trend amplified and sententialized in our time. Some recent writings on truth don't even treat the matter at all, as if the false is simply the truth value of the negations of what is true.[4] None of the analytic accounts treat falsity as part of our continuous and mostly right awareness. And none of them attend to our native, constant, but defeasible reality commitment (chapter 5) that enables false commitment.

We need to go into enough detail to avoid "sententializing" thought, and far enough to make it persuasive that imagination and memory combined with willing reliance to gain something wanted (the energy of rational belief) explains how false commitment is a natural by-product of our imperfect but effective cognitive abilities. It is mainly because present awareness and habitual commitment are full of reliance and expectation that can be defeated that false judgment is likely.

The reasons why truth of judgment, and falsity, taken item-by-item, is only an obtuse abstraction from something psychologically more complex and dependent on active imagination are probably well known. And the key observations below about the phenomenology of awareness have further support to be found among phenomenologists (like Merleau-Ponty 1945; Sokolowski 2000; Cobb-Stevens 1990; Follesdal [in Dreyfus 1982]), and such support can be further developed by inquiries like the recent ones by A. Noe, S. Kelley, M. Martin, T. Williamson and others into perception. Still, this is a discursive beginning of what needs a new phase of philosophical attention.

My observations aim to fit with the general position that truth and falsity are the outcomes of right and wrong thinking, and that judgment—as thinking that can be right or sometimes wrong as to what is or is not—is a constant and continuous native human activity (like sensation and breathing, imagining and remembering), enabled by conceptions, by which we commit in action, expectation, and understanding to the existence, the sorts, the employments, the natures and behavior of things and processes (chapter 5), and also do so in abstract reflection about them and ourselves as well.

So we need to know something more about how we can take something to be the real, along with the rest we are so taking, when we can in principle, instead, recognize that it is not the real. An opposed line of explanation, representationalism, has already been explored by philosophers for a long time, and its limitations are known. We need to look at falsity by presentation instead.

1. Right and Wrong Thinking

It is not right to say that understanding (as comprehending) is inseparable from language. Some of it is inseparable, but some of it is prior to the originating development of languages, and some of it is developmentally prior in individuals, say, by an infant's playing and crawling and exploring and first understanding baby words (cf. chapter 8.2.6). And some judgment exists only in our actions, like reaching for things, tying a shoe, eating with tableware, and singing, even hearing, a tune. Such awareness is usually automatic and unreflective, and includes background reliances, just as does our habitual and continuous conviction that we are saying and doing what we want. We can judgmentally apprehend something that only words we learn later can describe, as Jane Gardam's (1981) description of a child's experience conveys. See also Schooler and Fiore 1996.

Just as learned morality saves dithering about what to do, and mastery of words and circumstance saves fumbling in speech, and emotional, aesthetic, and social refinement reduces the need for calculated evaluation, so too expertise obviates item-by-item attention about the ordinary. Expertise enables right commitment without calculation, indeed, even attention, except as triggered by anomalies. We are all experts at the ordinary for us. The unreflective commitments in which we live are, for the most part, either so or not. When not so, the thinking is not done right, though that fact may not be accessible to us just then, and the cause may lie beyond what we can know about then.

How often in a day's ordinary moving around and living among objects and people is recognition and memory noticeably wrong? Not very. (That's similar to Donald Davidson's observing that most of our beliefs are true.) Wrong thinking shows up more with interpretation, prediction, reliance, and estimation than with ordinary recognition and action amid the familiar. A person's day may littered with false convictions, not often about ordinary things, but about the meanings, explanations, relationships, likelihoods, histories, real natures of, intentions of, and motivations of others and of oneself, and about various values and causal relations of events, persons, and social, political, and other realities, including money. But that's still a small portion of one's daily commitments. If we include our ordinary perception, most of the time we know many, many things, both occurrently and dispositionally.

If we think of experience as a moving and interactive vista—the world by way of awareness—we can see that the refractions of awareness itself can have imperfections (like a lens that makes edges crooked or makes parallel lines intersect—especially memory), or have reflections, scratches, and smudges that we take to be part of the scene. Such takings, usually by reliances, are false commitments, as are some of the material inferences we employ—the automatic transitions from one reliance to another—and the explanations, predictions, and expectations we may make up that rely on them. Those are not, of course, the only kinds of false judgments, but they are the sorts that I take to be explanatorily basic to the many other kinds there are. If we can explain those, I think we can explain the rest.

Thinking can be right about whether something exists, about the condition of things, about features of made-up objects, and about anything we can think about at any level of abstraction. Thinking can also be wrong, sometimes frequently and habitually, about most of those things, but not all. For not every judgment of every kind that you or I can make has a shadow judgment that is false, as "I exist," "I am here," and "I'm alive," and some others indicate. However, the practical use of such judgments seems very limited.

There are variations of true and false judgments ranging from judgments of existence ("There are wombats") and of relation ("Garages are usually near houses") to universal judgments like "Lead is unmagnetizable" and negatives "There aren't any witches in Salem," as well as to judgments that remote physical and historical events are or are not so, like "Cleopatra died from an asp bite," "The Romans colonized Ireland," and "There are clusters of galaxies within the Milky Way." There are many other sorts besides. But describing the mistakes by way of sentences that would express them does not explain how we make such mistakes, or even are able to. For one thing, we often do not use sentences at all, but rather make mistakes by our ready reliance in action, expectation, and reasoning from, and explanations for what is not so.

Anything we think, if we notice it, can be made something to think about. The range of what is so is a variety, not just of formal and empirical realities or of kinds of sentences or statements, but of kinds of empirical realities as well, like "He's jealous," "The dean is unsympathetic to our proposal," "The building leans to the left," "Gold won't dissolve in vinegar," "The tower moves in the wind," "The play's badly directed," "He's inconstant," "That's slipping," and "Rome was corrupted by greed and immorality"—and more. What is false is what you think when you think one of those things that is not so. How do we do that?

Kinds of false judgments tag along with what we can get right, but not like shadows or negations; that's a construct. Furthermore, what "is so" adapts to context as appears below, and so does "is not so." And do not, in particular, forget money. It is a social construct, but uncontestedly real, and something about which wrong thinking of many sorts is obvious. And yet it is paradigmatically something about which what is so is constitutively dependent on what is right, or not, to think.

False judgment involves one's going wrong in thinking aimed at what is so, particularly by mistaken construal, like taking a reflection to be the thing. Such mistaking is usually by habitual reliance, especially reliance on expectation. By reliance we commit to things that aren't so, things not expressed to oneself or attended to, even to things relied on in action whose falsity may never even appear to us. We talk of a person's habitual and subconscious true and false beliefs, and even of his unconscious true and false beliefs, because we infer those commitments from the actions and from the explanations we are offered. So something beyond sentential expressions or intervening representations is needed to explain how what is not so may be thought to be so. That's further complicated because what is not so is not individuated the way what is so is.

Imagination. — Imagination operates with memory and want in complex animals, and in humans it operates by way of understanding as well; it enables fit of action to what might happen and to what won't and can't happen, and to what is expected or not. It presents what is *not* so for planning and anticipation, along with what is usually so but is not in sight (hearing, etc.). Such expectations or fears or dreads can be defeated or just fail, and thus the commitments may be rendered false.

Imagination, like all of human and animal cognition and action, operates by targeted desire, usually by willing reliance aimed at something wanted. It is a philosophical fiction to suppose cognitive commitment is caused, even compelled, by evidence or reasons, except for the rare and uncharacteristic cases I mentioned, like "if I err I am" or "some of my beliefs are false," or when we are figuring things out or explicitly solving some problem by deliberation. The rest is by willing reliance of various sorts. Even what is beyond reasonable doubt can be willingly disbelieved (sometimes pathologically, sometimes willfully, and sometimes by misplaced reliance). If you suddenly see that something you already know entails a conclusion you reject vigorously enough, you may become even more ignorant by now rejecting the premise you earlier knew to be true.[5]

Imagination furnished by memory is capable of various refinements from experience and training. You can see that even in the anticipatory and responsive movements of a cutting horse's isolating a cow or in a sheep dog's turning a herd, as well as in the movements of humans playing hockey and basketball, and in the ingenious, spontaneous, counterexamples of skilled philosophers. Imagination, intelligence, and desire skate together. In humans imagination is constant, enveloping action, alight with understanding, not just an image maker, as Sartre deftly displayed.[6]

It is by imagination as medium for memory that the stability of objects, the density of solids, the weight of cups, and the steepness of stairs are expectations and reliances displayed in and modifying action without being articulated consciously. To climb stairs is a work of the imagination as well as of the limbs. The commitments involved operate as adjustments of action, awareness, and readiness. Objects and events have perceptible dimensions not presented to sense but relied on in action; and the more sophisticated the person is, the more dimensions not currently presented are part of one's operative reliances.

Imagination supplied with memory supplements the senses; it accommodates the backsides, tops, and insides of things, and our accumulated experience generally. It also supplies a medium for the solely thinkable, like the writing for "(p) (p $\supset$ p v – p)" and diagrams for geometry, and it combines things out of their natural order and behavior, like rainbow-colored baseball bats, for enjoyment and speculation. It is the indispensable means by which one can be aware of what is *about* to be (the wave about to capsize the boat) and what can't be (the boat turned away from the wave in time).

You may expect a chair to tip when it will not. The expected was imagined, anticipated in motor readiness and compensation. Your expectation that a friend will appreciate your gesture may show up in your feeling downcast when it is ignored. To handle a cup or a book, the feel has to be filled out, say, with readiness to lift it, how tight to hold it, how fast to move, and so on. That's all automatic, all reliant applications of past experience to provide readiness for the coming present. Each of those that can be disappointed in experiences amounts to a judgment that can be false. Imagination programs motor readiness. And all the senses are expectant too. We'd be visually surprised at a winking fluorescent red teacup, and surprised again at a daffodil that smelled like a sewer. We say, about mistakes and big oddities, "That's not how I imagined it, not at all."

Innumerably more features of things are actively expected and relied on than are registered by external sense (e.g., how easy to tip over, how hard to push, fragile or not, how far away, which side is up, how long it will last), and yet those features all together are vastly fewer than the real physical features of a perceivable real thing (e.g., how heavy a car is, the number of its windows, how thick its glass, or how many pocks in its paint surface, how many cylinders, the kind and age of its brakes—cf. chapter 1, "transcendent determinacy"). Besides, presentation and the way things are can deviate without disturbance of perception—for instance, as we walk around a table its visual presentation alters, but the perception remains constant. (Cf. Hatfield 2008 for discussion of perceptual constancy.) I think expectation plays an important adjusting role; for instance, though lines of telephone poles visually converge on a long straight country road, we don't conclude that the road narrows to a point. And we can still recognize tastes, of black cherries for example, though altered by others in Merlot.

For humans, the thing presented is co-presented abstractly by type(s) (structures) as well as by token, as a cat, a coon cat, a male, elderly, black, and bushy-tailed, not just that-one. For, the particular is perceived as it is understood. When perception goes wrong, often imagination has supplied some abstract and usual feature not in the object that we relied on or otherwise expected or adjusted to. That's one sort of falsity of judgment.

Imagination can be rich or poor. Inexperienced, it leaves one unrealistic and childish, like goslings following a mother-tractor. Limited or untutored imagination makes one impractical, unable to anticipate the obvious or surprised at the ordinary (e.g., how a sailboat will tilt or how tight a bottle cap is). Trained imagination is part of mastery in any form of action; that's why we hold disaster simulations, mock evacuations, fire drills, and so forth. Some people have "little or no imagination" not only in the obliviousness that invites error, but in the sense of "lacks inventiveness and originality," and even in the sense that marks stupidity where they can't anticipate outcomes and don't learn from experience.

Some people are victims of "overactive" imaginations prompted by greed, pride, and hate, and made liable to accidents by bravado (adolescent drivers) and gullible to scams and harm by greed. (I leave out for now how emotion and hormonal states can color the attractiveness of one's options.)

Imagination is treacherous because it is essentially incomplete. It *always* falls short of the real not only because the real is transcendently determinate (chapter 1), it does not even contain all of our own relevant experience. It is also unrestrained by natural necessity so that what seems possible may not be, for instance, to carry five plates unspilled up some stairs or to turn a screw with just a little more pressure. No matter how tutored and inventive it is, imagination never gets the whole of the particulars anticipated, so things can be impossible because of unimagined factors or difficult for reasons not known of, as happens even in space engineering and in philosophical reflection. And sometimes imagination is just inadequate to what is experienced, as with real love, beauty "beyond my imagining," grief, embarrassment, or an encounter entirely transcending (cf. 1 Cor. 2:9).

Because we can imagine what is not so, and have to be able to in order to plan and act, and have to rely on what is not yet at hand, we have space to mistake the imagined for the real. That usually happens by habitual reliances that don't hold up for particular cases. Because commitment is typically the product of reliance aimed at things we want (we rely on the brakes to stop our cars), when the reliance fails or is not sufficient, our commitment is false.[7]

Reliance. — Willing reliance provides ready and constant commitment to what is so, and frequently to what is not so, as presented by imagination and recall. Reliance is the energy of ordinary cognition (Ross 1993a; 1995). In fact, most of the coherence of one's self-understanding and of the worthwhile in life is the result of reliance aimed at fulfillment (presented in concrete imaginings). Mistakes of self-appraisal happen that way too, especially about what one really wants and about one's own virtues and vices. And mistakes about ordinary and more elaborate things come from habitual reliance on regularities experienced and expected, on associations taken as likely, and on various estimations of oneself and others.

Even rational aims can trigger mistakes: you may think a train on the next track is moving away, back from you, when in fact yours is rolling forward. The impulse for coherence (with no felt motion) motivates false commitment (and then dislodges it once you feel the motion of your train). The effectiveness of theatrical magic lies in our reliance on coherence in our experience.

So, imagination, suffused with understanding, employed in willing reliance as well as in deliberated judgment, is an indispensable element of cognitive success and also the conjurer for thinking wrongly that something is so or not. Imagination is indeed the master of falsity. It is also the conjurer of invention and art.[8]

2. Differences among Sentences, Statements, and Judgments

Peter Geach (1957, 104–5)[9] warned against equating statements and judgments because they are not the same; for one thing a judgment has to be present all at once to be made at all, not spread out as statements are. Further, (i) there can be falsity in the sense of *falsehood* in statements, but not in judgments,[10] (ii) expressed judgments require a background of unexpressed judgment, and (iii) judgments in focused awareness, like statements, require unfocused background commitment(s) unstated. Here are further differences.

(1) You can't falsely judge "I do not exist"; nor can you lie on the point. The sentence is grammatical, but you can't think that nonmetaphorically. We can judge, or think "No judgment is true" only by mistake, but we can lie, or try to, by saying so. Judgment, as continuous thought that is right or not as to what is so (like the dynamic view through a moving window) is explanatorily prior to the truth or falsity of sentences, statements, utterances, and even propositions (apart from formal contexts where "truth" is, for instance, operationally defined).[11]

(2) Time and space don't have parallel relationships to judgments and to sentences or even to statements. St. Augustine remarked that utterances take time but understanding is all together, not in pieces like the utterance you hear. A judgment may happen before the statement is finished and last long after the statement or be abandoned while one

is stating it. We often agree or disagree recognizing the judgment well before another's utterance is finished.

(3) A judgment can be true when the statement is false. Otherwise we couldn't lie by saying something. Also, someone's statements may have definite truth values when he has no relevant judgment at all, perhaps, speaking thoughtlessly or only manipulatively or without regard to truth or falsity. You can also lie by stating as truth a truth you do not believe. You can't do that with judgment. We cannot make certain self-referring judgments like "This judgment is false" or "All judgments are false," though we can formulate and express the sentences.

(4) Stringing sentences or statements together validly, say, is not, nondenominatively, reasoning; a machine can do it. A textbook can display it when no one is thinking at all. Neither is true judgment underivatively a pairing up of parts of ordinary sentences with parts of the world, or a paring up of whole sentences with parts of the world (say, truth conditions; cf. chapter 4). Nor is it merely a certain match-up of statements to reality, as Roderick Chisholm and J. L. Austin suggested (cf. chapter 4). There can't be statements without thought. And although thought is commonly dressed in statements, most of it is in action, feeling, imagination, and expectation. Besides, there is no sentence that cannot be used to express different judgments in different contexts (cf. R. Cartwright 1987, 33 ff, 55 ff).

(5) Only judgment is intrinsically true or false—that is, not by a relation to something else (e.g., match-up, coherence, or work-out) as philosophers keep telling us—but by being done right or wrong, so as to be the intentional presence, the *inesse*, of something that is so.

(6) Other Considerations. — Philosophers after the seventeenth century, despite their differing accounts of it, thought of consciousness as continuous awareness, some of which is genuine knowledge, but thought, in schema, of the latter, the knowledge, as the part of awareness that *matched up* to the physical world (representationalism) or *constituted* it (the phenomenalisms of Leibniz, Berkeley, Hume, Kant, and then Idealism, and even of some positivists like A. J. Ayer). There is no explanatory gain in that over saying perceptual consciousness is at core awareness of the world directly (perhaps even with physicalist-reductionist aims in mind). For in either case one would still want to

explain how an animal's electrochemical neural state changes can cause or be the same as states of conscious awareness of its midrange (animal-specific) world, and eventually to go further to explain how human comprehension is some vast refinement of the former. To persist in a story that the world is somehow the *outcome* of the conscious states not only does not address the underlying scientific question mentioned, it makes answering it irrelevant.

What I know can be a recalled sunny childhood moment on a wide beach with red pungent seaweed, or that ancient Egyptians believed in bodily afterlife, or that the sun will become a red giant far in the future. It can be something personal and close, like "My eyes hurt," or something far away, "The sun circles the center of the Milky Way every six hundred years." That is for most of us something known *by report*, and not "a reality known apart from report," as it may be for some astrophysicists who calculated it. But even so, that knowledge is not about a *sentence*, that it is true, but *of* a reality through report, the way I could know what someone said about me. Such knowing is *of* realities; it is a kind of mediated awareness. Remote realities, like "Napoleon was a general when Washington was too," and universals like "gold is a metal" (not the same as "everything that is of gold is also of metal") are known, mediated by words and images (that may be merely conventional). All those are phenomenologically different from knowing *about* sentences that they are true or even *that* certain assertions or statements (reports) are true (chapter 5); for the realities are what we know.

(7) Moreover, perceptual awareness is ordinarily continuous and multimodal, as I said, like the image on a moving mirror but filled with emotion and sensation, sound, smell, space, depth, and propensities, like a downtown crowd seen as I walk in it wearing glasses. We couldn't decompose all of a continuously changing perception into discrete sentences, even by obtuse abstraction as if we were taking speed photos of a horse race. Most of our background conviction that bulks out present knowledge is never put into words because it is too complex and multifarious for articulate expression and there is no need. Still, it is formative of what is experienced and its presence may be revealed when foreground judgment goes wrong, or when an expectation is defeated or surprised, or even by the way we modulate a gesture or our gait.

In reading and speaking as well, judgment vastly exceeds what can be stated. For example, there is continuous enveloping awareness that cannot itself be expressed, because it is *of* the judging thought, for instance, that we think that. That's indicated by our occasional "that's not right" revisions of words and acts, and even more rarely, "Oh, I did not know that I thought that." We are in a defeasible default state of confidence that we are expressing our thoughts and doing what we want. A paradigm single judgment is the driver's disgusted finding his tire is flat. His confident expectation is falsified. And a paradigm single false judgment is "Oops, I forgot my keys on the desk" (when they are in the next pocket). But of course even those occur in a flowing texture of awareness that is a mixture mostly of what is so.

We can't read music after the very beginning stages by explicit judgments identifying the written note and then finding the position to sound it. That has to be automated and then obviated by experience. That's true of reading words as well. Most of our judgments in action are like that, whether walking, reaching for a book, writing a word, shaking hands, singing, speaking, reading, discoursing, and doing any kind of automatic work with words. The knowledge is in the comprehending doing, not in something we say to ourselves.

(8) Our flowing commitments, feelings, actions, and resistances envelop real things, conventional arrangements, synthetics, manufactures, social constructs, arbitrary objects, and mere projections of desire and advertising. Moreover, awareness shades from crisp attention and reflective attentiveness to habitual automatic meta-awareness (e.g., of the language we are speaking) inhibition (and repression), to subconscious awareness, collective consciousness (socially conditioned approval and distaste, desire, and habitual beliefs), and perhaps even to universal, inaccessible consciousness (usually called "the unconscious"), for example, grasp of certain death and of the futility of pride and fame. Commitments in all those modes of awareness are what are primarily true and false.

(9) Wilfred Sellars, Donald Davidson, Robert Brandom, and John McDowell seem to have described the dependence of thought on one's language community in a way that makes the experiential foundation of knowledge perplexing, because they make abstract thought posterior

to language acquisition. No doubt much of it is; but it can't all be because the development of language in a community presupposes the ability for and activity of abstract thought, just as the acquisition of language by a child does. Their explanatory order seems backward, and seems to be prompted by the physicalist reductions some of them aim at or expect.

Instead, natural languages develop for cooperative action about what is not at hand and what might not be so, and acquire their other far more elaborate functions from that basis. Making a language, even out of little bits of communication, requires understanding. Consider the sign languages that are independent of spoken languages in some deaf communities. It is not that I doubt that abstract judgment is embedded in and unfolds in lived community, and is affected in scope and capacity by community. It is that intelligence, understanding, explanatorily *precedes* language and creates its social necessity, providing the possibility for it and its elaborations, and is not constituted by language ability, however much it is amplified and expanded by it.

Humans think abstractly and understand intelligently by nature, and natural languages develop as versatile and adaptive tools for intelligent living and communal cooperation, but are tools nevertheless. This is not something one needs to prove, since it is accessible in experience. One who alleges there is a reductive account of intelligence/understanding is the one who bears the burden to show it is so, not just to promise it. Expressive capacity belongs to the medium, but expressive ability belongs to the thinkers. Abstractive ability is native, not learned, but abstractive practices are learned and are socially refined.

3. On Some Ways of Going (Right and) Wrong: Custom and Context

It is trivial but useful to note that there are no actually false judgments no one makes. To say of some form of assertion, "q and not q," that it is always false is to use a derivative notion of "false" that applies to a form of sentence or statement and does not depend on anyone's actually judging anything. To say, "'Some things both exist and do not exist' is always false" is also a derived notion of "false," more like "would be false to say or think." In the latter sense, there are potentially false sentences no one ever uses. Also, some people idly use assertoric expressions without any definite judgment ("That's ok," "What goes round comes round"), the way students sometimes "go with the words" (computerese) with no definite thought; those utterances could be called "trivially" true or false, but that is also a derivative notion since no definite judgment is involved.

We cannot be wrong about everything we can be right about. Nor is there anything we *have* to be wrong about except from limited vantages, though we know that each of us is wrong about some things. Can we be right about everything about which we can be wrong? In principle, yes, we can, but not in practice; sometimes, as mentioned earlier, what makes the judgment false lies beyond what anyone can know at the time. For example, most people suppose a person who is gunshot hears the firing first (probably from old movies) and for centuries it seemed obvious that one cannot heat a liquid without heating its container as a means (before microwave cooking). The idea of cooking somehow with sound would have seemed absurd.

Right and wrong judgments that something is so, or not, do not mirror one another. They diverge because not every true judgment has a contrary false judgment, as remarked above. Further, "'p' is false just in case not-p" does not distinguish "there is no fact of the matter" from "the reality is otherwise." That presupposes bifurcation where there may be none (cf. chapter 3 on counterfactuals), as do disquotational theories if applied outside formal contexts. Interpretative, diagnostic, and prognostic judgments may fail to be true because there is no definite fact of the matter at all. We usually consider such failing as "being false" because things are not *as* thought to be. That seems to be another sense of "false." In fact, there is a broad notion of the false as just "not true"[12] while false as "erroneous" more closely tracks "what is or would be wrongly thought to be so." So, "not rightly thought to be so" is not co-extensive with "is or would be wrongly thought to be so."

Not everything that can be said to be true or false is either true or false. Sometimes it depends on whether we could in principle find out[13] and sometimes it depends on whether there is a reality about the matter, as with some of the counterfactuals discussed in chapter 3, and also with some evaluations and diagnoses (to be illustrated below). Sometimes the "independent fact of the matter" is a well-grounded thought construct like the horsepower of an engine, shopping centers, world travel, corporate profits, compound interest, and grade point averages. There weren't destination districts, streetscapes, vistas, scenes, traffic jams, corporations, churches, lawsuits, or charities, as such, before humans conceptualized them. But they are among the realities about which there is right and wrong thinking as to what is so, and thus, truth and falsity of judgment. So, to assume that "fact," "reality situation," and "state of affairs" univocally designate the de re conditions for true judgment is a metaphysical confusion (probably by extension from the belief that the existential quantifier in *formal* contexts is univocal for first-order quantification). The ways of the world form families, not a picket fence.

Going wrong in judgment varies with the sort of thinking. There are too many ways of thinking and ways of going wrong to list, and they can't all be explained in the same way. For instance, some kinds of thinking *make* their judgments true, and being false in such cases involves inconsistency, the result of breaking a rule or of bad rules, or of misunderstanding, inattention, or distraction. Whereas what one rightly or wrongly thinks perceptually usually, but not always, concerns what is independently so in the variety of ways of being-so mentioned above (especially the ways that include social constructs). Other thinking may go wrong in other ways, for instance, "Heating and cooling consists of caloric-fluid exchange" was a bad theory about heat.

No matter how thin a layman's notion of a flu virus may be, the de re conditions for a virus are the same as for the expert. That's true for parrots, plastics, metals, and everything else that has overflow necessary conditions. So, as I said, a judgment can be false on account of conditions not being satisfied that are not even remotely thought of, or knowable, by the person who makes the mistake. One may be acting, even for a whole career or lifetime, on reliances that conflict with what is so because of truth conditions one cannot access (overflow conditions hidden in nature), just as the causes of tuberculosis were for most of human history.

Sometimes a judgment can't be true if it can't in principle be something known. (What about, "One has no life after one's death"?) Other times, cognitive accessibility is not required; so we can make a mistake about the number of molecules in the Milky Way, even though we can't find out the correct number at some definite time (assuming there is such a smallest interval for the whole galaxy in which the number is determinate). And some thinking that something is so (or not) seems to have no thought-independent conditions for being right or wrong, like somebody's thinking, "Those people have a family life of neuroses," and other cases below.

Diagnostic and prognostic judgments are plentiful cases in point. Suppose an evangelist concludes that the United States is "a culture of death and oppression" for allowing assisted suicide, tolerating drug abuse, homelessness, a high death rate of young African American males, the widespread sale of guns and illegal drugs, and leaving 47 million people without health insurance. Is that enough to make the claim true? Or is the claim false because we don't have human sacrifice like the Aztecs, nor do we bury our dead under the household floor like the Mayans, or keep them in houses and on verandas like some South Pacific island tribe, or even provision the dead for travel as did the Egyptians? If the expression "a culture of death" does not belong to some well-regulated anthropological craft, is it just too vague for the claim to be true? Would that make it false? Is its truth a matter of construal by some audience? Whatever right thinking is in such contexts, it is not some kind of match-up with independent facts.

Another kind of right thinking? Suppose I think I am writing a book on jurisprudence though I have not written anything in months (or at all yet). Would the truth of that depend on what I *think*? Is this a truth by fiat? Or is it by what I *would* have done had I not become deflected by a new project? (What determines that?) Is there any individual state of mind, maybe a counterfactual one, that makes such a self-description true? It seems to be an item of self-interpretation, nothing very definite, though definite enough that one can be mistaken or lie about it. Right or wrong thinking is not all of one kind or some correlation, or failure of it, with a one-flavored reality.

The day of the week is determined by convention. So, to mistake Tuesday for Wednesday is to think wrongly as determined by an objective convention, not by some fact about time. Every day starts a new thousand years, but convention determines the (nearby) millennia. To get the wrong sum when adding is to think what is not so, but not in the same sense of "not so" as to misjudge someone to be honest who is deceptive, or a performance to be finished at a dramatic pause. The requirements for "being so" differ with the kinds of realities involved. Getting the judgments right involves different sorts of thinking for different modes of reality. Often enough, what counts as right thinking determines what counts as reality in the matter, rather than the reverse, for example, the umpire's close calls in baseball, your weight on a doctor's scale versus your home scale, even what a court finally finds to be the fact of the matter as to negligence, or intent, or malice, or foreknowledge.

Though right thinking[14] is what makes truth, there is not one encompassing analysis of what right thinking consists in or of what "is so" includes.[15] Suppose someone thinks that the more pieces required to assemble an object the less rigid it becomes over time," where the person has cars, bridges, and trucks in mind. Then what he thinks is not made false by the fact that C-60, a geodesic molecular ball with sixty pieces ("Buckyball"), is more stable than C-3, graphite (with fewer parts). The scope of reference is implicit by custom and context. That's the story about word meaning and thought in general: *custom and context.*

We take up lots of general commitments without consciously adverting to the realms that don't count and without having any explicit rule to exclude them; they are just not within the scope of our thought. Not that they are overlooked either. Such omissions of reality have no privative role; they don't make the thinking go wrong; they are just "beyond the contemplation" of the thoughts, beyond the custom and the context. It is a mistake to look for some feature in the world that is supposed to draw the boundary.

Authorized thinking and associated social practice *constitutes* various realities, over and beyond formal disciplines already mentioned. In complex societies like ours, the social construction of reality is pervasive.[16] In an ordinary office building, there are rooms (a social construct) in which besides people, if there are not insects unnoticed, the perceptible objects are all synthetics and/or social constructs, from plastics to plaster, carpets and computer systems. Consider this social construct: "big box" stores, four acres in area (about 170,000 square feet), grouped with "superstores" (60,000 to 100,000 square feet—1.5 to 2.5 acres) and their satellites, specialty stores or services, set around fields of parking so big one drives from one store to another that constitute super-shopping centers or life-style centers. It is all a construct. Those stores are legal and economic social constructs, as well as physical buildings made mostly of synthetics like concrete, steel, and plastics; but not just the buildings, the roads and signs, the employment systems, the stock and accounting systems, the debts, the profits—all are realities by social construction, in effect, by institutionalized public agreement backed with various forms of coercion. That's especially true of money.

Some judgments seem to deploy idealized constructions, like Freud's division of ego, superego and id, that make frameworks for reflection, analysis, and prediction projectively justified by their fertility for inquiry and therapy along with supporting cultural and historical construals, perhaps with no further reality required (despite Freud's and some followers' certainty that there is such, even material, independent reality). Jung found other divisions of the human psyche to have superior explanatory utility for theory and therapy, supported by other historical and cultural data. He too claimed to be describing what is independently so. What determines what is right to think about these matters? Is whether there is a collective unconscious chiefly a matter of the usefulness of such suppositions in theory and therapy, or is it a matter of how the world really is independently of what we think? What would settle that? It seems that it is more likely the former, and that such constructs are like zoning divisions of a modern city where the boundaries among residential, commercial (wholesale, retail, franchised, unfranchised, small business), industrial (light, heavy, clean, pollution controlled), and so on, are a consequence of the sorts of things to be grouped (well-grounded constructs themselves) for efficient regulation, commodious life, and efficient economics (differing from a medieval city that would need different divisions, say, by parishes and guilds). It other words, it seems as if truth in such matters as Freud and Jung addressed is a pragmatic mix of revealing theory and efficient therapy, a manner of right thinking and efficient practice aimed at certain optional objectives. What determines what is right to think about that last claim? Isn't that a further question of what is the right way to think?

4. The Master of Falsity

How does something that is not so get to be something we think to be so? Strictly, it does not. There aren't independent realities, things, or situations that aren't so—say physical antifacts. Chapter 2 offered reasons that there are no impossible things or states of affairs, and reasons why negations are intentional derivatives of physical and psychological realities, for instance, why a stone's not being two inches to the left of where it is, or a foot to the right, or my not being a painter, is a well-grounded cognitive derivative of what is independently and/or conventionally so. The particularity of what is not so turns out to be thought dependent. Things really are *not* certain ways we can think of (and the consequences of that). How then can what is not so be thought to be so? The key lies in the fact that intelligent awareness of what is so includes some imaginative awareness of what is not so, and of what is not so yet, and even of what can't be so, as I've already said. The readiness that bulks out present awareness is from imagination (outfitted from experience).

In one respect, false judgment is the same as getting the judgment right, except that what is thought to be is not what is so. That takes imagination. Imagination, as I've said, makes planning and anticipation possible, especially for taking account of what does not happen and of what cannot happen. It is a means of speculative and of negative awareness too. So what does not happen can be presented for judgment that it will not happen. (Probably other animals cannot do that as such, though they do respond by tiring or nosing about aimlessly to what is not so [food not in its regular place] or to what is not doable [a horse's refusing to jump or a dog's giving up the hunt].)

Because awareness of what might be so by itself does not compel commitment, judgment can go wrong if commitment is sufficiently motivated by habit, or by willing reliance, or by active desire, or negatively motivated by aversion, disgust, and the like. We can think we remember some childhood situation that an elder sibling knows is wishful thinking. We can deny that some imagined situation is to happen when others know we are deflating the evidence. The common phrase, "He lets his imagination run away with him," is pretty much on the mark sometimes for everyone.

Thought is projective because what we recognize is typically something that continues. Even to think a clock has stopped is to attribute a continuing state to it. We expect things to go on and to behave according to kind, to which we adjust present action. So imagination and memory infest present perception. All perception involves futurity. There is room for error because complex animals supplement the external senses both with sensory information not in the signals or organs (cf. Goodman 1968; 1978) and with expectations, by way of imagination with experience, not presented to sense. Phenomenologists from Husserl and Merleau-Ponty onward explored such features of experience, especially the way what is "absent" is present in and formatively part of experience. Analytic philosophers are beginning to take note.

Sometimes after a perceptual error we can just notice the holographic misapprehension flit away, "mouse," say, as we recognize the dust ball we mistook momentarily. Sometimes we can with our eyes open recall an emotionally charged occasion, say, an annoyance, with a holograph-like presence, as if it were at some distance away in direct awareness, even while the current scene stays right there. We can imagine in the same way absent and even impossible things and situations with our eyes open.

Open-eyed imagining is something like the continuous imagination that envelops perception too. Try this experiment: look steadily at a distant thing while imagining the table set for dinner with the food there. The distant thing should remain present, not directly attended, while we conjure the before-us presence of the merely imagined. It is not like a picture, as I said, it is more like a hovering hologram spectral and usually, as Hume remarked, less vivid than the real, and less determinate too. Something like that is coincident with and unnoticed in veridical perception as well, undergoing change as we change positions while perception remains constant.

Because imagination envelops our awareness of what is so, even with what is relevantly not so, and because expectation is usually by habitual imaginative reliance, concurrently with sensation, what is not so is sometimes taken to be real, along with what really is.[17] It is like mistakenly taking there to be a person on your left, when a person to your right is reflected on a clear-glass partition in an unfamiliar store, before you've had time to process the context.

Sometimes false belief consists in a rational expectation (action readiness) that fails: you flick a switch and the light does not go on as expected. If we mistake the shadow of a tree branch on a window to be a person—too quick a reliance on similarity of movement—or take tectonic plate theory to be false, or take there to be no blameworthy choosing at all, we construe things as they are not. Sometimes a pattern does not hold, or our reasoning is unreliable or we are inattentive to what is at hand. Sometimes falsity originates in sensory illusion too, though genuine illusions are not very common in familiar contexts.

Taking what seems so, the imagined, for what *is* so is more common, especially when "seems so" is understood broadly to include things like "seems to be wood," "seems honest," "seems to know what he is talking about," "seems cheap," "seems old," "seems nice," and other seemings to fit a pattern of our reliances. Minor perceptual errors are also common, like misreading the ledger lines in music, thinking a word is spelled a certain way, not noticing missing letters or extra ones, and thinking there is more space than there is. Those are by unfamiliarity, distraction, fatigue, tired senses, or careless not noticing. People bump into one another, or scrunch their tires against the curb, and miscount the number of traffic lights to an intersection. I might think I recall someone you mention, but recall someone else, neither of us noticing my naming error. I might confuse the color names you use, say, "taupe" and "teal." Some errors involve limitations (blurry vision, wandering attention in counting, poor coordination of steering with vision, etc.), factors other than imagination. It is, however, in our taking of what is *not* so to be so that imagination presents the situation and habitual reliances (some of which may be imprudent, indeed) explain the commitment.

Of course there are other very common sorts of false judgments, typically involving utterances or statements we have heard or read, or things we've been told. The fault in that thinking has to do with willing reliance on untrustworthy sources, or insufficient evidence or carelessness or simple ignorance, or negligent discipleship, but does not primarily trace to imagination. Those are usually from vices of commitment. I am instead concerned with taking what is not so to be what is so, because that raised the question of how what is not so can be presented for commitment. That might not be a distinct problem for a representational or sentential theory of cognition; but for a theory of the real sameness of what is known and what is so, there has to be an explanation of how what is not so can be taken to be what is so.

In a word, the ability to commit to the reality-to-be of what is not yet grounds the ability to commit to the present reality of what is not so. Without active imagination we could not know what might happen but does not, or what might have happened but did not. Fallibility is a by-product of the veridicality and the limitations of our cognitive system, which operates mainly on willing reliance, where only occasionally is there "belief compelled by the evidence."[18]

False judgment tends to originate from the cooperation of imagination, abstraction, background suppositions, and volition. And most of our erroneous judgments are not perceptual errors but errors about general, remote or interpretative, or explanatory things we imagine and particularly expect to be so. For instance, many think humans lived in the days of the dinosaurs, and that people are poor because they are lazy, immoral, or impaired, and that science and religion are necessarily in conflict. Without abstractive imagination we wouldn't even be able to conjure such situations, and without critical reflection and key information we might willingly, habitually, and uncritically commit to such cases of what is not so.

We tend to see what we want to see, and tend to project what we fear or hope for. Small coins look bigger to poor children than they do to well-off children. Basketball hoops look bigger and more easily accessible to star athletes, especially after they make difficult shots, than to others. White-coated actors in pharmacy advertisements seem authoritative to viewers. A child hears a creak in the dark with the terrified, "There's a wolf under my bed," projected from a story.

Imagination envelops experience with emotions too. And emotions—fear, pride, anger, cupidity, contentment and comfort, studiousness and curiosity—color perceptions and are modes of being willing (or resistant) and reliant. Sartre was right to say an emotion is an affective transformation of reality. Feelings like awe, wanting, loathing, hatred, and especially love and even capriciousness motivate imaginative, transforming construal that may invite wrong commitment. Feelings are the stage lighting of experience, always there and changing, and to some extent abstracted, mostly unnameable, but constantly pressuring or inhibiting commitment. Imagination joins curiosity to fill out one's expectations and make temptations, say, to test the paint's being dry on a door with a "wet paint" sign.

Getting judgment right isn't just avoiding getting it wrong. That's like explaining driving as avoiding accidents (cf. David Braine's [1993] similar reasoning). The explanatory order is the reverse. There are no wrong notes if you can't play at all. Falsehood is an outcome of imperfect cognitive ability. It is the ability to make what is not yet or is not at all a modifier of present action and judgment, and further the ability to reflect on our awareness, that makes the room for false judgment.

5. Conclusion

The fallibility of our cognitive system derives from its efficiency, particularly because humans do not need compelling or even conclusive evidence to know what is so. Mere seeming, other than the perceptual illusions and ambiguities, is made by imagining that operates constantly in aid of cognition. Humans can conjure situations at hand, remote, and universal that are not what is so (either not yet, not still, or not at all), and have to do so in order to recognize and act competently on what is right in front of them. So, given their various, even conflicting, reliances and desires, goals and intentions, vices and virtues, cognitive and moral limitations, humans have the ability (in the derivative sense of a runner *able* to stumble), and the inclination,[19] to take what is not so to be so, and thus to judge wrongly.[20] In every such case, they are not getting the thinking right.

Enchanted by what we want, especially by the order, meaning, and even beauty we desire, we fall under the spell of the master of falsity and magician of art. (See Robertson Davies's 1976 novel *World of Wonders*.)

Notes

Introduction: Structural Realism

1. Descartes (Adam and Tannery III, 506), letter to Regius, Jan. 1642, says, "The second proof is drawn from the purpose or use of substantial forms. They were introduced by philosophers solely to account for the proper actions of natural things of which they were supposed to be the principles and bases, as was said in an earlier thesis. But no natural action at all can be explained by these substantial forms, since their defenders admit that they are occult and that they do not understand them themselves. . . . So these forms are not to be introduced to explain the causes of natural actions."

And Descartes (Adam and Tannery IV, 401), letter to Mersenne, 20 April 1646, says, "Finally it is a most absurd suggestion that in all the particles of the matter in the universe, there resides some property in virtue of which they are mutually drawn towards and attract each other; and that in each particle of terrestrial matter in particular there is a similar property in respect of other terrestrial particles which does not interfere with the former property. For in order to make sense of this, one has to suppose not only that each particle of matter has a soul, and indeed several different souls, which do not impede each another, but also these souls are capable of thought, and indeed divine, to enable them to know without any intermediary what was happening in those distant places, and to exercise their powers there."

2. In fact, professional magicians work by constant conjunctions in experience, repeatable as often as one likes, that hold counterfactually, but that are not cases of real causation. See George Johnson, "Sleights of Mind," *New*

York Times, August 2, 2007, science sec. So the Humean analysis even supplemented with counterfactuality is insufficient.

3. Mackie 1974; Salmon 1984; Tooley 1987; Armstrong 1983. See the instructive survey by Jonathan Schaffer in "Metaphysics of Causation," *Stanford Encyclopedia of Philosophy*, avail. at http:plato.stanford.edu, and James Woodward, "Causation and Manipulability," there as well. See also Niiniluoto 1999 for the current options for grounding the sciences.

4. Nature, it seems, operates like that, with biological, chemical, and physical underlying structures, perhaps with structures "all the way down without end." See chapters 3 and 7.

5. Descartes (Adam and Tannery III, 506), reasoned there are no minds in physical things.

6. "Software" stands in contrast to "hardware," which is the physical system it operates. So the software may be regarded as emergent relatively to the physical base, though of course in human inventions it has a distinct cause.

7. The succeeding images—hydraulic (early-nineteenth-century), electrical (late-nineteenth-century), electronic (mid-twentieth-century), and information (late-twentieth-century)—each served their purposes and then needed replacement by more encompassing ideas. I am proposing the software notion for now. It will, perhaps, be succeeded as well.

8. Descartes realized that the late Scholastic accounts of how physical causation produces effects (influxus theory, eduction-emergence theory, etc.), as far as their resources went till then, failed to explain the quantitative regularities of nature.

9. Carl Zimmer, "Search Is Urged for Life Not as We Know It," *New York Times*, July 7, 2007, science sec., wrote: "The report, which is posted on the Web site of the National Academies, www.nationalacademies.org, even explores the possibility of life based on silicon, not carbon, though Dr. Meyer, who had no role in the work, thinks that astrobiologists should limit their search to carbon-based life forms. 'When we look in the universe,' he said, 'the only compounds we see with more than six atoms are all carbon chemistry. So there's a hint that looking for carbon chemistry may be a better bet. There we have some idea of what to look for.'" Can there be life with compounds less than six atoms? Imagining and conceiving are not enough to determine possibility.

10. That's what Aristotle and others regarded as analogy.

11. "Non-indexed" de re necessity (e.g., your being made of flesh and bone, your being both animal and rational, water's not being homogeneously infinitely divisible) contrasts with "indexed" de re necessity, say, of origin: your having had the very parents you had. The latter involves indexical reference to individuals, or in some cases to natural kinds (e.g., animal).

12. For instance, there are properties of light just discovered and previously unknown but necessary all along. Kenneth Chang reported in *New York Times*, May 16, 2006, science sec.: "In other experiments, scientists have shown that it is possible to make light at least appear as if it is traveling faster than the speed of light. . . . For Dr. Boyd's trick, the scientists used an optical fiber of glass with small amounts of the metal erbium, which acts as an amplifier. In the experiment, a pulse of laser light was fired into the fiber. Even before the peak of the pulse entered the fiber, another pulse appeared, seemingly out of nowhere, at the far end of the fiber. This new pulse then split in two. One, a twin of the original pulse, moved forward, while the other moved backward through the fiber. The backward pulse, which traveled faster than the speed of light, and the original pulse met at the front end of the fiber, where they canceled each other. Even though one pulse momentarily became three, the experiment did not violate the law mandating conservation of energy because the amplifying effect of the erbium added a temporary surge of energy. . . . At first glance, the experiment appears to flout the usual speed limit on the transmission of signals as the original pulse jumped to the forward-moving pulse on the other side of the fiber. However, the pulses were in a shape known as Gaussian, which is, in principle, infinite in width, though in practice not quite that wide. Thus, the outgoing pulse was actually just part of the original pulse that was reshaped by the fiber's unusual properties."

13. The critical state of a liquid is the temperature above which increased pressure fails to prevent its turning into a gas. Water above its critical temperature, 705.6F, has no definite volume, will fill its container, and yet will also dissolve salt and sugar and wet the walls.

14. Apparently the sonoluminescence of water droplets is a recently discovered de re necessity. And a boiler of 30 gallons of water heated above 50 pounds per square inch, without pressure release, explodes with the force of a pound of dynamite—sometimes right through the roof. Analogously, even some mathematical objects have features unpredictable from what we know of them, at least at a given stage, hidden necessities, some so startling that mathematicians like Roger Penrose (1989, 124 ff.) think we are discovering features of independent realities, like the Mandelbrot sets. I don't explore how to distinguish the "hidden necessities" of formal objects from those of natural objects here, though, the hidden necessities of natural objects are certainly independent of what humans think.

15. Some think the idea is only magic because we don't have a naturalistic account of it; but if we don't examine what it is and how it is related to the rest of knowledge, we never will explain how animals can do it. So, I suggest, leave the reductionist enterprise aside for now until we can explain consciousness at all, and concentrate here on the philosophy.

16. As, say, the ability to play a Chopin Etude is to actually play it.

17. Sublimation is the property of some solids (like diamonds) of passing from solid to vapor without intermediate state (liquid), so that solids (real diamonds) can be made by a carbon vapor deposit process.

18. So, Aristotle's two notions of definition (*Posterior Analytics*) have a place in present thinking (prescientific to scientific), though that distinction is not the same as Locke's also useful one between nominal and real definitions (more like "definition of the word" and "conditions for the thing").

19. D. P. Henry (1984) explains some of the history of "empty names."

20. For instance, Kenneth Chang, "Black Holes. Gravity Quivvers," *New York Times*, May 2, 2006, wrote: "The equations of general relativity can be easily written down but are notoriously hard to solve. Astrophysicists were able to simulate the head-on collision of two black holes three decades ago, but computing the paths of orbiting black holes and their violent merger proved much harder. . . . Dr. Centrella's simulations still contain some simplifications that do not reflect attributes of actual black hole pairs: the two black holes have the same mass, and neither is spinning. The calculations predicted, for example, that 4 percent of the mass of the black holes should be converted into gravitational waves."

21. There's a lot more to be considered that doesn't fit in here, for instance, whether all the animal operations in humans are eminently performed by the intelligent psyche. See Braine 1993 for related discussions.

22. Those relations are variously called "correspondence," "coherence," and "pragmatic verification."

23. This is not negatively to prejudge whether animal awareness may be emergent; we can consider that separately. For the moment, let us assume that it has a "naturalistic" explanation yet to be discovered.

24. Referential rooting is a matter of the pragmatic traction of discourse modifying action and is not a feature of words or phrases by themselves.

Chapter 1. **Necessities: Earned Truth and Made Truth**

1. The truthmaker (as productive cause of truth) is thought alone (chapters 4 and 8), but different sorts of thinking produce judgments true in different ways, for example, by inflation, by inheritance and by earning truth.

2. Such notions were traditionally called "analogous" by Aristotle and later writers well past the medieval period.

3. The pliant general notions are consequent on the diverse particular ones.

4. I later distinguish statements, propositions, situations, and reality. For now, a statement is "what is meant by an assertion expressed in words."

I acknowledge that some deviant cases will come up later where the sentence is grammatically and semantically normal but fails to express a definite statement (see chapter 2).

5. The term "experience" is not to be taken narrowly, because most deep and general scientific generalizations are made up to fit data that has been manipulated (by obtuse abstraction) and then justified by mathematical neatness. In Kantian terms, natural necessities are conditions for the possibility of experience, and do not have their content determined by the categories of thought, but are, rather, known from experience; they are "synthetic a priori." For my purposes, because the explanatory relation runs from things to thoughts (on the whole), and not from thought to things, such necessities do not amount to cognitively a priori conditions for experience.

6. We ignore or circumvent or compensate for the variance of abstractions from real values—sometimes with catastrophic results like bridge failure.

7. See Goodman 1961 and Elgin 1983, 169–81. In fact, there are various kinds of "being about," of which denoting (in the simple positivist sense of "being the label on") is only one. Peter Geach (1980) explored the perplexities of reference in intentional contexts.

8. Whether "exists" occurs univocally in a range of claims like "numbers exist," "accidents exist," "properties exist," "individuals exist," and so on, is an empirical matter; yet there is usually no discussion of tests for univocality. See some proposals in Ross 1981, 37–47. It is a vexing situation in philosophical dialogue when one person says a word is used only in one sense over a range of cases, and another insists it has varied senses in the same range and they do not share a common test of sameness. Yet a lot of important philosophy depends on attending to such cases, especially about "exists."

9. I oversimplify a bit. The sense in which formal objects have to be "comprehended in their conceptions" is normally "that every relevant proposition about such objects is determinately true or false by virtue of the conception of such objects and the embedding system." That will do for many purposes; but formally incomplete systems may require a specialized notion of "contained."

10. There are two issues here. One is how our "constructions" can exceed our logic, so that truths can be "contained" that are not logically derivable from axioms that do not express them. The other concerns implications, say, theorems, that will never be discovered. With invented systems—for instance, modal systems, deontic logics, paraconsistent logics, and various branches of mathematics—the form of the thinking determines what is so by constituting it.

11. That is, the thinking that authorizes it to be said provides its complete certification.

12. In a dispositional sense, what is right to think, whether thought actually or not, is what is true. That of course would imply that there are no actual mathematical truths before there are finite intellects.

13. For that would require the referents to exist necessarily, whereas material things and conditions exist only contingently.

14. Those are obviously different truth conditions, and they are meaning relevant. So, "is true" and "is necessary" apply to necessities of nature and to formal truths in different senses (i.e., with different meaning relevant truth conditions).

15. "Fully grounded physically" is itself a plastic predicate with context-varying conditions; often we can "see" that it is "there," without being able to provide it. For example, the shine of paint and fabrics is visible, but most of us have no idea what physical basis it has (which varies, of course, with the material).

16. J. Gorman, in the *New York Times*, April 26, 2006, wrote that "the measuring of ants, in particular the heads of ants, which can be done by holding an ant in forceps steady under a stereomicroscope and judging its size with a scale built into the scope's eye piece" is a rite of passage for budding myrmecologists; he opines that it is "maddening."

17. Are materialists going to say there can be no being without truth, and commit themselves to the existence of intelligence as a condition for any sort of being, or commit themselves to providing an analysis of truth that does not require thinking?

18. The notion of "construction" is interesting here because there is no physical production and yet we cannot analyze the idea into "entailment" or the like, because such notions normally involve logical derivability, whereas some of the propositions in some formal systems are not derivable from distinct axioms.

19. "There is no truth without thought" has sometimes been twisted into its opposed, "Reality is made by truth." French philosophers (see Descombes 1980, 55–60) have argued that reality is the product of truth, a patent exaggeration. Richard Rorty blended American materialism with Continental phenomenology (post-1960) into the idea that science is a kind of literature that carries the "lived-world" (the world of business, love, farming, family, manufacture, illness, and death) "with it," whereas fiction is isolated in our experience so as to carry only fragments from the rest of our lived and scientifically interpreted world. "Truth," in this hybrid view, is a pragmatic success at prediction, encompassment, expression, communication, and so on, with science having no special privilege or access to truth over poetry or fiction (Rorty 1979; 1982; 1991[a]; and 1991[b]). Goodman (1968) also said truth is more important in art than in science where fit will do. Many philosopher Americans and Europeans think that the compliant reality for necessities of nature and truths other than formal truths is made by our thinking.

20. There might seem to be for "triangles have three sides and three angles" in three geometries, but that's because the statement is ambiguous if not anchored into its space: plane, spherical, and so on.

21. Numbers and geometrical figures are only equivocally individuals. "Socrates is human" is not just "Socrates is one of the individuals called 'human'" as quantification would represent it. That turns prediction into mere class membership and is an imperialistic replacement of what we mean.

22. There might seem to be exceptions: geometries with replacements for the fifth postulate, and logics that accept the principle of excluded middle and reject the principle of bifurcation. But the latter involve changes of meaning in the connectives so that different assertions are involved. In the case of geometry, either the diverse systems are equivalent or there are also changes of meaning.

23. Some people call these features "presuppositions." I do not object, as long as it is understood that the relation is not to be defined logically, because it is not a logical relation but a linguistic or pragmatic and variable one.

24. This is like what John Searle called "the background" of a statement (Searle 1992, 175–96).

25. That is, occurrences that differ in those features differ in meaning.

Chapter 2. Real Impossibility

1. See Gabriel Nuchelmans's (1973) historical comments on propositions. Philosophers sometimes talk as if there were an abstract treasury of such truth-bearers, a domain of propositions. That's a construct. Such suppositions are inventions for the sake of logic and can be treated instrumentally, not as real. The same holds for the extensional talk of possible worlds.

2. Suppose some humans had so used their language that nothing *counts* as inconsistent, say, because they have no use for the notion (never talking or thinking about their own or one another's *sayings*). Would nothing be impossible then?

3. What kind of argument, except the deduction of an inconsistency in the view, could be used to refute that?

4. If there is no circumstance when everything that is necessary is supplied, then there is no sufficient condition.

5. The idea (held by Chisholm, Plantinga, and others) that there are infinities of states of affairs that are impossible, and infinities that are necessary, and infinities that are merely possible, reenacts Platonism in a new vocabulary modeled on Carnapian state descriptions.

6. Logically, negation is a transformational relation. Physical things and states don't strictly stand in logical relations, mainly because physical relations are always formally indeterminate among contradictories (ontological grueness), while logical relations cannot be. The key arguments for that are below in chapter 2.2 and again in chapter 6.

7. The notion of "states of affairs," if broadened beyond the actual and potential conditions of existing things, introduces a merely conceptual artifact that if taken as real distorts the ontology without any basis except the demands of extensional logical notation. See David Armstrong's (1990) quite opposed view.

8. Indexed necessities de re involve physically particular individuals, for example, my having the parents I had. Non-indexed necessities can be shared, for instance, "being rational."

9. John Wiley (1995) quotes a definition: "Hydrogen is a light, odorless gas, which, given enough time, turns into people."

10. That's what C. I. Lewis (1946) called the "signification" of a word, and what others sometimes call "truth conditions" for the terms.

11. Notice "synthetic gems" has split into two related notions: (i) stones of the same composition as the natural ones, but fabricated in a laboratory, and (ii) fabricated stones of different composition that at the macrolevel look or behave "very much" like real ones (e.g., synthetic diamonds, zircon). In either case the hidden necessities scooped up by practices of reference are the overflow signification.

12. That would be sameness of necessities at each included order of magnitude from the perceptible to the subatomic. Perhaps there will turn out to be nothing that pure, though I think the pure elements may do.

13. Kripke 1982, 36: "Any concrete physical object can be viewed as an imperfect realization of many machine programs." That's not quite as strong as my claim, but close to it.

14. See Wittgenstein 1953, secs. 195–97, and Kripke's (1982, 70 n.58) comment, about the whole function being present at once all together.

15. See Kripke 1982, 35–36 n.24, quoted above note 13.

16. If there are no logical relations among physical objects and events, how can it be a logical truth that a pure function cannot be, or be realized by, a physical condition? The reply is that negations, for example, "not being addition," are denominative. They are real enough, but their content is intentional. There is no such physical condition as "being impossible," or "not being male," for instance. They are *consequent* intentional features of things, in the latter case fully grounded physically.

17. For instance, the possibility of artificial muscles (for robots) is not ensured by conception or imaginability but by physics and chemistry, and perhaps discourse practice too; consider artificial muscles. "One is a nickel-titanium alloy coated with platinum, which causes the fuel—currently methanol, but hydrogen or alcohol could work too—to react with oxygen, producing heat. The metal shrinks; the muscle flexes. The artificial muscle can apply 100 times as much force as real muscle.... The second artificial muscle, currently less

powerful, is made of a sheet of nanotubes, tiny but superstrong cylindrical molecules of carbon. The reaction of fuel and oxygen releases electrical charges that repel each other and cause the nanotube sheet to expand." *New York Times*, March 23, 2006. Yet what determines that those are "muscles"? Is it not discourse practice and similarity of function?

18. That's a consequence of the overflow necessities of nature. So, unless we are willing to postulate a divine being, there can be no real thing that is "possible no matter what." Saving those principles by postulating necessarily existing surrogates for contingent things, like properties and individual essences, gets nowhere as an explanation, anymore than David Lewis's postulating that there are many physical worlds of internally relative actuality, and comparative possibility, does. For what is the status of the worlds? Are they collectively the analogue of Spinoza's infinite attributes of the one divine substance?

19. Someone asks, pointing to a wooden rocker, "Could that chair have been made of glass?" (cf. Kripke 1972) "No," is the reply. "Not unless it is made of glass and we mistake it for wood." Why not? Because the material composition of a thing is indexically de re necessary in that without it, that thing would not have been at all. But could it by replacement of parts come to be made of glass? Maybe, but I don't think there is anything to settle the matter for all similarly structured examples; it depends on customs and contexts of discourse. Usually the matter of a thing is de re necessary for it, but sometimes discourses differ. Sorites problems have particular answers according to the practices of craftbound discourses, not some general metaphysical resolution. (cf. Williamson 1994 and Keefe 2000 for other views of the matter).

20. If there were no free divine creator, there would be no domain of possibility beyond the power of nature, no merely metaphysical possibility because there are no independently real abstract objects, and we've already shown that logical possibility (consistency or imaginability) is not the same as real, metaphysical, possibility. If the divine being were as Avicenna or as Spinoza described, there would be no unrealized possibility at all. And even on the supposition of a free creator, the merely metaphysically possible (ad extra) would have no content because of untaken divine elections. See Ross 1986, 1989, and 1990.

21. It is unreliable in principle to conclude something is really possible because it is conceptually consistent or imaginable, say, that there might be an evil demon, or that we might be brains in a vat, or that there might be water with a different atomic structure (not merely deuterium or the like), or that we could transfer a brain/spine from one living body to another (Parfit 1984). There may be no such real possibility because of vacuous or conflicting overflow necessities.

22. It will turn out later that there is no direct referring without the intentional presence of what is referred to. There is, however, piggybacked referring,

where my reference is by way of someone else's (I am talking about whatever he is, or thinks he is, talking about), and there is purported reference, the way parents talk of Santa Claus.

23. One of the defeating challenges to phenomenalism in any form is to explain the overflow de re necessities of things, some of which always lie beyond what we know.

24. See Ross 1981, chap. 5.

25. But, of course, it would not have been at all had not the latter come to be.

26. "Sometime" and "Somehow" in these contexts mean "under some actual condition not necessarily temporal."

27. Again, the illusion that the overflow (say, for "flying pigs") is determinate is projected from the assumption that things are laminates of properties and that there is a real universal treasury of them, so that everything is a "layer" of some of them, and any consistent layering (What would make it completed and unified into *one* thing?) can amount to an existing thing. Russell once thought of objects as laminates of universals co-present in space-time loci. Other philosophers still talk as if things are laminated properties without an explanation of what the co-occurrence consists in.

28. One should keep these related notions of vacuity separate: (i) one is vacuity of a referring term, that is, there is nothing definite that it picks out, so what is said lacks content. The other (ii) is vacuity of alternate situations, for example, where there are no contraries with determinate overflow content to what is really necessary. In fact, such latter "alternatives," even to be stated, have to suppose the actuality of what is necessary, just as denials of singular existentials also, by the proper names, have to suppose the existence of what is denied, for example, "Quine never existed."

29. Note that "kind" in conjunction with "cases" is the same as infima species in that such kinds are immediately individuated into cases, though they can be natural or artificial. Besides there are sorts, both naturally and artificially, that are not strictly individuated.

30. Russell thought of individuals as the spatiotemporal intersection of a cloud of properties—an idea that still resonates even among philosophers like Armstrong (1983) and D. Lewis (1983). Russell's "complete complex of compresence" idea lacks a principle of unity, something Leibniz had emphasized. What makes *one* thing out of the intersection of universals or properties?

31. The notion "is really the same but not formally identical" is further explicated in chapter 7.3.

32. If you assume there are a finite number of distinct de re necessities, you might also think there are finite distinct combinations (but is that so?). Skipping that question, there is no compelling reason to suppose the de re ne-

cessities for things are finite in principle; maybe nature is recursively structured, with no bottom of ordered magnitudes or structures.

33. I skip for now immaterial kinds with material cases, ranging from "The First Letter of the Alphabet" to "the diatonic scale," and immaterial species, like "The Angel Gabriel," which, strictly, are not individuated, and abstract particulars, like Mahler's Symphony No. 5, plays, and novels.

34. Will you let this suffice? If there is an explanation for the being of everything that is physical, it has to be by something that is not, in its explanatory aspect, physical (e.g., as Spinoza also reasoned)? That's because physical explanations that are not reductions always end with "and why is that so?"

35. That reasoning is like Plato's and Avicenna's and was adopted by Aquinas in *De Ente et Essentia*. It can be expressed as "unless there is something that exists because of what it is, there is no final explanation for the existence of anything at all." I read Scotus's *De Primo Principio* as an a posteriori rationale for why such a final explanation for the existence of things is possible, indeed necessary, and so, actual.

36. As I mentioned, one could devise a restricted interpretation of formal modal logic to express relations of real, metaphysical, possibility, and so on, midway between "logical possibility" (some form of thought consistency) and "natural possibility" (possibility relatively to the potentialities of nature), where further things beyond the naturally possible would be metaphysically possible, as products of untaken divine elections but without any prior content, perhaps, like works of artists that have no prior templates (Ross 1993b). That further indicates that a de re interpretation of formal modal logic requires a cognitively independent ontological justification.

37. That reopens an old question about the relation of logic to metaphysics. For it seems that one's ontology of necessity and possibility may restrict the formal logic one uses, just as one's account of what might have been (see chapter 3) may affect what one thinks about bifurcation and thus about classical logic (cf. Dummett 1991).

38. "Somehow" here is to be understood as including something existing a-temporally and independently. Cf. note 26. To accommodate one's conviction that there are possibilities whose content is inaccessible to us in principle, we may postulate a cause within whose ability such beings do lie, a free creative cause of whose power the order of the cosmos is a single (or part of a single) disposition, the ordained power of God (see Aquinas, *Summa Theologica*, I, q.25), that might have been disposed wholly otherwise.

39. Some might prefer "intentional" since the supposed possibility does not have to be expressed.

40. To say something is within the power of remote ancestors related to it by random natural selection is an equivocation because the conditions of

real possibility for a *particular* thing are not realized until the outcome is not random.

41. I skip the refinements in which some worlds stand in various accessibility relationships to others, since the ontological problems are comparable to the case presented.

42. Divine power, relatively to our concepts for things, is constrained by the ordained divine power as a whole (the whole order of the cosmos), and the absolute divine power apart from any particular divine elections is inaccessible in content beyond what is actually made and beyond our knowledge that what is made is not equivalent to it.

43. I do not mean that genus to species is the same as determinable to determinate, but that this feature is common to both.

44. This division traces roughly to Francis Suarez's "On the Various Kinds of Distinctions" (Suarez 1976).

45. Leave out for now any effort at distinguishing conditional possibility determined by other abilities like invention from already actual abilities that may be time bound.

46. This reasoning supposes that whatever is really possible is either actually existing or within the capacity of something existing (tenselessly). Are there things that just happen, that is, happen without an antecedent account in nature? You might think of the random, or think whatever is not prevented might (with some probability) happen. But even quantum phenomena are sortally, just not individually, regular. A relative frequency notion of probability will not allow us to establish that any phenomenon, taken singly, is genuinely at random.

47. If not sure that notion is deficient, try "chronons, the minimal units of physical time." Can there be such a thing? What about "spatons, the minimal units of cosmic distance"?

48. We don't know that there could be rabbucks (deer-sized evolutionary descendants of rabbits [Dixon 1990]). That's not like "a rational animal with left-handed amino acids," for which some think there is a determining formula and that it would be a different species from humans.

49. I don't have a recipe to determine whether a conjecture ("pictures by phone in 1950" or "teleportation of humans in 2035") amounts to a real possibility. Still, philosophy is unreliable if it relies on, rather than is merely enriched, by conjectures not known to be real possibilities.

50. David Lewis's account of the naturally necessary as what happens in all the suitably similar worlds and the naturally impossible as what does not happen in any of them seems to be a ramified Humean account (allowing for counterfactuals) that proposes a logical shadow but not an explanation of the naturally impossible.

51. For convenience I skip the miracles that are outside the order of nature (like divine revelation) or contrary to it (like bodily resurrection) because they can be known only ex post facto, though they do support the idea that there are metaphysical possibilities (possibilities beyond the order of nature) that, if not also actualities, lie only within untaken divine elections and are antecedently to creation without definite content (analogously to the possibilities that gain content along with actuality within musical artistry, but were nothing definite before [Ross 1993b]).

Chapter 3. What Might Have Been

1. I am not distinguishing "strong" from "weak" modal fictionalism here or either of those from modal instrumentalism, which Daniel Nolan (2002) does neatly. For I think one can treat a possible-worlds interpretation of modal logic as an abstract model for various areas of modal discourse in natural languages where it is an empirical matter how well the formal structures map and illuminate such discourse. So the interpreted formal system would be analogous to a mathematical model of a physical system.

2. D. P. Henry (1984) explored some inventive medieval treatments of empty names.

3. That makes it difficult to establish a key principle: that what does not exist on account of what it is, might not have existed at all. Avicenna held that all things in nature, none of which exist on account of what they are, exist necessarily by divine emanation. Maimonides and Albertus Magnus, Aquinas and Scotus, reasoned that any such thing might not have existed at all and, so, requires a cause of being (ultimately, a creator). They supported that with the deduction that a perfect divine being has to be free (with liberty of contradiction) with respect to everything else; so, it does not emanate but elects its creatures. Still a central metaphysical question depends on whether it can be shown that "not existing on account of what it is," as is proved by a thing's beginning to be or ceasing to be, ensures that it "might not have been at all" without already supposing the existence of a free creator. That same question applies especially to the material cosmos as a whole. There is also a further question as to whether, when all vestiges of Platonism are put aside, the notion of a thing that exists because of what it is, where that is unknowable, has explanatory content.

4. See the 2001 survey by Peter Menzies in *Stanford Encyclopedia of Philosophy*, on the web at http://plato.stanford.edu/entries/causation-counterfactual/.

5. It may be epistemically ("for all we know") possible that some humans are reduced to a state of quasi-rational and voluntary action without reflective self-awareness. It would be like a lasting state of parasomnia (e.g.,

sleepwalking), and it may even be for-all-we-know-possible that some evolutionary prehumans were by nature in such a state of reasoned and voluntary action without reflective self-awareness; but whether either is really possible depends on the way of the world, not on our thinking.

6. You might neatly conceive of a cabbage we made to think by the application of electricity to it. But it can't happen.

7. An argument merely from imagined possibilities is a material non sequitur. The same thing goes for typical conclusions by David Parfit (1984) about personal identity based on thought experiments about brain transfers and the like. They illicitly assume from the consistency of descriptions that there *really* could be such situations.

8. I mean here "naming" in the sense of "what we *call* a thing."

9. Of course, if you are a neo-Platonist about individual essences or about determinate individual possibilities a priori, you'd say no to that.

10. Ross 1985 offers a brief discussion of emergence. It seems as if Aristotelian forms are emergent, "educed" as some called it, from the capacities of matter.

11. Let "kind" here do duty for "property," "universal" (in current parlance), "real nature," "sort," and whatever other general formulas are fully realized materially.

12. That would appear, at least when joined with "nothing comes from nothing," to entail that if there are possibilities beyond the capacities of nature (metaphysical possibilities broader than natural ones), there exists something whose abilities exceed the cosmic ones.

13. Social constructs and their consequential features are not less real because they are thought and action dependent. They are just not independent of thought the way bacteria are. But they can be public and perceivable realities, like a hospital.

14. Some philosophers call that relation "supervenience." But that seems not to be an explanatory notion, but more a correlation one, as I understand it (cf. Kim 2005),whereas emergence may be a natural necessity among natural systems with their own organizing principles that are not reducible to the quantitative principles of energy transition within the base system from which they originate and on which they depend. So, for all we know so far, there may be principles of biological organization that are not reducible to the physics of their components. Kim (2005), like many others, including Sellars, concluded that qualia are not reductively analyzable and explicable. Is that an emergence theory?

15. Hume's denial of that is based on supposing that we cannot perceive natural necessity, when it is obvious that we can, for instance, if your foot is caught in a bear trap, or your head caught in a window, or your breath is knocked out. Hume had too narrow a view of the perceptible.

16. The *Columbia Encyclopedia* (1983) states: "A constellation, in common usage is a group of stars (e.g., Ursa Major) that is imagined to form a configuration in the sky; properly speaking, a constellation is a definite region of the sky in which the configuration of stars is contained" (194).

17. Hume's idea that you can't experience necessity was a verbal kidnapping. His "impressions of sense" was merely an imaginative projection of "simples" from our complex experiences. As was becoming obvious by the time of C. I. Lewis (1929), we don't have such experiences and "impressions."

18. That is a change that not only unseated Hume's claim that necessities are not known through experience, but also Kant's thesis that necessities are only known a priori. The argument, something Thomas Reid recognized in the eighteenth century, is that natural sameness, which is necessary, is discovered.

19. Philosophers argued *whether* there really are analytic truths (Quine 1951; White 1950); yet, from a linguistic point of view based on usage, the answer is obviously "yes," but is of no consequence except as a map of the "quick circuitry" in our vocabulary and beliefs, and without a guarantee of truth.

20. The ancestry of the idea of analytic truth (that Leibniz adapted) is that arithmetic and geometry and ordinary talk contain statements where truth can be explained as an inclusion of one idea in another. It is an old idea involved with explaining how we know certain things, like "triangles have three interior angles"; Thomas Aquinas, for instance, said there are judgments that are true because the predicate is contained in the definition of the subject (*Summa Theologica*, I, q.17, a.3, *ad* 2). Such statements can be true de dicto and false de re, however, for example, if there were no real Euclidean space at all.

21. Perhaps Peter Strawson had in mind a linguistic analogue of Kantian transcendental reasoning: to draw metaphysical conclusions from the conditions of the possibility of our conceptual organization. Even Nelson Goodman (1968) moved in the direction of constructive phenomenalism when he said that "the world is the product of art and discourse," and later adopted irrealism.

22. Beliefs, for instance, that spiders are not insects, (a "spider" is an "eight-legged arachnid") and evaluations (a "ragamuffin" is a "dirty or unkempt child") often become parts of word meanings.

23. David Hume proposed that meaning inclusions ("relations of ideas") are the only necessary truths, having contradictory denials. Immanuel Kant, instead, proposed that there are a priori judgments that are pre-formative of perception, some of which are analytic (meaning inclusions) and some of which are synthetic a priori (like Euclidean geometry, arithmetic, and the Newtonian principles); the latter were offered as important necessities that structure experience and thus, the experienced world. Even positivistic philosophers, and other empiricists, but not all, right through to the late-twentieth-century, thought analytic truths and stipulations were the only "necessary" (namely, verbal) truths, effetely neither forming, nor resting upon experience.

24. More strictly, bundles of belief, and sometimes, just habitual ways of talking like "cars run on gas."

25. Do chocolate and butter qualify? Whether chocolate is a thermoplastic does seem to be a matter of convention as to how far from industrial products one extends the reference. On a test by meaning alone, the answer would be "yes"; but custom advises otherwise, and maybe that's because of overflow features not contained in the meaning but by the chemical paradigms for which the term was invented.

26. Which is disjunctive in a way that only a pawn's first move is, but otherwise is quiddative (what it is), but for a made up object.

27. For a while, Peter Strawson (1959) pursued descriptive metaphysics on the assumption that the real ontology of things is reflected in our conceptions. And Dummett's proposed (1991) to settle certain disputes about realism in science by determining whether the logic of our discourse about such things, as revealed in a theory of meaning adequate for the whole language, is classical or intuitionistic.

28. "Iron" means "a lustrous, ductile, malleable, silver-gray metal, good conductor of heat and electricity, attracted by magnets and easily magnetizable, atomic number 26, atomic weight 55.847, with 2/8/14/2 electronic configuration, that flows at 1,538 degrees Centigrade." How could you tell that by looking or hefting a frying pan?

29. Ross (1981) offers a general account of adaptation of meaning to context; chapter 7 there develops the idea of craftbound discourse versus unbound discourse and there is a general sketch of semantic relativity in Ross 1992.

30. See "Semantic Contagion" (Ross 1992) for remarks on the pragmatic traction of language in action. Broad meanings, like "water is a liquid" (even when all water on Jupiter may be solid forever), make efficient connections even when strictly false.

31. With vat minds (Putnam 1992), the overflow significations of their verbally coincident beliefs would differ radically from ours. So, we could not have had all the same beliefs as we do, absent the real physical world.

32. I adapted C.I. Lewis, on the modes of meaning (1946), something Roderick Chisholm once suggested to me.

Chapter 4. **Truth**

1. Thinking can be constitutive or efficacious or performative, as well as responsive, say, perceptive. Right from the start, I am discarding the idea that underivative truth (not just formal constructs) is a relation between sentences and the world without any element of understanding in it.

2. A similar idea is Anselm's in his dialogue *De Veritate* (1998).

3. By "discourse" here and throughout I mean practices of expressed judgment used to modify action, whether sailing, carpetmaking, architecture, musical composition, philosophy, or physics. David Wiggins (1998, 332) says "the only way forward is for us to treat it as a methodological assumption, pending disproof, that there is only one relevant sense of the predicate 'true'; to take this as the sense of the word in ordinary English." That does not seem necessary at all and seems not responsive to contextual adaptation of meaning (see examples in note 4) with which we are all adept.

4. And I don't mean trivial contrasts like "true sentence" and "true Englishman," but contexts like: "There are unprovable truths of arithmetic"; "It is true that there might have been cold-blooded dinosaurs"; "It is true that the first Western/Latin university was founded in Paris around 1215 AD"; "It is true that the Son of Man will come again, to judge the living and the dead"; "It is true that there are three outs per inning in baseball"; "It is true that Gary Carter hit the winning run in a World Series"; "It is false that had I been born in 1025, I would have been part of the Norman Conquest."

There are not the same substitutable expressions, the same co-applicable expressions, or the same opposed expressions for all those cases of "is true that"—they differ in meaning. Generally, words acquire meaning by contrast of meaning with other words and further differentiate with use (with the exception of proper naming expressions). See Michael Dummett 1991, 14, line 25, for explicit acknowledgment of multiple concepts of truth; similar observations are in Davidson 1990 and many other writers. Crispin Wright (1992) opted for a "core notion" of truth that acquires "accidentals" in diverse discourses. That's a good start, but I don't think the differences are mere accidentals. Further, none of those who make similar observations about the multiplicity of our conceptions of truth offers a linguistic theory, like that of semantic contagion (Ross 1981; 1992) to explain how the adaptation to context occurs as a linguistic phenomenon.

5. Aristotle's idea in *Metaphysics* 1011b25, "To say of what is that it is not, or of what is not that it is, is false, while to say of what is that it is, and of what is not that it is not, is true," might seem to be a match-up idea until one takes into account that he holds that the knower *becomes*, in an accidental way, what is known. What is known, the very thing under abstraction, becomes the actuality of one's ability to judge.

6. I have in mind J. L. Austin's "correlation" account, explained by Kirkham (1995, 124), and similar theories, considered below, that do not take correspondence to be a part-by-part match-up, but an overall match-up by correlation of expressions with what is so.

7. Michael Dummett (1991) talked as if truth were a meta-linguistic, rather than a meta-judgmental, notion and proposed to make advances in the philosophy of thought by advances in the philosophy of language. "True" is very

commonly treated as a *semantic* feature, one that Davidson uses as the basis for his account of meaning, and others propose to explain through their accounts of meaning.

8. Notice in "I swear to tell the truth" the relevant notion of "truth" has an overriding belief element, rather than a dominant "is so" element. Similarly, sometimes when I might say, "Everything you say is the truth," I am not committing to the accuracy of everything you say but to its honesty; and there is a similar form of expression, "Yes, everything you say is true," that has a suppressed condition "according to your lights." There is no escaping the contextual adaptation of "is true."

9. David Wiggins (1980) made a similar objection.

10. Besides, there would have to be a universal semantics for all 6,319 or so extant natural languages (according to a 2005 count).

11. Austin 1950. Richard L. Kirkham (1995, 124–30) explains and employs Austin's self-characterization of his theory as a correspondence theory.

12. That's because the actual reality, my typing this endnote, say, becomes, immaterially, the operative state of my ability to understand (classically of the *intellectus possibilis*, my capacity to grasp, judge, and reason), just as the seen is the actuality of my ability to see when I am seeing it. So too, my saying the words "ineluctable confoundment" is the actuality (the exercise) of my ability to say them.

13. In fact, to say there is truth by thick coherence, but that it does not suppose another notion of truth (e.g., by postulation), generates a contradiction.

14. For instance, performative judgment by enactment ("I take you for my lawful wedded . . ." "I promise . . ."), by legislation, "murder is unjustified killing of a human with malice aforethought."

15. Aristotle said, "to say of what is, that it is and of what is not, that it is not, is true" *Met.* 1011b25. Aquinas, *Summa contra Gentiles*, I, 59, n.2, said, "veritas est adequatio intellectus et rei, secundum quod intellectus dicit esse quod est, vel non esse quod non est." I read *adequatio* as equality or sameness, not as a match up. For like Aristotle, Aquinas holds that knowing is immaterially becoming what is known (as the actuality of the ability to know). Medieval writers also spoke of the truth of propositions in a way more like John Austin; "sicut significant, ita est."

Chapter 5. Perception and Abstraction

1. Note that abstraction as understood here is our constant, native, departicularization of things. I repeat that numerous times because it is so widely missed.

2. Even though the name "Caesar" has to travel backward by chains of reference to the very person, still, Caesar the referent gets into the thought as subject of attribution only through abstractive conception (e.g., Roman dictator), just as "assassination" does. We can talk about Julius Caesar, the very individual, just as we can talk about our living president.

3. Of course, some of one's past may be presented clairvoyantly in vivid particularity, like posttraumatic stress experiences but without the conviction of presentness. Both sorts of presence are enabled by abstraction; the difference lies in the vivid sensory quality and particularity of the clairvoyant memory.

4. Note the discussion of the "given" from C. I. Lewis, *Mind and the World Order* (1929) onward through Sellars 1956 and McDowell 1994. Of course, there are subjective appearances, imaginary objects, and judgments subsisting in linguistic and other representations. But they are outputs and extensions of other awareness, not the core of transparent awareness on which an explanation of animal perception as well as abstractive human judgment has to be grounded. The manner of things' presence in animal awareness is species specific. Colors of things are not just our subjective *responses,* nor are the definite sounds (say, a low C, F, or G of the singing sands of Oman) merely our and similar animals' response. They are real, though they are dynamic, happenings with light or sound waves.

5. James Gibson (1950; 1966; and 1979) made major contributions to the empirical psychology of perception and set psychologists and philosophers (some are mentioned here) on the path to rejecting old representationalism and devising new understandings of direct awareness of external things without an intervening theater of subjective experience.

6. This viewpoint is similar to the direct realism of Gibson (see note 5). There are related more recent views; see, for example, Tim Crane (2006), M. Martin (1998); and see R. Sokolowski's (2000) reading of Husserl. See also Marion 2000. Some think chimps and some birds (ravens and crows) and other animals have at least something approaching abstraction. I doubt that is abstraction as I use the notion, but some animals (ravens, for instance) do seem to have nonreflexive perceptive and adaptive awareness that enables complex contrivance. See essays in Hurley and Nudds 2006 for even stronger claims.

7. There are many musical illusions. See http://psy.ucsd.edu/~ddeutsch/psychology/deutsch_research1.html.

8. DiSpezio 2002. There are also Web sites with dynamic visual illusions.

9. I got this term and the idea from George Marvodes, who later published and applied the expression "input alignment" in his *Belief in God* (1970). He reasoned that aligned causes that produce a single effect that is entirely dependent on each as ordered are each directly perceptible by way of the effect.

I modify and adapt the notion here. The example of seeing the moon or the moon image on a reflecting telescope is his, as is the telephone example.

10. See the reason given in chapter 5.9. It is indeed startling that molecules can be so arranged that living things, thousands of species of them, can be sentient, and so, able to perceive. But it is a fact. So why can't molecules assemble into things that make brain states with which to perceive distant objects by sensory modifications without intervening perceived phenomena (without "the representations")?

11. An HHUD is a "holographic heads-up display," like that used by supersonic jet fighter pilots, where there is a computer-generated and abstracted presentation of the terrain such that by flying according to that display they fly better than they could even if they could look ahead for themselves.

12. See Hatfield 2002 on how B. Russell, W. James, and E. Mach dealt with sense data.

13. Husserl 1970; Merleau-Ponty 1945; and Sokolowski 2000.

14. Paul Churchland (1979; 1995) speculated on an eventual recalibration of consciousness that would bring the units of experience into closer correlation with those of physical science, gradually making the manifest image resemble the scientific image.

15. That, later on, got confused with "being in the mind," a subjective state, rather than "being in mind," a condition of the thing: *inesse*. That's a fundamental difference in notions of animal perception. Cf. the analysis of *inesse* in Sellars 1968, 63–66. Sellars tried to accommodate the notion within a basically representational, post-Kantian, scheme.

16. Does the decedent's living belief that she would have grandchildren *become* true with the birth of children to her children, even after she no longer holds the belief?

17. In fact, we distinguish seeing the following car in one's mirror from seeing the reflection on the mirror.

18. Some ancients held an extromission view of vision, a kind of flashlight notion of the eye as emitting rays to make things visible.

19. Those are made-up numbers; real ones can be approximated, though.

20. That's somewhat like the backward causation mentioned above. For, of course, if none were born her belief would have been false. Or is it that if her thinking is right, the belief was true, though events will not conform till later? (Aquinas, in *De Veritate*, seems to adopt the latter view.)

21. By "intelligence" I do not mean some quality that comes in degrees, like cleverness, but an absolute difference between "intelligent" and "not intelligent" (able to judge abstractly by considering the "what" of things).

22. If we think of concepts as both abilities and as what is disclosed (and can be thought about), it is obvious that they belong in a network of contrast dependence.

23. Aquinas (*Summa Theologica*, I, q.79, c) speaks of "some power derived from a higher intellect whereby it is able to light up the phantasms." That suggests that our constant abstractive ability lights up what is sensibly presented to disclose formative structures in it.

24. The idea that a person or a cat gets to be subject of judgment by "reference" as a kind of verbal pointing—as a kind of inclusion in a row by pointing—is misleading. The things we think of are themselves elements of the thoughts and the words in sentences about objects go in place of the things in expressed transformations; medieval logicians called that "personal supposition," whereas if the word goes proxy for its own meaning, that was called "simple supposition"; and if the word goes proxy for its inscription, that was called "material supposition." But words in sentences go in place of things in thought. You can only point to what you are otherwise, even if indistinctly, aware of. Cf. Kneale and Kneale 1962. The thing has to be intentionalalized in order to be within the judgment.

25. Robert Brandom (2000) has a similar notion for our inference proclivities, "material inference." (I call them expectations or implicit reliances.) There are many other sorts of concepts, for example, as presenters for remote things, as classifiers, and so forth.

26. I have linguistic meanings for those words but not sense meanings (operative conceptions) by which I could recognize cases; it is the latter that are operative concepts.

27. They did not make explicit the distinction of the native continuous activity of abstraction from the focused, conceptually modified instant-to-instant states of that abstraction. Yet I think their statements apply to the latter as well.

28. "I love the velvet feel, the bee sound, the lavender smell, your touch." It may be pleasure for animals; for humans it can be love (delight) and a means of expressing love.

29. Hatfield (2008) explains that the geometry of the visually perceived is not the same as the projective geometry of the relationships of the real objects. The relatively uniform human visual geometry by which we maintain visual constancy during our movements is, I conjecture, one form of the automatic supplementation of sense responses to enable effective vision.

30. I think that was called *vis cogitativa* by Aquinas, who says (*Summa Theologica*, Ia, q.78, a.4), "furthermore for the apprehension of intentions which are not received through the [external] senses, the estimative power is appointed...; for other animals perceive these intentions only by some natural instinct, while man perceives them by a coalition of ideas. Therefore, the power, which in other animals is called the natural estimative, in man is called cogitative which by some sort of collation discovers these intentions."

31. That feature is counterintuitively called "plastic flow."

32. Such explanations, along with a general grasp of the features of light and optics, resulted in thermometers, Polaroid lenses, Polaroid photography, liquid crystal displays, cathode ray tubes, color television, high-definition television, night glasses, and thousands of other things.

33. I don't think philosophers who read Brentano as if intentionality is mere aboutness that might be analyzed into some kind of reference (cf. Nelson Goodman's [1961] notion of "about") grasp the continuity between his writing and his medieval predecessors who thought real things are within perceptual awareness, the way you can see your own hand. Husserl, as Sokolowski interpreted him, was a lot closer to the views I advance here than, say, Sellars's (1968) representational analysis.

34. Animals do that too, but without the "what?" mode of human awareness. Again I note that some scientists now think the latter, too, is not exclusively human (cf. essays in Hurley and Nudds 2006).

35. A merely "Cambridge change" as Peter Geach called your getting farther from me as I walk away from you.

36. There is an analogue for mere animals. When two cats see a ball from opposite sides, what they see, *optically,* lacks insides and a side opposite from where each sits, though the two see the very same thing. The real ball is distinct and separable from their seeing; and both rely unknowingly on the same unseen features to poke it, or roll it. Indeed the visual aspects by which it is seen may differ for the two cats, so one can see the spotted ball (spotted on the opposite side) without seeing the spot, whereas the other sees the spotted side (perhaps also not seeing the spot, but in a different sense). That indicates that what is seen is not the appearance, but that what is seen is seen by means of the (supplemented) appearance (like adjusted refraction) in input alignment with the thing.

37. See note 11.

38. Wilfred Sellars (1968, 63 ff, and 90–115), with historically literate grasp of the notion of *inesse,* and employing a basically post-Kantian representationalist dualism of thought "contents" and "attributes" of things, tried to work out how one could, by a two-name reduction, make sense of "the hypothesis of the identity of general contents with attributes," and said it "requires, in other words, a dualism of two modes of in-esse, the in-esse of attributes in representings and the in-esse of attributes in things" (92). He was trying to find a way to explain "the in-esse of attributes in representings" (a Kantian reformulation of the medieval *esse intentionale* of things) within a two-name framework. Describing the project (93), Sellars wrote: "The general strategy was to construe the in-esse of contents in representings on the model of standing for as a relation between linguistic expressions and their senses. . . . The hypothesis is that the relation of representings to their contents is to be construed on the model of the relation of linguistic expressions to their senses . . . ." Sellars uses "in-esse" once

to indicate presence of a content as representation in thought and explicitly in a second sense to indicate the occurrence of the attribute in particulars.

Neither is the sense of *inesse* I use here, though Sellars's explaining the "in-esse of attributes in representings" is closer to what I mean by the "*inesse* of objects in awareness," the intentionality of things. I am using *inesse* for the presence of real particulars in awareness; they become modifications of our awareness; for consciousness is the making present of things (Sartre: "the being of consciousness is the consciousness of being"), whether it is animal awareness or human intelligent awareness.

It is a strange by-product of Cartesian dualism that so many philosophers, even physicalists, resolutely say that the presence of physical things in cognition does not, indeed cannot, happen. But no one has ever shown that to be so. Instead, assumptions are repeatedly, perhaps unthinkingly, made that exclude it (like the immediate awareness principle, that we are immediately aware only of our own ideas).

39. Perhaps "being perceived" and "being understood" need in our present-day philosophical context to be regarded as real relations (in contrast to "not real") to preserve the idea that the thing perceived or otherwise known is the reality itself that is included in awareness, not a replica or representation. We may get something into thought, say, Apostle Peter's starting to walk on water, by surrogates like a Bible story, but if what we believe is what happened, then that event is present abstractly in thought (probably mediated by the story or a picture), unless we have a case of knowledge merely *by* report (see chapter 8).

40. A Greek Orthodox theologian said belief, to be deep conviction, has to descend from the head to the heart. An eighteen-year-old driver's, "I might get killed," is often a merely notional belief in contrast, say, to an adult's finding out, "This time I really fouled up." Seventeenth-century English divines said things like, "I believe in my bowels that Christ is risen," indicating the depth of their certitude.

41. Cf. Hoffman 1983. The idea that we could have the same brain states absent a body and the external causes of its states, as if the body and the world could be like "a phantom limb," is a fantasy. Brains are, in nature, neural-cognitive centers of animal being and animal awareness, for which action, environment, perception, and feeling are the point and naturally necessary.

42. It turns out that there is not *understanding* directly of mere particulars, but of particulars only through the universal (by way of abstraction), just as the long tradition before Berkeley and Hume had held.

43. Similarly, is it de re or de dicto that you know you had great^4-grandmothers who had your mitochondrial DNA? How about "There are more than 110 chemical elements"?

44. There is a different sense of "about" in one's saying "Freshmen are eager" and in one's saying "Being a beginner is embarrassing."

45. Both Locke (*Essay*, II, xi, 10, p. 59: "I think I may be positive . . . that the power of Abstracting is not at all in them . . . a perfect distinction betwixt Man and Brutes") and Hume thought other animals do not think. On the opinions of Descartes, Locke, Leibniz, and Hume concerning animal cognition, see Wilson 1995. For the recent and extensive dispute about that, see the essays in Hurley and Nudds 2006.

46. Sometimes it is not clear whether one's belief is really de re rather than de dicto. Nevertheless, it is impossible to explain how the remote, the universal, and the entirely abstract can be what we know de re, say, that Rome (image: arches, gladiator breastplates, and swords) lasted longer than the British Empire (image: sails and red patches on world map), or that there are nonmetallic elements, unless it is by abstract presentation, particularized by conventional images or subvocalized words, as illustrated above. The only alternative is a replacement analysis, the effect of which is to tell us we do not mean what we are sure we do mean.

Chapter 6. Emergent Consciousness and Irreducible Understanding

An earlier version of this chapter appeared as "Immaterial Aspects of Thought," *Journal of Philosophy* 89, no. 3 (1992): 136–50, © *Journal of Philosophy*.

1. Some call that "supervenience," though strictly, as I understand it, supervenience is a logical relationship between systems, for example, of neural and perceptual states, whereas emergence is supposed to be a real and explanatory relation among systems that develop out of one another, without intermediaries or reductions, under a universal natural (or rationally constructed) order.

2. Such reasons trace back to considerations both Plato and Aristotle employed and that were shared by their Arabic and scholastic adapters.

3. The formal underdetermination of the physical (cf. Quine) seems to be among the twentieth-century conceptual breakthroughs along with space-time relativity (Poincaré and Einstein), physical indeterminacy (Heisenberg), and arithmetic incompleteness (Gödel).

4. Distinguish reasoning that the form of thought is definite in the way the physical cannot be (the main line of argument) from the epistemic version that we can know that thought is determinate in form though we cannot ever know that a physical process is similarly determinate. The latter would also imply that thought and the physical are different in principle. But it hasn't the same weight as the reading I rely upon.

5. "Thought" here means "judgmental understanding capable of truth or falsity"—what Aristotle thought was related to the ability to understand the way one's actual singing is related to one's ability to do it. *De Anima,* III, 4, 429b, 30: "Mind is in a sense potentially whatever is thinkable, though actually it is nothing until it has thought." (Remember, for Aristotle mind is just a power [a naturally active definitive ability] of the human psyche, that indicates and requires the incorruptibility of the psyche.) There are many kinds of thinking; some are realized as bodily doings, like my carefully pouring a liquid or walking up stairs. But it is only the understanding element that I am now trying to show cannot be wholly physical; understandings that involve sensation or feeling cannot be entirely nonphysical either, any more than my going for a walk can be a mere willing.

6. See Aristotle's argument in *De Anima,* III, 4, 429a, 10–28, and Aquinas's (1951) commentary on *De Anima,* sec. 684–86, that the understanding cannot have an organ as sight has the eye, the optical system, and as philosophers nowadays suppose thinking has the brain, because the limited physical states of an organ would fall short of the contrasting states of understanding that we know we can attain. (Perhaps we should note that some, like Roger Penrose, recognizing the computation problems, have suggested that the human brain is probably a quantum computer, thus not limited in its states as was previously supposed.)

7. Philosophers should not recoil with distaste at such remarks about thought, because they attribute even odder features to propositions, such as being infinite in number, and belonging to a tight logical network with formal features like "excluded middle," and being such that every one is determinately either logically related by implication or exclusion, or is logically independent of any other.

8. Of course, Plato was the first to emphasize that no physical thing ever realizes a pure form. But it still seemed like a novelty in its new twentieth-century dress, especially in its applications to induction, measurement theory, and confirmation theory.

9. A pure function is one satisfied by an infinite number of functors, and determinate for each n-tuple, like "+", and complete in each and every instance (that is, it does not consist in a relationship among its cases, but explains them).

10. The qualification is presumed hereafter in each appropriate context without repetition. For any valid reasoning or process is also a case of some invalid or otherwise incompatible form at some level of generality, for instance, modus ponens is also a case of "if the premises are true, then the conclusion is," an invalid form, but not an "equally most particular" one.

11. But in part, yes, in the sense that my utterances and actions are physical. Moreover, human thought is not possible apart from feeling or sense, just

as a gesture is not possible without bodily movement or inhibition. The target here is theories that thoughts are "no more than" functions determined physically; for, of course, they are "at least physically mediated" for humans. That's a reason why there can be no personal survival of death without a miraculous resurrection.

12. There is a difference between thinking in accord with the operation and doing the operation, a distinction Wittgenstein made between acting in accord with a rule and following it.

13. Valid reasoning is, of course, also a case of invalid forms, for instance, "P, therefore, C." So we have to speak of there being no equally most particular invalid form.

14. Logically equivalent but nonsynonymous functions would give the same arrays from inputs to outputs. Besides, a device that went to an address for the answer, and took it out in an envelope (encoded), which it did not open (decode), but handed to you (displayed for you to decode) could be made to produce the same array of outputs as addition. Yet it would not be adding; cf. J. Searle's Chinese box example. Furthermore, look at this function:

```
10 Z = X*X*X
20 Print Z
30 X = X + 1
40 GO TO 10
```

This is a machine function for an endless loop to print the cube of every number beginning with zero. You can see that no matter what outputs the machine gives, it might have been doing something till then other than printing successive cubes, unless it produces all cubes—which cannot be done. The machine wears out first.

15. Some conjunction tasks seem possible that are not—for instance, to conjoin all statements that can be expressed in English. That's not because of some fuzziness about the function "conjoin," but because the supposed totality is incoherent as an extension.

16. That does not, however, block the main position of this book that nature is rich in intelligible, active structures for which humans have a natural abstractive aptitude. For such structures are materialized and not pure functions. Humans can find pure functions that many such processes approximate. So, as I remark elsewhere, there are no logical relations in nature, any more than there is genuine addition as leaves pile up.

17. Instead, it is a feature of the individuation of the physical by its multiplicity of quantitative dimensions. Further, individuation is difference from every other actual thing of any sort whatever, along with a principle of internal unification, but not an a priori or transworld property of anything physical—a point not further explored here

18. I also disagree about that outcome too. I think Wittgenstein was showing the "meaning" of a word is not a rule for its use, and that in practice, knowing the meaning is not knowing and following a rule; and certainly, he was not reasoning that we are always in a skeptical quandary about what a word means; for he thought the whole meaning is present in each use.

19. An automatic pilot is a different matter. If we define flying as operating the machine to take off, travel, and land safely, the machine may do even better than the human. But the machine does not do the human activity.

20. What is "the direction" in which the object is traveling? There are no real "point-masses." That is an idealization, as is a photon's rest mass (photons and neutrinos are always moving). No object falling to earth is in a pure vacuum and under no gravitational attraction to other bodies. Physical phenomena often come close to our mathematizations that, of course, are invented to represent them. But those mathematizations are idealizations; see N. Cartwright 1983; and Hacking 1983.

21. General natures, say, biological structures, are organized matter or energy, not pure functions. Such structures can be formulated and classified too, as can be found in compilations; cf. *Scientific Tables* (Basel: Ciba–Geigy, 2005).

22. Of course, you can indeterminately deny yet include what is determinate, as when one might say, "no one can really add" without being specific as to what is denied, in effect meaning "do anything *you* would mean by 'add,'" without supposing there is such a thing.

23. Augustine (1973) used a similar argument, in book 2 of *Contra Academicos*, against a "verisimilitude" (mere likelihood) notion of all truth.

24. Thought, as content, is immaterial in other ways. For instance, it lacks the transcendent determinacy of the physical. A true judgment "someone is knocking on my door" requires for its physical compliant reality a situation with many features not contained (or logically implied) in the true judgment: thus various determinate but incompossible physical situations might make the same statement true (cf. chapter 1).

Further, some thinking is as much physical as it is immaterial. My walking, as an action, is as much a mode of thought as it is a mode of movement, yet no movement, however complex, could ever make a thought. Leibniz, in section 17 of the *Monadology* (Loemker 1969, 644), says that if perception were supposed to be produced by a machine, we could make the machine on large scale and walk around in it like a mill; we would never find a perception, only the movements of wheels, gears, and pulleys. See also Leibniz's "Conversation of Philarete and Ariste" (Loemker 1969, 623).

Further still, machines do not process numbers (though we do); they process representations of them (signals). Since addition is a process applicable only to numbers, machines do not add. And so on for statements, musical themes, novels, plays, and arguments. Machines process only representations, but the pure functions are among the represented.

25. Roughly, things can be really the same without being identical if they are naturally co-occurrent, at least one cannot exist without the other, they are conceptually distinct, and, usually, the causes sufficient to produce one of them are sufficient to produce the other, or causes sufficient to produce one of them depend for effectiveness on the existence of the other. That is not intended to be a strict definition because "is really the same thing as" is a contextually pliant notion, but the focal idea is that one thing is not strictly identical with the other, and at least one relatum is not able to exist without the other, but that there is one reality. See chapter 7.3 for more.

26. It also goes in reverse: with practice, deliberate gestures (in sport or music) become directly media of thought.

27. In fact, that is a reason personal survival of death requires some kind of resurrection that is sufficient for continuity of one's character and distinctive personhood.

28. Of course, a physical effect is in its overflow truth conditions more determinate than the thought, as explained earlier.

29. A medium in-which understanding is realized may limit our access to reality, just as the senses limit our access to the micro and macro cosmic. So I can't do modus ponens in Portuguese, not knowing that language; but I could, if I did.

30. It will turn out in chapter 7 that the cosmos is organized that way too, with various internested systems some of which are in obediential potency as means or media for other active capacities. This is a stronger relationship than mere supervenience, which is usually explained as a logical relationship, because there are orders of natural necessity and (nonreducible) emergence.

31. That point is neither a reason for Cartesian dualism nor an argument for personal immortality. It was used by major interpreters of Aristotle to support the idea of one intellect for all mankind, analogous to the sun. For the Christians it became an argument for the natural incorruptibility of the psyche but left open the need of a miracle for personal survival of death, and left an anomaly as to what would be the outcome had there not been a divine gift of resurrected life.

Chapter 7. **Real Natures: Software Everywhere**

1. Of course, there need not have been words for that relationship. I also skip for the present that some chimps and ravens make what appear to be

tools, like stretching a wire into a probe, or using a string to pull out something that had been hidden from view (cf. essays in Hurley and Nudds 2006).

2. Descartes vigorously rejected forms as explanatory of any change. See this book's introduction at note 1. Aristotle, too, had thought physics is the science of changing (moving) things, though he did not regard that as entirely a system of (mathematizable) quantitative relationships, but instead as a system of active substances with substantial and accidental forms—a conception Descartes was replacing.

3. I omit the details of further distinctions that are canvassed with citations in Jonathan Schaeffer, *Metaphysics of Causation,* avail. at http://plato.stanford.edu/.

4. The amount and pattern of the chair's rocking, as potentiality, is determined by the length of the rockers, the height of the chair, and so on—namely, the design (structure). The rocking is by a different sort of causation, efficient causation.

5. One thousand trillion mathematical operations per second—a rate expected to increase to ten petaflops by 2013 (*New York Times,* August 19, 2005).

6. Tunes (melodies) are forms, intelligible structures, but more than that because they as compositions are complete works. They, like sonatas, novels, plays, and other allographic works of art (Goodman 1968) are abstract particulars, that is, complete things that require some materialization in order to exist at all, but not any particular one because their identity is not dependent on one kind of material, though they require some suitable material to exist at all, whereas structural forms are not complete things because they are constitutive of something else.

7. I do not here mean what Keith Campbell meant by abstract particulars, namely tropes, but such things as musical compositions, novels, plays, dramas, soap operas, and the like that can have many diverse materializations but can't exist without one.

8. Aristotle remarked that some forms can be received by many kinds of matter.

9. For instance, in deep water waves, Wavelength, L, depends on period, T [$L = (g/2\pi)T^2$ ($g = 9.8$ m/s^2)] and Velocity = C = L/T, so, therefore, C = 1.56 m/s^2 x T (T is in the units of seconds, L is in meters, and C is in meters/sec).

10. Geach and Anscombe (1963) used the example of waves in water to convey Aristotle's idea of constitutive and repeatable form that is really distinct from its matter. Further, see Greene 2004, 419–22, on gravitational waves' stretching objects.

11. This is a partial paraphrase of information in an article by Margaret Wertheim, "Celebrating Puzzles," *New York Times,* July 26, 2006, D3.

12. Chapter 5 discusses how abstraction is required for their cognition.

13. Cf. Suarez 1976, on distinctions. Sandra Edwards (1974) surveyed the notions in several medieval philosophers with ample translated passages.

14. A functional kind, say, bread or concrete, may be real in contrast to other relevant kinds, though the domain, like bread, is not one of uniform constitution or of fixed bounds, and does not occur on its own in nature.

15. It seems that at some point nature has to be emergent since, when reductions run out, there will not always be some further transformational intermediate between a resultant and its cause.

It may also happen that some phenomena are not naturally emergent but produced by special divine creation, like individual humans, as many Christians and Orthodox Jews have long believed.

16. Some consequent natures (that is, characteristic behavioral propensities on account of what the thing is) are resultant, like the outcome when you mix ammonia and detergent; some natures are emergent, as when you put ink dots into a meaningful pattern to make a message; and some are constructed, a mixture of resultants and conventional metrics, like "rotational laterality"— not the less important scientifically for all that. How much a cereal box will turn on its base and how much it will tilt in the first blast from a hair dryer three feet away may be arbitrary in all its metrics, and trivial to know, but it is real and much like what a hundred-story building in New York City does on its axis in a hurricane.

17. The resultant natures of things are as real as their microconstituents. That holds at every order of natural magnitude, though I am uncertain about how far into microphenomena scientific realism extends because of the doubtful borders between finding and making. Cf. Hacking 1983; Devitt 1996; Van Frassen 1980; and Wright 1992.

18. How Leibniz is to be interpreted is disputed. For instance, see Garber 1995 and Duarte 2004.

19. Niiniluoto (1999) lays out the varied diet of options philosophers have invented to explain that.

20. John Zeis (2003, 69–90) said the notion of structure/form is needed to fill a gap in Hilary Kornblith's (1993) account of induction within a materialist/naturalist framework. For Kornblith had said, "our conceptual and inferential tendencies jointly conspire, at least roughly, to carve nature at its joints and project the features of a kind which are essential to it" (94), where real kinds are "homeostatic property clusters," like the biological species, "such that we may reliably infer the presence of some of these properties from the presence of others" (36); that, he thinks, is the basis of induction (89). Kornblith claimed (61), "The human mind is well provided for; it has an innate structure which is conducive to the possibility of such knowledge." But Zeis argued that one needs a version of Aristotelian formal causation to explain the unity and natu-

ral replication of the kinds, and proposed treating perception as direct in the way James Gibson had explained (1966, 1979). That would be like the idea I develop here.

21. There has been recent, I think compatible, discussion of real structure and its explanatory base among philosophers of science, for instance, Saunders 1993, 295–326.

22. See the interesting survey of options in Niiniluoto 1999, 144–59.

23. Things do what (and as) they do because of what they are: protons, neutrons, mesons, muons, neutrinos, and so on. There are no outside laws, like divine shouts, that direct matter. And the laws are not like grooves in space that determine what things do by being the paths they follow. There have to be, as Hilary Putnam (1987) recognized, active dispositions in things. Otherwise our science explains nothing. See the discussion of dispositions by S. Armstrong, U. T. Place, and C. B. Martin in Crane 1996.

24. Arthur Fine (1984, 83–107) expressed a similar approach that he called the "Natural Ontological Attitude"; and the critical scientific realism Niiniluoto (1999) advocated is close in spirit as well, though neither explicitly commits to intrinsic intelligible, constitutive, and repeatable structures. But see the *Stanford Encyclopedia of Philosophy* on the Web, entry on "Structural Realism," for similar lines of thought.

25. The scripting of nature is compatible with there being statistically random phenomena or phenomena that at some included magnitude may be random, relatively to an including magnitude. I am not venturing into that area of special expertise.

Chapter 8. **Going Wrong with the Master of Falsity**

1. Aristotle (*De Anima*, III, 3, 328a11) says "imaginations are for the most part false."

2. For instance, in *Summa Theologica*, I, q.17, a.3, 4 and q.85, a.6c.

3. Inquiry into the false usually falls below philosophical notice. For instance, the *Cambridge Dictionary of Philosophy* (Audi 1995) contains no entry for "falsity" or "the false" or "false," and the main article on "truth" by Paul Horwich does not mention any general theory of falsity. Similarly, *A Dictionary of Philosophy* (Flew 1979), under "false" directs the reader to "see Truth and Falsity," and under the latter offers no reference to anyone's treatment of how false judgments, sentences, or whatever get to be false. It is as if everyone knows that being false is a kind of failing at being true, or nothing other than the logical opposite of being true, despite the fact that true and false as predicates can diverge from mere negations of one another. *Blackwell's Dictionary of Philosophy* (Mautner 1996, 147) says "anything which is capable of assertion or denial can be

said to be true or false." That tells us what can be *said* to be true or false (or part of it), but, it alerts us that we can *say* of what has to be true that it is false, but we cannot always so judge.

4. Implicitly, "not-true" is for classical, bifurcated, logic the same as "false." In a whole anthology, *The Nature of Truth* (Lynch 2001), there are only a few pages that mention the false and falsehood, with nothing that treats the subject as a matter of genuine puzzlement, and most philosophers, including Michael Dummett, treat the matter as if it only concerns whether the negation of a true proposition is the same as the false.

5. A philosopher once said that if he came to see the existence of God followed from the principle of noncontradiction, he would reject that.

6. Sartre (1991) dissociated imagining from mere picturing, and like other phenomenologists explored its rich resources that are inextricably merged with understanding and action. Aristotle (*De Anima*, III, 427b9–429a9) tied imagination more narrowly to the making of images that are mostly false (i.e., not of what is actual), though he must have meant that judgment that relies on imagination is prone to falsity, for falsity resides in judgment, not in fantasy as such.

7. Thinking something to be so that is not is more like confidently expecting what does not happen than it is like mistakenly checking "true" on a list of sentences.

8. Aquinas, commenting on Aristotle's *Metaphysics* 1010b–1011a, remarked, "First, the proper cause of falsity is not the senses but the imagination which is not the same as the senses" (citing *De Anima*, III, 3, 428b, 10). I saw that comment someplace rendered as "the imagination is the master of falsity, not the senses." I adopt that here but add "it is also the magician of art and invention."

9. Curley 1974, 177, mentions this too.

10. I skip the matter of self-deception here, though "lying to oneself" is of considerable interest, as is the phenomenon of pathological false judgment where the falsity is suppressed from consciousness. Additionally there is the phenomenon of falsifying awareness, where a happening that fits one description (say, one's illicit enjoyment) is conceptualized defensively and judged quite differently, say, to be intellectual curiosity.

11. Knowledge (broadly, cognition) seems to be explanatorily prior to "belief," "truth," and "justification"; for if there were no animal and human cognition at all, there would be no ecological role for any of those others. People who think we could live in a life of mere belief, without knowledge, are slighting the role of animal cognition generally and its specific function as platform of human cognition. Think of animal cognition as species specific (e.g., cat vs. dog vs. woodpecker), continuous presentation of eco-niche realities that via

instinct, memory, habit and imagination enable and produce variable animal action, usually involving motion, that on the whole is beneficial to the animal (either functioning toward preserving life or enabling reproduction) and originating from its species programmed desires.

12. For a suitable expression or thought, not just for a stone or an event.

13. See Dummett (1991) on pragmatic verification, as well as on constructive formal proof.

14. In *De Veritate* (ca. 1080), Anselm (1998) remarked that truth is a matter of right thinking and reasoned that the truth of statements (propositions) is just a subcase.

15. It helps to think that true belief, even justified, that is not knowledge, is explanatorily posterior to knowing.

16. This idea is largely the same as John Searle's (1995) realism about social constructs. It is much broader in scope than the earlier sociologists' notion, for instance, Berger and Luckmann 1966, and includes physical objects like temples and shopping centers and any other thing that stands in causal relations on account of its status by human institution.

17. From this basis, there develop many other routes to taking what is not so to be so, some from negligence and ignorance—bad habits—and some from just bad luck, where the most reasonable thing to believe is what is simply not so.

18. And even there, we assent willingly; for we are sometimes willing even when internally compelled, otherwise we could not willingly pursue happiness.

19. I am rejecting an Empiricist cash-register model of knowledge as true belief caused by "enough" evidence. If the belief (commitment, in my terms) is not caused, compelled, by the evidence, then something else must cause it: for the most part, that is willing commitment (usually aimed at some good to be gotten from it—see Ross 1986c). The Empiricist tradition, and even Descartes (*Meditation IV*) and his objectors, were to an extent cognitive-voluntarists because they held that one could by unrestrained commitment get *false* beliefs and that one is responsible for proportioning belief to the evidence (Locke, Hume), and for restraining belief on insufficient evidence, and so on (William Clifford).

20. I explore the role of willing reliances in rational belief elsewhere, see, for example, Ross 1986c; 1995; and 1993a. Because commitment typically follows such patterns, false judgment is invited by the very abilities by which we anticipate and conjecture and entertain options for action.

Works Cited

Anscombe, G. E. M. 1969. *Intention*. Oxford: Basil Blackwell.
Anselm. 1998. "On Truth." In *Anselm of Canterbury: The Major Works*, ed. B. Davies and G. Evans. Oxford: Oxford University Press.
Aquinas, T. 1948. *Summa Theologica*, 3 vols. Trans. Fathers of the English Dominican Province. New York: Benzinger Brothers.
———. 1951. *Commentary on Aristotle's De Anima*. Trans. K. Foster and S. Humphries. New Haven: Yale University Press. Reissued 1994, Notre Dame, Ind.: Dumb Ox Books.
———. 1952. *Quaestiones Disputatae de Potentia Dei* (Disputed Questions on the Power of God). Trans. English Dominican Fathers. Westminster, Md.: Newman Press.
———. 1954. *Quaestiones Disputate De Veritate, Questions 1–9*. Trans. Robert W. Mulligan. Chicago: Henry Regnery.
———. 1961. *Commentary on the Metaphysics of Aristotle*. Trans. J. P. Rowan. Chicago: Henry Regnery.
———. 1965. *Aquinas on Being and Essence: A Translation and Interpretation*. Ed. and trans. J. Bobik. Notre Dame, Ind.: University of Notre Dame Press.
Aristotle. 1984. *The Complete Works of Aristotle: The Revised Oxford Translation*, 2 vols. Ed. J. Barnes. Princeton: Princeton University Press.
Armstrong, D. 1983. *What Is a Law of Nature?* Cambridge: Cambridge University Press.
———. 1990. *A World of States of Affairs*. Cambridge: Cambridge University Press.
Asimov, I. 1972. *Asimov's Guide to Science*. New York: Basic Books.

Audi, R., ed. 1995. *Cambridge Dictionary of Philosophy.* New York: Cambridge University Press.
Augustine. 1973. *Against the Academicians.* Milwaukee: Marquette University Press.
Austin, J. L. 1950. "Truth." *Proceedings of the Aristotelian Society* 24: 111–28. Reprinted in *Philosophical Papers,* ed. J. O. Urmson and C. J. Warnock. Oxford: Oxford University Press, 1970.
Ayala, F. 1985. "The Theory of Evolution: Recent Successes and Challenges." In *Evolution and Creation,* ed. E. McMullin. Notre Dame, Ind.: University of Notre Dame Press.
Ayer, A. J. 1952. *Language, Truth and Logic* (reprint of 2d ed., 1946). New York: Dover.
Bach, K. 1993: "Meaning, Speech Acts, and Communication." In *Basic Topics in the Philosophy of Language,* ed. R. M. Harnish. Herts, England: Harvester Wheatsheaf.
Bealer, G. 1982. *Quality and Concept.* Oxford: Oxford University Press.
Berger, P. L., and T. Luckmann. 1966. *The Social Construction of Reality: A Treatise in the Sociology of Knowledge.* Garden City, N.Y.: Anchor Books.
Black, Max. 1954. "The Identity of Indiscernibles." In *Problems of Analysis.* Ithaca: Cornell University Press. 204–16.
Blanshard, B. 1941. *The Nature of Thought,* vol. 2. New York: Macmillan.
Bohm, D. 1980. *Wholeness and the Implicate Order.* Boston: Routledge and Kegan Paul.
Braine, D. 1993. *The Human Person.* London: Duckworth.
Brandom, R. 2000. *Articulating Reasons.* Cambridge: Harvard University Press.
Carroll, J. 1994. *Laws of Nature.* Cambridge: Cambridge University Press.
Cartwright, N. 1983. *How the Laws of Physics Lie.* New York: Oxford University Press.
Cartwright, R. 1987. *Philosophical Essays.* Cambridge: MIT Press.
Cavell, M. 1993. *The Psychoanalytic Mind.* Cambridge: Harvard University Press.
Chalmers, D. 1996. *The Conscious Mind.* Oxford: Oxford University Press.
Cherniak, C. 1986. *Minimal Rationality.* Cambridge: MIT Press.
Chisholm, R. 1977. *Theory of Knowledge,* 2d ed. Englewood Cliffs, N.J.: Prentice-Hall.
Churchland, P. M. 1979. *Scientific Realism and the Plasticity of Mind.* Cambridge: Cambridge University Press.
———. 1995. *The Engine of Reason, the Seat of the Soul.* Cambridge: MIT Press.
Cobb-Stevens, R. 1990. *Husserl and Analytic Philosophy.* Boston: Kluwer Academic.
Crane, T. 1996. *Dispositions.* London: Routledge.

———. 2006. "Is There a Perceptual Relation?" In *Perceptual Experience*, ed. T. Gendler and J. Hawthorne. Oxford: Oxford University Press.
Curley, E. M. 1974. "Descartes, Spinoza and the Ethics of Belief." In *Spinoza: Essays in Interpretation*, ed. M. Mandelbaum and E. Freeman. LaSalle, Ill.: Open Court.
Davidson, D. 1986. "A Coherence Theory of Truth and Knowledge." In *Truth and Interpretation: Perspectives on the Philosophy of Donald Davidson*, ed. E. LePore. Oxford: Basil Blackwell.
———. 1990. "The Structure and Content of Truth." *Journal of Philosophy* 87: 279–328.
Davies, R. 1976. *World of Wonders*. New York: Viking.
Dennett, D. 1978. *Brainstorms*. Montgomery, Vt.: Bradford Books.
———. 1987. "The Intentional Stance." In *The Intentional Stance*. Cambridge: MIT Press.
Descartes, R. 1897–1913. *Ouevres de Descartes*, 12 vols. Ed. Charles Adam and Paul Tannery. Paris: Cerf.
Descombes, V. 1980. *Modern French Philosophy*. New York: Cambridge University Press.
Devitt, M. 1996. *Realism and Truth*. Oxford: Blackwell.
DiSpezio, M., et al., eds. 2002. *Book of Optical Illusions*. New York: Sterling.
Dixon, D. 1990. *Man after Man: An Anthropology of the Future*. New York: St. Martin's.
Dretske, F. 1977. "Laws of Nature." *Philosophy of Science* 44: 248–65.
Dreyfus, H., ed. 1982. *Husserl, Intentionality, and Cognitive Science*. Cambridge: MIT Press.
Duarte, S. 2004. "The Metaphysical Foundations of Philosophy in the Light of Aristotle, Descartes, and Leibniz." Dissertations in Philosophy. Van Pelt Library, University of Pennsylvania.
Ducasse, C. J. 1944. "Propositions, Truth, and the Ultimate Criterion of Truth." *Philosophy and Phenomenological Research* 4: 317–40.
Dummett, M. 1991. *The Logical Basis of Metaphysics*. Cambridge: Harvard University Press.
———. 1994. *Origins of Analytical Philosophy*. Cambridge: Harvard University Press.
Duns Scotus, J. 1950. *Opera omnia*. Civitas Vaticana: Typis Polyglottis Vaticani.
Edwards, Sandra. 1974. "Medieval Theories of Distinction." Dissertations in Philosophy. Van Pelt Library, University of Pennsylvania.
Elgin, C. 1983. *With Reference to Reference*. Indianapolis: Hackett.
Field, H. 1980. *Science without Numbers: A Defense of Nominalism*. Princeton: Princeton University Press.
Fine, A. 1984. "The Natural Ontological Attitude." In *Scientific Realism*, ed. J. Leplin. Berkeley: University of California Press.

Fine, K. 1985. *Reasoning with Arbitrary Objects.* Oxford: Basil Blackwell.
———. 2002. "The Varieties of Necessity." In *Conceivability and Possibility*, ed. T. Gendler and J. Hawthorne. Oxford: Oxford University Press.
Flew, A., ed. 1979. *A Dictionary of Philosophy.* New York: St. Martin's Press.
Follesdal, D. 1982. *Husserl, Intentionality, and Cognitive Science*, ed. H. Dreyfus. Cambridge: MIT Press.
Garber, D. 1995. "Leibniz: Physics and Philosophy." In *Cambridge Companion to Leibniz*, ed. N. Jolley. New York: Cambridge University Press.
Gardam, J. 1981. *God on the Rocks.* London: Abacus.
Geach, P. 1957. *Mental Acts: Their Content and Their Objects.* New York: Humanities Press.
Geach, P., and G. E. M. Anscombe. 1963. *Three Philosophers.* Oxford: Blackwell.
———. 1967. "Identity." *Review of Metaphysics* 21: 3–12.
———. 1973. "Ontological Relativity and Relative Identity." In *Logic and Ontology*, ed. M. Munitz. New York: New York University Press.
Gendler, T., and J. Hawthorne, eds. 2002. *Conceivability and Possibility.* Oxford: Clarendon.
Gibson, J. 1950. *The Perception of the Visual World.* Boston: Houghton Mifflin.
———. 1966. *The Senses Considered as Perceptual Systems.* Boston: Houghton Mifflin.
———. 1979. *The Ecological Approach to Visual Perception.* Boston: Houghton Mifflin.
Goodman, N. 1955. *Fact, Fiction and Forecast.* Cambridge: Harvard University Press.
———. 1961. "About." *Mind* 70: 1–24.
———. 1968. *Languages of Art.* Indianapolis: Bobbs-Merrill.
———. 1978. *Ways of World Making.* Indianapolis: Hackett.
Greene, B. 2004. *The Fabric of the Cosmos.* New York: Knopf.
Grice, H. P. 1967. "Logic and Conversation." William James Lectures, reprinted in Grice 1989.
———. 1989. *Studies in the Ways of Words.* Cambridge: Harvard University Press.
Hacking, I. 1983. *Representing and Intervening.* Cambridge: Cambridge University Press.
———. 1994. "Entrenchment." In *Grue!*, ed. Douglas Stalker. Chicago: Open Court.
Hatfield, G. 2002. "Sense Data and the Philosophy of Mind: Russell, James and Mach." *Principia* 6(2): 209–30.
———. 2008. "On Perceptual Constancy." In *Perception and Cognition: Essays in the Philosophy of Psychology.* Oxford: Oxford University Press. Forthcoming.

Henry, D. P. 1984. *That Most Subtle Question.* Manchester: University of Manchester Press.

Hoffman, D. D. 1983. "The Interpretation of Visual Illusions." *Scientific American* 249(6): 154–62.

Holden, A. 1965. *The Nature of Solids.* New York: Columbia University Press.

Hopcroft, J. E., and J. E. Ullman. 1974. *The Design and Analysis of Computer Algorithms.* Reading, Mass.: Addison-Wesley.

Hoyle, F. 1957. *The Black Cloud.* New York: Harper.

Hume, D. 1957. *An Inquiry concerning Human Understanding,* ed. C. Hendel. New York: Liberal Arts Press.

Hurley, S. 1998. *Consciousness in Action.* Cambridge: Harvard University Press.

Hurley, S., and M. Nudds, eds. 2006. *Rational Animals?* Oxford: Oxford University Press.

Husserl, E. 1970. *Logical Investigations.* Trans. J. N. Findlay. London: Routledge and Kegan Paul.

Johnson, W. E. 1927. *Logic.* Cambridge: Cambridge University Press.

Joseph, G. 1980. "The Many Sciences and the One World." *Journal of Philosophy* 77: 773–90.

Keefe, R. 2000. *Theories of Vagueness.* Cambridge: Cambridge University Press.

Kim, J. 1990. "Supervenience as a Philosophical Concept." *Metaphilosophy* 21: 1–27.

———. 2005. *Physicalism as Something Near Enough.* Princeton: Princeton University Press.

Kirkham, R. L. 1995. *Theories of Truth: A Critical Introduction.* Cambridge: MIT Press.

Kneale, W., and M. Kneale, 1962. *The Development of Logic.* Oxford: Clarendon.

Kolers, P. 1968. "Bilingualism and Information Processing." *Scientific American* 218(3): 78–86.

Kornblith, H. 1993. *Inductive Inference and Its Natural Ground: An Essay in Naturalistic Epistemology.* Cambridge: MIT Press.

Kripke, S. 1972. "Naming and Necessity." In *Semantics of Natural Language,* ed. D. Davidson and G. Harman. Dordrecht: D. Reidel.

———. 1982. *Wittgenstein on Rules and Private Language.* Cambridge: Harvard University Press.

Leibniz, G. W. 1969. "Conversation of Philarete and Ariste." In *Philosophical Papers and Letters,* 2d ed. Trans. L. Loemker. Dordrecht: D. Reidel.

Lewis, C. I. 1929. *Mind and the World Order: An Outline of a Theory of Knowledge.* New York: Scribner's.

———. 1946. *An Analysis of Knowledge and Valuation.* LaSalle, Ill.: Open Court.

Lewis, D. 1986. *On the Plurality of Worlds.* Oxford: Basil Blackwell.

Locke, J. 1975. *An Essay concerning Human Understanding.* Ed. Peter Nidditch. Oxford: Clarendon.
Lynch, M.P., ed. 2001. *The Nature of Truth.* Cambridge: MIT Press.
Mackie, J. 1974. *The Cement of the Universe.* Oxford: Oxford University Press.
Marion, M. 2000. "Oxford Realism: Knowledge and Perception." *British Journal of the History of Philosophy* 8(2): 299–338.
Martin, M. 1992. "Perception, Concept, and Meaning." *Philosophical Review* 101: 745–63.
———. 2002. "The Transparency of Experience." *Mind and Language* 17: 376–425.
Mautner, T., ed. 1996. *Dictionary of Philosophy.* Cambridge: Blackwell.
Mavrodes, G. 1970. *Belief in God.* New York: Random House.
Maxwell, J. 1865. Philosophical Transactions of the Royal Society. London. Series A:CLV, 459.
McDowell, J. 1994. *Mind and World.* Cambridge: Harvard University Press.
Merleau-Ponty, M. 1945. *The Phenomenology of Perception.* London: Routledge.
Mitchell, R.W., N.S. Thompson, and H.L. Miles, eds. 1996. *Anthropomorphism, Anecdotes and Animals.* Albany: State University of New York Press.
Molnar, G. 2003. *Powers.* Oxford: Oxford University Press.
Mumford, S. 1998. *Dispositions.* Oxford: Oxford University Press.
———. 2004. *Laws In Nature.* London: Routledge.
Niiniluoto, I. 1999. *Critical Scientific Realism.* Oxford: Oxford University Press.
Noe, A. 2002. "Direct Perception. In *Macmillan Encyclopedia of Cognitive Science.* London: Macmillan.
———. 2004. *Action in Perception.* Cambridge: MIT Press.
Nolan, D. 2002. "Modal Fictionalism." In *Stanford Encyclopedia of Philosophy,* Summer 2002, ed. E.N. Zalta. Avail. at www.plato.stanford.edu.
Nozick, R. 2001. *Invariances.* Cambridge: Harvard University Press.
Nuchelmans, G. 1973. *Theories of the Proposition.* Amsterdam: North-Holland.
Parfit, D. 1984. *Reasons and Persons.* Oxford: Oxford University Press.
Passmore, J.A. 1985. *Recent Philosophers.* LaSalle, Ill.: Open Court.
Penrose, R. 1989. *The Emperor's New Mind.* New York: Oxford University Press.
Pierce, C.S. 1966. "Some Consequences of Four Incapacities." In *Charles S. Pierce: Selected Writings,* ed. P. Weiner. New York: Dover.
Plantinga, A. 1974. *The Nature of Necessity.* Oxford: Clarendon.
———. 1993. *Warrant and Proper Function.* New York: Oxford University Press.
Polanyi, M. 1966. *Tacit Dimension.* New York: Doubleday.
Prior, A.N. 1971. *Objects of Thought.* Ed. P.T. Geach and A.J.P. Kenney. Oxford: Clarendon.
Putnam, H. 1975a. "Philosophy and Our Mental Health." In *Mind, Language and Reality: Philosophical Papers,* vol. 2. London: Cambridge University Press.

———. 1975b. "Philosophy of Language and the Rest of Philosophy." In *Mind, Language and Reality: Philosophical Papers*, vol. 2. London: Cambridge University Press.
———. 1987. *The Many Faces of Realism*. LaSalle, Ill.: Open Court.
———. 1992. "Brains in a Vat." In *Skepticism: A Contemporary Reader*, ed. K. DeRose and T. A. Warfield. Oxford: Oxford University Press.
Quine, W. V. O. 1948. "On What There Is." *Review of Metaphysics* 2: 1.
———. 1951. "Two Dogmas of Empiricism." *Philosophical Review* 60: 20–43.
———. 1953. *From a Logical Point of View*. Cambridge: Harvard University Press.
———. 1960. *Word and Object*. Cambridge: MIT Press.
Rorty, R. 1979. *Philosophy and the Mirror of Nature*. Princeton: Princeton University Press.
———. 1982. *Consequences of Pragmatism*. Minneapolis: University of Minnesota Press.
———. 1991a. *Essays on Heidegger and Others*. Cambridge: Cambridge University Press.
———. 1991b. *Objectivity, Relativism and Truth*. Cambridge: Cambridge University Press.
Ross, J. F. 1981. *Portraying Analogy*. Cambridge: Cambridge University Press.
———. 1985. "Christians Get the Best of Evolution." In *Evolution and Creation*, ed. E. McMullen. Notre Dame, Ind.: University of Notre Dame Press.
———. 1986. "God: Creator of Kinds and Possibilities." In *Rationality, Religious Belief, and Moral Commitment*, ed. R. Audi and W. Wainwright. Ithaca: Cornell University Press.
———. 1989. "The Crash of Modal Metaphysics." *Review of Metaphysics* 43: 251–79.
———. 1990. "Aquinas' Exemplarism, Aquinas' Voluntarism." *American Catholic Philosophical Quarterly* 64(2): 171–98.
———. 1992. "Semantic Contagion." In *Frames, Fields and Contrasts: New Essays in Semantics and Lexical Organization*, ed. A. Lehrer and E. Kittay. Hillsdale, N.J.: Lawrence Erlbaum.
———. 1993a. "Cognitive Finality." In *Rational Faith*, ed. Linda Zagzebski. Notre Dame, Ind.: University of Notre Dame Press.
———. 1993b. "Musical Standards as Function of Musical Accomplishment." In *The Interpretation of Music*, ed. M. Kausz. Oxford: Clarendon.
———. 1995. "Rational Reliance." *Journal of the American Academy of Religion* 62(3): 769–98.
Russell, B. 1948. *Human Knowledge: Its Scope and Limits*. London: Allen and Unwin.
Salmon, Wesley. 1984. *Scientific Explanation and the Causal Structure of the World*. Princeton: Princeton University Press.

———. 1990. *Four Decades of Scientific Explanation.* Minneapolis: University of Minnesota Press.
Salvadori, M.G. 1980. *Why Buildings Stand Up.* New York: McGraw-Hill.
Sartre, J-P. 1940 [1991]. *The Psychology of Imagination.* Seacacus, N.J.: Citadel Press.
Saunders, S. 1993. "To What Physics Corresponds." In *Correspondence, Invariance, and Heuristics: Essays in Honor of Heinz Post,* ed. S. French and H. Kamminga. Dordrecht: Kluwer Academic.
Schooler, J., and S.M. Fiore. 1996. "Consciousness and the Limits of Language: You Can't Always Say What You Think or Think What You Say." In *Scientific Approaches to Consciousness,* ed. J. Cohen and J. Schooler. Hillsdale, N.J.: Lawrence Erlbaum.
Searle, J. 1983. *Intentionality: An Essay in the Philosophy of Mind.* Cambridge: Cambridge University Press.
———. 1992. *The Rediscovery of the Mind.* Cambridge: MIT Press.
———. 1995. *The Construction of Social Reality.* New York: Free Press.
Sellars, W. 1956. "Empiricism and the Philosophy of Mind." *Minnesota Studies in the Philosophy of Science,* ed. Herbert Feigl. 1: 253–329.
———. 1963. *Science, Perception, and Reality.* Atascadero, Cal.: Ridgeview.
———. 1968. *Science and Metaphysics.* London: Routledge and Kegan Paul.
Shoemaker, S. 1969. "Time without Change." *Journal of Philosophy* 66: 363–81.
Smart, J.J.C. 1959. "Sensations and Brain Processes." *Philosophical Review* 68: 141–56.
Sokal, A. 1996. "Letter to the Editor." *New York Times,* July 22, 1996, sec. A, p. 18.
Sokolowski, R. 2000. *Introduction to Phenomenolgy.* Cambridge: Cambridge University Press.
Strawson, P. 1959. *Individuals.* London: Methuen.
Suarez, F. 1597. "Disputationes Metaphysicae #31." In *Opera Omnia,* 26 vols. Published 1856–66. Paris: Vives.
———. 1976. *On the Various Kinds of Distinctions.* Trans. C. Vollert. Milwaukee: Marquette University Press.
Tooley, M. 1977. "The Nature of Laws." *Canadian Journal of Philosophy* 667–98.
———. 1987. *Causation: A Realist Approach.* Oxford: Clarendon Press.
Van Fraassen, Bas. 1980. *The Scientific Image.* Oxford: Clarendon Press.
Walker, R. 1989. *The Coherence Theory of Truth.* London: Routledge.
White, M. 1950. "The Analytic and the Synthetic: An Untenable Dualism." In *John Dewey: Philosopher of Science and Freedom,* ed. S. Hook. New York: Dial Press.
Wiggins, D. 1980. "What Would Be a Substantial Theory of Truth." In *Philosophical Subjects,* ed. D. Van Straaten. Oxford: Clarendon.
———. 1998. *Needs, Values, Truth.* Oxford: Clarendon.

Wiley, J. P. Jr. 1995. "Phenomena, Comments and Notes." *Smithsonian* 26: 26–31.
Williamson, T. 1994. *Vagueness.* London: Routledge.
Wilson, M. D. 1979. "Superadded Properties: The Limits of Mechanism in Locke." *American Philosophical Quarterly* 143–50.
———. 1995. "Animal Ideas." Presidential Address, Proceedings and Addresses of the American Philosophical Association 69(2): 7–25.
Wittgenstein, L. 1953. *Philosophical Investigations.* Trans. G. E. M. Anscombe. New York: Macmillan.
Worrall, J. 1989. "Structural Realism: The Best of Both Worlds?" In *The Philosophy of Science,* ed. D. Papineau. Oxford: Oxford University Press.
Wright, C. 1992. *Truth and Objectivity.* Cambridge: Harvard University Press.
Young, J. O. 2001a. "The Coherence Theory of Truth." In *Stanford Encyclopedia of Philosophy,* Summer 2001, ed. E. N. Zalta. Avail. at www.plato.stanford.edu.
———. 2001b. "A Defense of the Coherence Theory of Truth." *Journal of Philosophical Research* 26: 89–101.
Zanstra, H. 1962. *The Construction of Reality.* New York: Pergamon Press.
Zeis, J. 2003. "Completing Kornblith's Project." *International Philosophical Quarterly* 43(169) March.

Index

abstraction, 9, 20, 22, 195n.39
  Aquinas on, 96, 193n.23, 193n.27
  Aristotle on, 8, 13, 25, 96, 97, 189n.5, 193n.27, 196n.2
  defined, 190n.1, 191n.6
  domains of abstract entities, 32, 33, 34–36, 42, 46, 53, 61, 64, 74, 75, 140, 181nn.18, 20
  as focused by conceptions (operative concepts), 62, 85–86, 87–88, 93–95, 98, 102, 109–10, 146–47, 191n.2, 193nn.26, 27
  formal objects/pure abstractions, 13, 15, 61, 79–80, 116–18
  innate ideas vs. abstractions, 69–70
  of intelligible structures, 85–86, 93, 94, 95–96, 100–103, 112, 130, 139, 143, 146–47, 148, 198n.16
  laws of nature as abstractions, 7, 13, 131, 143–44, 176n.20
  as native and continuous activity, 69, 85–86, 89, 93, 94, 115, 126, 147, 156, 161–62, 162, 190n.1, 193n.27, 198n.16

obtuse abstractions, 7, 13, 68, 143, 150, 151, 169, 177n.6
  relationship to judgment, 65, 69, 89, 93–94, 98, 110–12, 151, 192n.21, 193n.24
  relationship to language, 161–62
  role in knowledge, 61, 69, 77, 79, 83, 85, 110–12, 196n.46
  role in perception, 6, 26, 61, 65, 83, 85, 87–88, 89, 94–98, 111, 191n.3
  subject of, 96–98
abstract particulars, 133–34, 136, 140, 141–42, 183n.33, 201nn.6, 7
activity names, 38
Albertus Magnus, 185n.3
analogy
  analogous definitions, 60
  analogous realities, 142
  Aristotle on, 174n.10, 176n.2
  contrast dependence, 3, 12, 14, 22, 76, 177n.8, 189n.4, 192n.22
analyticity, 55–61
  grounds of, 57–58
  and necessary truth, 187n.23
  Quine on, 55, 60, 187n.19

217

analyticity (*cont.*)
   relationship to truth, 56, 57, 58–60, 187nn.19, 20
   true by definition vs. false in supposition, 59–60, 62, 187n.20
animal awareness
   vs. human awareness, 7, 8, 52–53, 69, 70, 78–79, 87, 89, 90–91, 92, 104, 105, 107–8, 112, 115, 116, 141–42, 154, 160, 168, 191nn.4, 5, 192n.15, 193nn.28, 30, 194nn.34, 36, 196n.45, 204n.11
   as resultant/emergent from physical processes, 115, 176n.23
Anscombe, G. E. M., 201n.10
   on intentional being, 104
Anselm, St., 83
   De Veritate, 188n.2, 205n.14
Aquinas, Thomas
   on abstraction, 96, 193n.23, 193n.27
   on causation, 130
   commentary on *De Anima*, 197n.6
   on conceptual inclusion, 187n.20
   De Ente et Essentia, 183n.35
   De Veritate, 192n.20
   on essence, 6
   on falsity, 150
   on God as creator, 185n.3
   on imagination, 204n.8
   Summa contra Gentiles, 190n.15
   Summa Theologica, 127, 183n.38, 193nn.23, 30, 203n.2
   on truth, 190n.15, 192n.20
   on understanding, 127, 197n.6
   on *vis cogitativa*, 193n.30
Aristotle
   on abstraction, 8, 13, 25, 96, 97, 189n.5, 193n.27, 196n.2
   on analogy, 174n.10, 176n.2
   De Anima, 8, 125, 197nn.5, 6, 203n.1, 204n.8
   on definition, 176n.18
   on desire, 89
   on essence, 50, 96
   on falsity, 150
   on First Mover, 130
   on form, 9, 186n.10, 196n.2, 201nn.2, 8, 10
   on imagination, 89, 203n.1, 204nn.6, 8
   on knowledge, 189n.5, 190n.15
   on mathematics and geometry, 13
   on matter, 132–33, 201nn.8, 10
   Metaphysics, 189n.5, 204n.8
   on mind, 127, 197n.5
   on natural necessities, 42
   on phantasms, 97
   on physics, 201n.2
   on possibility, 51, 186n.10
   Posterior Analytics, 176n.18
   on science, 50
   on senses of being, 14
   on sensible experience, 25
   on truth, 189n.5, 190n.15
   on understanding, 125–26, 127, 189n.5, 190n.15, 197nn.5, 6, 200n.31
arithmetic, 5, 15, 67, 187nn.20, 23, 189n.4, 196n.3
   addition, 117, 118, 119–20, 121, 122, 125–26, 199nn.22, 24
   numbers, 12, 14, 79, 80, 117n.8, 118, 179n.21, 192n.19, 199n.24
   squaring, 117, 118
Armstrong, David, 145, 174n.3, 180n.8, 182n.30
   on dispositions in things, 203n.23
   on empty universals, 31
Asimov, I., 62
Augustine, St., 25, 158, 199n.23
Austin, J. L.: on truth and correspondence, 6, 72–75, 159, 189n.6, 190nn.11, 15
Avicenna, 127, 181n.20, 183n.35, 185n.3

Ayala, F., 52
Ayer, A. J., 142, 159

Bach, K., 57
being, 32–36
　contingent existence, 29–30, 178n.13
　existence as *ens rationis*, 5, 14
　"exists" as context-sensitive, 14, 177n.8
　"exists" as contrast-dependent, 14, 177n.8
　explanation for existence, 32, 183n.35
　explanation for physical being, 43, 183n.34
　as first object of awareness, 99
　intentional being (*esse intentionale*), 86, 90–91, 94, 99–100, 103–6, 109–13, 147, 159, 192n.15, 194n.38
　relationship to causation, 8
　relationship to possibility, 34–35, 39–40
　vs. seeming, 107
　sentence "I do not exist," 158, 162–63
　"to be" vs. "to be an F," 32–34
belief
　"believe" as context-sensitive, 3
　"believe" as contrast-dependent, 3
　certitude of, 195n.40
　justification of, 6, 205n.15
　reality commitments, 68, 69, 94, 98–99, 150
　relationship to evidence, 20–21, 154, 171, 172, 205n.19
　relationship to judgment, 68–69
　relationship to knowledge, 8, 204n.11, 205n.15
　relationship to meaning, 54–55, 58–60, 187nn.16, 22, 188n.24, 190n.8

　webs of, 20–21
　See also judgment; knowledge
Berger, P. L., 205n.16
Berkeley, George, 24, 70, 131, 142, 145, 159, 195n.42
Bernoulli's principle, 145
Black, Max, 49
Blackwell's Dictionary of Philosophy, 203n.3
Blanshard, Brand, 77–78
Bohm, David, 42
bosons, 59
Braine, David, 172, 176n.21
Brandom, Robert, 21, 77
　on language, 161–62
　on material inference, 57, 193n.25
Brentano, Franz, 194n.33
British empiricism, 25, 69–70, 99, 103, 131, 205n.19
　See also Berkeley, George; Hume, David; Locke, John

Cambridge Dictionary of Philosophy, 203n.3
Campbell, Keith, 201n.7
Carnap, Rudolf: on state descriptions, 35–36, 179n.5
Carroll, J., 145
Cartwright, Nancy, 143, 199n.20
Cartwright, R., 159
causation, 55, 116, 174n.3
　"cause" as context-sensitive, 3
　"cause" as contrast-dependent, 3
　as directly perceived, 100–103
　Hume on, 1, 131, 132
　indeterminacy/determinacy in, 124–25
　among intelligible structures, 101, 142
　Kant on, 1, 131
　necessity of causal connections, 49

220 Index

causation (*cont.*)
  occasionalism regarding, 55, 130, 135
  as quantitative transition, 130
  and real impossibility, 23
  as regular succession, 1, 6, 131, 132
  relationship to being, 8
  relationship to counterfactuals, 1, 48, 131, 173n.2
  See also efficient causation; formal causation
Cavell, Marcia, 74
cellular construction, 136, 144
Chalmers, David, 50
Chang, Kenneth, 175n.12, 176n.20
Chinese rings, 136
Chisholm, Roderick, 179n.5, 188n.32
  on truth and correspondence, 6, 72, 73–75, 159
Churchland, Paul, 192n.14
Clifford, William, 205n.19
Cobb-Stevens, R., 151
common names, 12, 51, 72
computers
  Big Blue, 120
  Blue Gene (IBM 2006), 3, 126
  Deep Blue, 3
  operating systems, 129
  See also software
conceptions
  abstractions focused by, 62, 85–86, 87–88, 93–95, 98, 102, 109–10, 146–47, 191n.2, 193nn.26, 27
  conceptual inclusion, 54, 55–56, 60, 62
  as contrast-dependent, 192n.22
  as refined, 100, 101–2
  relationship to judgment, 87–88, 93–96, 100–103, 151
conceptualism, 55, 77, 80

consequent natures, 37–39, 40, 52–53, 107–9, 139, 140–42, 145, 202nn.15–17
convention, 47, 53–55, 58, 62, 73, 82, 127, 161, 164, 165–66, 168, 188n.25
conventional kinds, 4, 16, 27, 37, 38–39
  regarding images, 111, 112, 160
  regarding measurement, 14, 16–17, 101, 202n.16
  See also social constructs
counterfactuals
  and crafts, 7, 47, 48
  as lacking truth value/de re vacuous, 4, 5, 45, 46, 47, 48, 49, 64, 65, 163, 164
  relationship to causation, 1, 48, 131, 173n.2
  relationship to natural necessities, 5, 46, 47, 49, 50, 51, 53, 64, 65
  relationship to possible worlds, 33, 46–47, 64, 131, 184n.50
  as true or false, 7, 45, 46, 47–48, 49, 53, 65, 67
crafts, 22, 26, 38, 39, 57, 68, 181n.19, 188n.29
  and counterfactuals, 7, 47, 48
  and perception, 87, 105, 144
  and truth, 77, 81–82, 165
Crane, T., 191n.6

Davidson, Donald
  on linguistic competence, 75
  on natural language, 161–62
  on true beliefs, 79, 152
  on truth and coherence, 77, 78
  on truth and correspondence, 72, 74, 75–76
  on truth and discourse, 189n.4
  on truth and meaning, 74, 75–76, 189n.7

Index 221

Davies, Robertson: *World of Wonders*, 172
death: personal survival after, 198n.11, 200nn.27, 31
definitions, 24, 57, 58–60, 61, 158
Democritus, 59
Dennett, Daniel, 70, 74
deontic logic, 177n.10
Descartes, René, 137, 139, 196n.45
　on causation, 174n.8
　on falsity, 150, 205n.19
　on God, 125, 130, 145
　on innate ideas, 25, 69–70, 140
　on laws of nature, 130
　on material being, 24, 42, 69, 125, 126, 173n.1, 174n.5, 200n.31
　on minds, 24, 125, 126, 174n.5, 200n.31
　on objective being, 90
　on physical science, 9, 69, 130, 131
　on substantial forms, 9, 69, 130, 173n.1, 201n.2
Descombes, V., 178n.19
desire
　and imagination, 96, 154
　and perception, 87, 89, 96, 103, 161, 171–72
　relationship to falsity, 150, 154–55, 157–58, 168, 171, 172
Devitt, M., 202n.17
dielectric polarization, 101, 142
discourse
　defined, 189n.3
　relationship to meaning, 54, 56, 61–62
DiSpezio, M., 191n.8
Dixon, D., 184n.48
Dretske, F., 70, 145
Dreyfus, H., 151
Duarte, S., 202n.18
Ducasse, C. J., 77–78

Duhem, Pierre, 145
Dummet, Michael, 61, 183n.37, 188n.27, 189nn.4, 7, 204n.4, 205n.13
Duns Scotus, John, 6, 20
　on causation, 130
　De Primo Principio, 183n.35

Edwards, Sandra, 202n.13
efficient causation
　as regular succession, 1, 131, 132
　relationship to formal causation, 1, 6, 130–31, 132–33, 135, 148, 201n.4
　as transactional, 132–33
Einstein, Albert, 13, 196n.3
Elgin, C., 177n.7
emergence, 105, 126–27, 130–31, 186n.10, 202nn.15, 16
　of animal awareness, 115, 176n.23
　defined, 52–53, 196n.1
　vs. supervenience, 113, 140–41, 186n.14, 196n.1, 200n.30
empty names/kinds, 7, 31, 176n.19, 182n.28
energy, 132–33, 135–36, 146
essences
　of individuals, 34, 140, 181n.18, 186n.9
　intelligible structures as, 6–7, 50
　See also structures, intelligible
Euclid, 24, 119, 187nn.20, 23
evolution, 39–40, 108, 109, 146, 183n.40, 184n.48
extrinsic changes, 137

facial expressions, 107
falsity
　and cognitive accessibility, 163, 164–65
　content of false judgment, 149
　disquotational theories of, 163

falsity (*cont.*)
   "false" as context-sensitive, 149, 153–54, 162–63, 164–67
   role of defeasible reality commitment in, 150, 160
   role of habit in, 98, 152, 154, 155, 157, 168, 170, 205n.17
   role of imagination in, 94, 150, 151, 154–58, 159, 168–72, 204n.6
   role of memory in, 150, 155, 157, 168
   role of reliant expectations in, 150, 152–53, 154–56, 157–58, 159, 160–61, 164, 168, 169, 170, 171, 172, 204n.7
   role of willing reliance aimed at reward in, 150, 154–55, 157–58, 168, 171, 172
   regarding self-appraisal, 157
   as taking what seems so for what is so, 170, 172
   vs. truth, 8, 149, 150, 153–54, 162–67, 168, 203n.3
   as wrong thinking, 151–58, 159, 162–67, 172
Field, Hartry: on ontological commitment, 14
Fine, Arthur, 203n.24
Fiore, S.M., 152
Flew, A., 203n.3
Fodor, Jerry, 70
Follesdal, D., 151
force fields: as intelligible structures, 129, 145
formal causation
   constitutive vs. accidental forms, 134
   relationship to efficient causation, 1, 6, 130–31, 132–33, 135, 148, 201n.4
   relationship to real natures, 6

formal necessities
   certification of, 15–16, 18, 22, 177n.11
   as conceptual/invented, 11, 17, 26, 59, 61, 79–80, 158, 178n.18
   examples of, 5, 11–12, 14, 15, 178n.20
   vs. natural necessities, 5, 11–16, 17, 18, 19–22, 42, 141, 175n.14, 178n.14
   See also mixed necessities
formal objects, 14, 18, 19, 22, 175n.14, 177n.9
   as abstractions, 13, 15, 61, 79–80, 116–18
   and coherence, 77, 79–80, 83
   and conceptual inconsistency, 26
   and truth by inflation, 5, 12, 15, 176n.1
Franklin, Benjamin: and electricity, 50, 51
Frege, Gottlob, 72
Freud, Sigmund, 167

games, 48, 77, 79, 188n.26
   baseball, 5, 16, 17, 93, 144, 166, 189n.4
   chess, 3, 5, 13, 46, 58, 120, 122, 148
Garber, D., 202n.18
Gardam, Jane, 152
Geach, Peter, 177n.7, 194n.35, 201n.10
Gendler, T., 4, 49
genetic codes, 7, 27, 52, 56, 64, 137
genus and species, 37–38, 52, 184n.43
geometry, 13, 15, 155, 178n.20, 179n.21
   Euclid, 24, 119, 187nn.20, 23
Gibson, James, 87, 191nn.5, 6, 202n.20
God/divine power
   as Creator, 42–43, 51–52, 130–31, 181n.20, 185n.3, 202n.15
   Descartes on, 125, 130, 145

existence of, 204n.5
as First Mover, 3, 130
relationship to real possibility, 30,
  33–34, 35, 36–37, 42–43, 51–52,
  125, 181nn.18, 20, 183nn.36, 38,
  184n.42, 185nn.51, 3
Gödel, Kurt, 82, 196n.3
Goodman, Nelson, 20, 46, 72, 81, 169,
  177n.7, 178n.19, 187n.21
  on aboutness, 194n.33
  on figure constancy, 108
  on "grue" cases and induction, 28,
    119, 144
  Languages of Art, 82
  on realism in art, 56
  on works of art, 201n.6
Gorman, J., 178n.16
Greene, B., 131, 201n.10
Grice, H. P., 57

habit, 161, 204n.11
  role in falsity, 152, 154, 157, 168, 170,
    205n.17
  role in perception, 87, 88, 94, 95,
    97, 98, 100, 108, 146–47
Hacking, Ian, 81, 136, 199n.20, 202n.17
Harvey, William, 4
Hatfield, G., 98, 108, 192n.12, 193n.29
Hawthorne, J., 4, 49
Heisenberg, Werner, 196n.3
Hempel, Carl, 78
Henry, D. P., 176n.19, 185n.2
HHUDs (holographic heads-up
  displays), 88, 89, 192n.11
Hick, John, 80
Hintikka, Jaakko, 60–61
Hoffman, D. D., 195n.41
Holden, A., 101
Hooke's law, 100–101
Hopcroft, J. E., 126
Horwich, Paul, 203n.3

Hoyle, F., 28, 36
human awareness
  vs. animal awareness, 7, 8, 52–53,
    69, 70, 78–79, 87, 89, 90–91, 92,
    104, 105, 107–8, 112, 115, 116,
    141–42, 154, 160, 168, 191nn.4, 5,
    192n.15, 193nn.28, 30, 194nn.34,
    36, 196n.45, 204n.11
  as continuous, 68, 149, 151–52, 159,
    160–61
  feeling and emotion, 99, 100, 107,
    110, 111, 123, 149, 152, 157, 159, 160,
    161, 169, 171–72, 197n.5, 198n.11
  See also human understanding;
    perception
human body
  brains in a vat supposition, 8–9,
    28, 63, 181n.21, 188n.31
  brain states, 70, 87, 109, 112–13, 123,
    126–27, 141, 192n.10, 195n.41,
    197n.6
  resurrection of, 198n.11, 200nn.27,
    31
human souls, 130–31, 202n.15
human understanding
  Aristotle on, 125–26, 127, 189n.5,
    190n.15, 197nn.5, 6, 200n.31
  diversity of thought, 188n.1
  intelligence defined, 192n.21
  intelligence vs. cleverness, 192n.21
  as irreducibly nonphysical, 4, 7, 8,
    65, 83, 88, 105, 108, 109, 112–13,
    115–27, 192n.10, 196n.4, 197nn.5,
    6, 7, 198n.11
  vs. mechanical simulation, 120,
    121–22, 199n.19
  media for thought, 106–7, 116,
    122–23
  of pure functions, 115–23, 196n.4
  relationship to language, 8, 70, 77,
    151–52, 161–62

human understanding (*cont.*)
  role in right judgment, 83, 87
  role of imagination in, 93, 112, 154–57, 168
  thought content vs. physical states, 116, 123–24, 125–27, 198n.11
  See also abstraction; human awareness; knowledge; perception; pure functions
Hume, David, 20, 159, 184n.50, 195n.42
  on animals, 196n.45
  on causation, 1, 131, 132
  on evidence for belief, 205n.19
  on imagination, 169
  on impressions of sense, 103, 142, 186n.15, 187nn.17, 18
  on laws of nature, 145
  on natural necessities, 54, 186n.15, 187nn.17, 18
  on relations of ideas, 57, 70, 187n.23
Hurley, S., 70, 88, 191n.6, 194n.34, 196n.45
Husserl, Edmund, 69, 169, 191n.6, 192n.13, 194n.33

Idealism, 81, 131, 159
imagination
  and desire, 96, 154
  and perception, 86, 87, 96, 97, 98, 106, 108, 149, 150, 155, 156, 169
  real possibility vs. imaginability, 3, 4, 24, 28, 42, 47, 49–50, 51, 64, 174n.9, 180n.17, 181nn.20, 21, 186n.7
  role in falsity, 94, 150, 151, 154–58, 159, 168–72, 204n.6
  role in human understanding, 93, 112, 154–57, 168
  role in knowledge, 110–11, 204n.11

indeterminacy of the physical vs. pure functions, 115–23, 124–25, 196n.4, 199nn.21, 22
individuals, 179n.21
  relationship to real kinds, 31–32
  unity/particularity of, 31–32, 182n.30
individuation, 154, 198n.17
  individual essences, 34, 140, 181n.18, 186n.9
  lacked by intelligible structures, 138–40, 146–47
induction, 19–20, 28, 144–46
  Goodman on, 28, 119, 144
infima species, 37–38, 182n.29

James, William, 80, 192n.12
Johnson, W. E., 32
Joseph, Geoffrey, 143, 145
judgment
  as constant/continuous activity, 68–69, 73, 149–50, 151–52, 158, 159, 160–61
  and default/defeasible reality commitment, 98–99, 150
  definite content of, 116, 123–24, 125–26, 126–27
  as false, 69, 85, 94, 96, 99, 149, 151–58, 161, 162–72, 197
  and *intellectus possibilis*, 190n.12
  interpretive, diagnostic, or prognostic judgments, 163, 164, 165
  as irreducibly nonphysical, 4, 83, 123–24, 125, 126–27, 197n.5, 199n.24, 200n.28
  "judgment" as context-sensitive, 3
  "judgment" as contrast-dependent, 3
  and media for thought, 106–7, 116, 122–23, 125, 200n.29

motivation for, 95
involving pure functions, 116–18
relationship to abstraction, 65, 69, 89, 93–94, 98, 110–12, 151, 192n.21, 193n.24
relationship to belief, 68–69
relationship to conceptions/operative concepts, 87–88, 93–96, 100–103, 151
relationship to intelligible structures, 93–94, 95
relationship to perception, 85, 156
relationship to understanding, 83, 87
the remote as present in, 69, 77, 85, 100, 109–12
as self-referring, 159
vs. sentences, 68–69, 70, 72, 73, 74, 76–77, 99, 110, 127, 149, 150, 152, 153, 158–63, 171, 189n.7
vs. statements, 149, 152, 153, 158–63
as true, 68–69, 70, 73, 74, 76–77, 94, 96, 99, 149, 151, 153, 158, 159, 161, 164, 168, 197, 199n.24
types of, 153
Jung, C. G., 167
Jung, Karl: on islands of consciousness, 20–21

Kant, Immanuel, 139, 159
on causation, 1, 131
on sense perception, 142
on structures of thought, 25
on synthetic a priori natural necessities, 54, 131, 145–46, 177n.5, 187nn.18, 23
Keefe, R., 181n.19
Kelley, Sean, 104, 151
Kim, J., 141, 186n.14
Kirkham, Richard, 74–75, 82, 189n.6, 190n.11

Kneale, W. and M., 193n.24
knowledge
cognitive accessibility, 163, 164–65
de re vs. de dicto, 109–11, 112, 160, 195n.43, 196n.46
prescientific vs. scientific, 6–7, 176n.18
of pure abstractions, 69, 106, 196n.46
and real sameness of what is known and what is so, 5–6, 7–8, 9, 85, 86, 100, 103–6, 109–12, 137, 138, 139, 147, 148, 171, 189n.5, 190n.15
relationship to belief, 8, 204n.11, 205n.15
relationship to intelligible structures, 3, 5–7, 9, 65, 93–94, 115
relationship to truth, 6, 8, 204n.11
of remote realities, 69, 77, 85, 86, 89, 100, 106, 109–12, 148, 160, 191n.2, 196n.46
by report, 67, 86, 109, 110, 160, 195n.39
role of abstraction in, 61, 69, 77, 79, 83, 85, 110–12, 196n.46
role of intentional presence (*inesse*) in, 109–13, 147, 159
role of memory in, 110–11, 160, 204n.11
role of sentences in, 86, 110, 111, 112, 160
of universality, 17, 68, 69, 77, 85, 86, 100–103, 106, 109–10, 111–12, 148, 195n.42, 196n.46
See also abstraction; perception
Kolers, Paul, 98
Kornblith, Hilary, 202n.20

Kripke, Saul, 40, 74, 118, 180nn.13, 14, 181n.19
  on general names as rigid designators, 37
  on necessary identities discovered a posteriori, 54–55, 60–61
  on pain and c-fiber stimulation, 49
  on physical objects and machine programs, 122
  "quus/plus" examples, 28, 116, 119–20, 122

lamination, 17
languages, natural
  language communities, 161–62
  polysemy of, 76, 80
  relationship to abstraction, 161–62
  relationship to human understanding, 8, 70, 77, 151–52, 161–62
  vs. sign languages, 162
  See also meaning; sentences; statements
laws of nature
  as abstractions, 7, 13, 131, 143–44, 176n.20
  as contingent, 49
  Descartes on, 130
  gravitation, 131
  as idealizations, 13, 120–21, 143–45, 199n.20
  and induction, 144–46
  as natural necessities, 28, 50, 102, 145–46
  relationship to intelligible structures, 6, 50, 144–46, 203n.23
Leibniz, G.W., 142, 159, 182n.30, 187n.20, 196n.45, 202n.18
  on identity, 55, 137, 139
  on perception, 199n.24

Lewis, C.I., 6, 95, 187n.17
  on the given, 191n.4
  on mind-world gap, 139
  on modes of meaning, 188n.32
  on phenomenalism, 142
  on signification of a word, 180n.10
Lewis, David, 33, 34, 39, 46, 131, 181n.18, 182n.30, 184n.50
linguistic reluctance, 61–62
Locke, John, 137
  on abstraction, 196n.45
  on animals, 196n.45
  on evidence for belief, 205n.19
  on God and arbitrary combinations, 36
  on matter, 59
  on nominal vs. real definitions, 176n.18
  on primary qualities, 59
logic
  conjunction, 116, 117, 118, 121, 198n.15
  disjunction, 117
  extentional logic vs. real predication, 28, 29
  modus ponens, 117, 118, 124, 197n.10, 200n.29
  modus tolens, 15
  physical relations vs. logical relations, 28–29, 138, 179n.6, 180nn.13, 16, 198n.16
  principle of bifurcation, 67–68, 77, 163, 179n.22, 183n.37, 204n.4
  principle of noncontradiction, 204n.5
  propositional calculus, 5, 15
  relationship to metaphysics, 183n.37
  set theory, 15, 79
  validity, 117–18, 197n.10, 198n.13
  See also modal logics

logical atomism, 71–72
logical positivism, 54, 78, 187n.23
Luckman, T., 205n.16
Lucretius, 24, 59
Lycan, William, 46
lying, 159, 204n.10
Lynch, M. P.: *The Nature of Truth*, 204n.4

Mach, E., 145, 192n.12
Mackie, J., 55, 174n.3
magic and trickery, 108–9, 158
magnitudes of reality, 1, 3, 37, 131, 132–33, 148, 182n.32, 202n.17, 203n.25
  atomic structure, 24, 26, 41, 50, 54, 55, 59, 60, 62, 64, 107, 108, 121, 132, 141, 147, 174n.9, 180n.12, 181n.21, 188n.28
  molecular structure, 4, 17, 26–27, 27, 50, 52–53, 62, 64, 75, 88, 102, 107, 109, 114, 121, 132, 137, 141, 166, 180n.17, 192n.10
  and perception, 107–9, 141–42
  subatomic particles, 59, 145
Maimonides, Moses, 185n.13
Malebranche, Nicolas, 130
Mandelbrot sets, 175n.14
Marion, M., 191n.6
Martin, C. B., 203n.23
Martin, M., 151, 191n.6
Marvodes, George
  Belief in God, 191n.9
  on input alignment, 191n.9
material implication, 21–22, 46, 47
material inferences, 57, 152–53, 193n.25
materialism, 49–50, 70, 178nn.17, 19
mathematics, 61, 101, 102, 116, 123, 175n.14, 177nn.10, 12
  See also arithmetic; geometry

matter
  Aristotle on, 201nn.8, 10
  definitions of, 59–60
  Descartes on, 24, 42, 69, 125, 126, 173n.1, 174n.5, 200n.31
  Locke on, 36, 137
  as overflowing conceptions, 14–15
  as structured energy, 132–33
  transcendent determinacy of the physical, 19, 123, 156, 157, 199n.24, 200n.28
Mautner, T., 81, 203n.3
Maxwell, J.: on dielectric polarization, 101
McDowell, John, 6, 77, 139, 161–62, 191n.4
meaning
  and analyticity, 55–61, 187nn.19, 20, 23
  as context-sensitive, 3, 12, 14, 22, 24–25, 39, 41–42, 54, 67–68, 74, 75, 83, 139, 149, 153–54, 162–63, 164–67, 177n.8, 178n.14, 189nn.3, 4, 190n.8, 200n.25
  as contrast-dependent, 3, 12, 14, 22, 76, 177n.8, 189n.4, 192n.22
  by definition, 57, 58–59, 60, 61, 188nn.25, 28
  as extension/denotation, 63, 177n.7
  as linguistic meaning, 63, 64, 74, 75–76, 193n.26
  and linguistic reluctance, 61–62
  as overflow signification, 3, 50–51, 52, 53, 56, 63–64, 102, 180n.11, 188nn.25, 31
  relationship to abstractions, 70
  relationship to belief, 54–55, 58–60, 187nn.16, 22, 188n.24, 190n.8
  relationship to discourse, 54, 56, 61–62

meaning (*cont.*)
  as sense meaning, 52, 63, 64, 95, 193n.26
  by stipulation, 58, 59, 188n.26
  as truth conditions, 75–76
  as use, 117–18, 180n.14, 199n.18
  See also reference
meaning inclusion, 46, 47, 50–51, 54, 55–61
  by idealization, 58, 60
  by paradigm case, 52, 57, 58, 60
memory, 107, 123, 124, 149
  as clairvoyant, 191n.3
  and perception, 86, 87, 96, 97, 98, 106, 108, 149, 152, 155, 169
  role in falsity, 150, 155, 157, 168
  role in knowledge, 110–11, 160, 204n.11
Menzies, Peter, 185n.4
Merleau-Ponty, Maurice, 69, 104, 151, 169, 192n.13
Mill, J.S.: on abstraction, 13
miracles, 43, 185n.51, 200n.31
mixed necessities, 11, 16–18, 22, 178n.15
modal logics
  interpretations/applied semantics of, 4, 28, 29, 32–36, 46–47, 183n.36, 185n.1
  modal fictionalism, 46, 185n.1
  modal instrumentalism, 33, 185n.1
  S-4, 28, 39
  S-5, 28, 33, 39
  truth in, 177n.10
Mumford, S., 145
music, 133–34, 136, 138, 140, 141–42, 144, 201nn.6, 7

natural necessities, 135, 200n.30
  certification of, 15–16, 18, 22
  constitutive vs. resultant de re necessities, 52–53
  de re necessities as overflow conditions of applicability/truth conditions, 3–5, 6–7, 9, 11, 18, 19, 22, 26–28, 30–31, 34, 35, 56, 75, 102, 103, 164, 174n.4, 175n.12, 180n.10
  as discovered by experience, 13, 100, 177n.5
  examples of, 4, 5–6, 11, 11–13, 15, 17, 18, 19, 26–27, 54–55, 57, 60–61, 64
  vs. formal necessities, 5, 11–16, 17, 18, 19–22, 42, 141, 175n.14, 178n.14
  hidden necessities, 3, 4–5, 6–7, 11, 18, 19, 21, 26–32, 34, 40–42, 50, 53, 56, 64, 65, 82, 103, 174n.4, 175nn.12–14, 180n.11
  as lacking de re contraries, 9, 18, 23, 41, 43
  laws of nature as, 28, 50, 102, 145–46
  and linguistic reluctance, 61–62
  as natural identities, 54–55, 57, 60–61, 62
  non-indexed vs. indexed de re necessities, 4, 14–15, 18, 51, 64, 174n.11, 180n.8, 181n.19
  number of de re necessities, 182n.32
  overflow necessities, 3–5, 6–7, 8–9, 11, 14–15, 18, 19, 22, 26–28, 30–31, 34, 35, 36, 40–42, 49, 50–51, 52, 53–55, 56, 57, 61–63, 64, 75, 82, 102, 103, 164, 174n.4, 175n.12, 180nn.10, 11, 181nn.18, 21, 182nn.23, 24, 188n.25
  relationship to counterfactuals, 5, 46, 47, 49, 50, 51, 53, 64, 65
  See also causation; mixed necessities; real kinds; structures, intelligible

necessity
    "necessary" as context-sensitive, 3, 12, 22, 39, 178n.14
    "necessary" as contrast-dependent, 3, 12
    and umbrella notions, 12
    See also formal necessities; natural necessities
negation, 25, 29, 150, 163, 168, 179n.6, 180n.16, 204n.4
Newton, Isaac, 13, 24, 61, 145, 187n.23
Niiniluoto, I., 121, 143, 174n.3, 202n.19, 203nn.22, 24
Noe, Alva, 88, 104, 105, 151
nominalism, 55
Nuchelman, Gabriel, 179n.1
Nudds, M., 70, 191n.6, 194n.34, 196n.45

occasionalism, 55, 130, 135
oxidation, 19

paraconsistent logic, 177n.10
Parfit, David, 181n.21, 186n.7
Passmore, J.A., 49
Peirce, C.S., 80, 81
Penrose, Roger, 126, 175n.14, 197n.6
perception
    animal vs. human, 70, 87, 89, 90–91, 92
    causation gap in, 91–92, 99
    and consequent/resultant realities, 107–9, 139, 141–42
    constancy in, 156, 169
    and desire, 87, 89, 96, 103, 161, 171–72
    direct perceptual realism, 88–89, 148, 159–60, 191n.6, 193n.28
    errors involving, 87, 94, 98, 107, 108–9, 156, 169, 170, 171, 172
    evolutionary development of, 108
    foreground/background visual ambiguity, 88
    of general structures, 85–86, 92–96, 100–103, 112
    hearing, 70, 87, 88, 97, 103, 104, 160
    illusions involving, 87, 94, 98, 107, 108–9, 156, 158, 172, 191nn.7, 8
    and imagination, 86, 87, 96, 97, 98, 106, 108, 149, 150, 155, 156, 169
    incorrigibility of the sensibly given, 20
    input alignment, 88, 191n.9, 194n.36
    intentional presence (*inesse*) in, 86, 90–91, 94, 99–100, 103–6, 192n.15, 194n.38
    and magnitudes of reality, 107–9, 141–42
    and memory, 86, 87, 96, 97, 98, 106, 108, 149, 152, 155, 169
    the perceived as directly presented, 6, 77, 83, 86–87, 92, 100–106, 109, 191nn.4, 5, 195n.39
    polarized awareness in, 97
    potentiality vs. actuality in, 91
    relationship to judgment, 85, 156
    role of abstraction in, 6, 26, 61, 65, 83, 85, 87–88, 89, 94–98, 111, 191n.3
    role of instinct in, 87, 88, 94, 97, 98
    role of learning/habit in, 87, 88, 94, 95, 97, 98, 100, 108, 146–47
    role of representations in, 86, 88–89, 149
    as selective, 87–88, 100, 109, 144, 156, 160
    and sensation, 87–88, 89, 96–97, 103, 104, 105, 155, 160, 169, 170, 191n.9
    sensus communis/unification of modalities, 97
    sight, 67, 70, 87, 88, 91, 97, 103, 192n.18, 197n.6
    smell, 88, 90, 97, 104, 160
    taste, 90, 97

perception (*cont.*)
　touch, 90
　as veridical, 8, 108–9, 150, 171
　See also knowledge
performatives, 83, 190n.14
phenomenalism, 56, 70, 140, 142, 146, 158, 182n.23, 187n.21
phenomenology, 89, 151, 169, 178n.19, 204n.6
physics, modern, 1, 39
　Big Bang, 146
　Descartes on, 9, 69, 130, 131
　Newtonian physics, 13, 24, 61, 145, 187n.23
　principle of inertia, 61
　quantum phenomena, 184n.46
　relativistic physics, 13, 131, 145, 176n.20, 196n.3
Piaget, Jean, 100
Place, U. T., 203n.23
Plantinga, Alvin, 33, 46, 179n.5
Platonism, 179n.5, 183n.35, 185n.3, 186n.9, 196n.2
　theory of Forms, 25, 28, 36, 42, 71, 74, 120, 134, 140, 145, 147, 197n.8
Poincaré, Henri, 61, 196n.3
Polanyi, M.: on tacit knowing, 21
possible worlds, 3, 4, 53, 179n.1
　applied semantics for, 29, 32–36, 185n.1
　and necessary truth, 59, 61, 184n.50
　relationship to counterfactuals, 33, 46–47, 64, 131, 184n.50
posttraumatic stress experiences, 191n.3
presuppositions, pragmatic, 21–22, 179nn.23, 24
primary qualities, 59, 72
promising, 83
proper names, 12, 54, 189n.4

properties
　as abstract entities, 34, 140, 181n.18
　individuals as laminates of, 71, 182n.27
　and laws of nature, 145
propositions
　as abstract entities, 34, 35–36, 197n.7
　as de re vacuous, 41, 42
　as inconsistent, 23, 24, 25, 26, 179n.2
　natural necessities as, 11–12, 16, 22, 41
　Nuchelman on, 179n.1
　"proposition" as context-sensitive, 3
　"proposition" as contrast-dependent, 3
　truth value of, 71, 150, 158, 205n.14
psychology, 6, 167
pure functions
　definition of, 121, 122, 197n.9
　vs. indeterminacy of the physical, 115–23, 124–25, 196n.4, 199nn.21, 22
　vs. machine functions, 122, 198n.14, 199n.24
Putnam, Hilary
　on brains in a vat, 63, 188n.31
　on central state materialism, 49
　on dispositions in things, 203n.23
　on science, 82
　on Twin Earth, 63
puzzles, physical, 136, 201n.11

Quine, W. V. O., 20, 21
　on analyticity, 55, 60, 187n.19
　on ontological commitment, 14
　on semantic ascent, 82
　on truth, 82
　on underdetermination of the physical, 28, 119, 196n.3

random phenomena, 183n.40, 184n.46
real impossibility, 5, 22, 157, 168
  and causation, 23
  of chronons, 27, 35, 47, 184n.47
  as context-sensitive, 24–25, 39, 41–42
  as defective conceptions, 9, 41–42, 47, 48, 50
  as deficient conceptions, 9, 23, 25, 41–42, 47, 48, 50, 148, 179n.4, 184n.47
  of ergons, 41, 47
  examples, 3, 23, 24–25, 27, 28, 30, 35, 36, 39, 41, 45, 47, 48, 174n.9, 184n.47
  vs. logical contradiction, 42
  relationship to conceptual inconsistency, 23, 24, 25, 26, 179n.2
  relationship to inconceivability, 23–24, 42
  relationship to overflow necessities, 27–28, 30–31, 35, 36, 41, 41–42, 49–50, 51, 181n.21
  relationship to unimaginability, 24
  of silicon-based life, 3, 24, 25, 28, 30, 36, 39, 45, 47, 48, 174n.9
  See also real possibility
real kinds
  basic natural kinds, 26, 27, 37, 180n.12
  borderline cases involving, 143–44
  common names for, 37
  mixed natural and conventional kinds, 38–39
  natural kinds, 3–4, 5, 18, 19, 26–27, 37–38, 40–41, 48, 50, 51–52, 54, 64, 96, 143, 148, 164, 174n.11, 182n.29, 186n.11

  non-indexed de re necessities for, 3–4, 18, 19, 26–27, 37–38, 40–41, 50, 51–52, 64, 164, 174n.11
  relationship to particular individuals, 31–32, 182n.29
  synthetic kinds, 5, 9, 26, 37, 38, 40, 48, 50, 52, 140, 143, 161, 167, 180n.11, 182n.29, 202n.14
  See also structures, intelligible
real possibility
  conditional possibility vs. actual possibility, 184n.45
  vs. consistent conceivability, 3, 4, 20, 23–24, 27–30, 34, 36, 41, 47, 49–50, 51, 174n.9, 180n.17, 181nn.20, 21, 183n.36, 185n.5, 186nn.6, 7
  as context-sensitive, 39
  vs. imaginability, 3, 4, 24, 28, 42, 47, 49–50, 51, 64, 174n.9, 180n.17, 181nn.20, 21, 186n.7
  relationship to actually existing things, 8, 29–30, 34–35, 39–40, 48, 49, 50, 51–52, 53, 65, 184n.46, 186n.12
  relationship to God/divine power, 30, 33–34, 35, 36–37, 42–43, 51–52, 125, 181nn.18, 20, 183nn.36, 38, 184n.42, 185nn.51, 3
  relationship to overflow necessities, 27–28, 30–31, 34, 35, 36, 41–42, 49–50, 50–51, 64
  See also real impossibility
real sameness
  of common substances and atomic components, 54–55
  as contextually pliant, 139, 200n.25
  defined, 31–32, 137–39, 182n.31, 200n.25
  as discoverable through experience, 54–55, 187n.18

real sameness (*cont.*)
  vs. formal identity, 6, 7, 31–32, 54–55, 70, 137–39
  mind-world gap closed by, 6, 104, 139
  of natural identities, 54–55, 62
  of real kind and individual, 31–32
  of structure and materialization, 7, 32, 134, 137, 138, 139, 146
  of what is known and what is so, 5–6, 7–8, 9, 85, 86, 100, 103–6, 109–12, 137, 138, 139, 147, 148, 171, 175n.15, 189n.5, 190n.15
  of what is perceived and what is so, 83, 85, 99–100, 137, 138, 139, 148
  of what is said and what it is said with, 106, 139
  of what is thought and its medium, 106–7, 122–24
  of what is thought and physical enactment, 125
  of what is thought and what is so, 7–8, 65, 67, 69, 70, 82, 83
reductionism, 4, 7, 8, 175n.15
reference
  and abstraction, 13, 177n.7
  chains of, 111–12, 191n.2
  defined, 63
  direct referring and intentional presence, 181n.22
  vs. linguistic meaning, 63
  piggybacked referring, 181n.22
  purported referring, 181n.22
  referential rooting, 176n.24
  relationship to truth, 30–31, 48, 50–53, 181n.22
  vs. sense meaning, 63
  vacuity of, 4, 5, 31, 35, 41–42, 43, 44–46, 47, 48, 49, 50, 51, 64, 65, 148, 163, 164, 182n.28
  See also meaning

Reid, Thomas, 49, 187n.18
representations, 86, 88–89, 192n.10, 195n.39
representationalism, 70, 72, 106, 151, 159, 170–71, 191n.5, 192n.15, 194nn.33, 38
Rescher, Nicholas, 46
resultant natures, 37–39, 40, 52–53, 107–9, 139, 140–42, 145, 202nn.15–17
resurrection of the body, 197n.11, 200nn.27, 31
Rorty, Richard, 81, 178n.19
rotational laterality, 16, 38, 52–53, 202n.16
Rubik's Cube, 136
rules of thumb, 62, 188n.30
Russell, Bertrand, 71, 182nn.27, 30, 192n.12
Ryle, Gilbert: on polymorphous concepts, 12

Salmon, Wesley, 131, 132, 174n.3
Salvadori, M. G., 17
Sartre, Jean-Paul
  on emotions, 171
  on imagination, 155, 204n.6
Schaffer, Jonathan, 174n.3
Schooler, J., 152
science, modern, 2–3, 26
  applied science, 5
  classification in, 22
  natural identities in, 54–55, 57
  relationship to real natures, 50
  truth in, 67, 178n.19
  See also physics, modern
Searle, John
  on background of statements, 179n.24
  Chinese box example, 198n.14
  on intentional being, 104
  on social constructs, 205n.16

self-deception, 204n.10
Sellars, Wilfred, 20, 77, 186n.14
  on belief elements of meaning, 58
  on the given, 191n.4
  on *inesse*, 192n.15, 194n.38
  on language, 161–62
  on mind-world gap, 139
  on myth of Jones, 89
  representationalism of, 194n.33, 194n.38
sentences
  vs. continuous human awareness, 149
  and falsity, 149
  vs. judgments, 68–69, 70, 72, 73, 74, 76–77, 99, 110, 127, 149, 150, 152, 153, 158–63, 171, 189n.7
  meaning as context-sensitive, 74, 75
  role in knowledge, 86, 110, 111, 112
  and truth, 70, 72, 73–77, 110, 159, 188n.1
Shoemaker, S., 49
signal vs. message, 53, 83, 98, 126–27, 141
Smart, J.J.C., 49, 142
social constructs, 22, 77, 86, 161, 164, 166–67, 186n.13
  law, 5, 12, 16, 17, 26, 38, 39, 47, 48, 58, 67, 144
  money, 52, 154, 167
  Searle on, 205n.16
  See also crafts; games
software, 174n.7
  intelligible structures as, 1–3, 7, 9, 129, 136, 144, 146, 148
  vs. physical systems, 2, 174n.6
Sokolowski, R., 151, 191n.6, 192n.13, 194n.33
Spinoza, Benedict de, 181nn.18, 20, 183n.34
Stalnaker, Robert, 46

Stanford Encyclopedia of Philosophy, 203n.24
statements, 11, 205n.14
  vs. continuous human awareness, 149
  defined, 176n.4
  vs. expression, 139, 140
  and falsity, 149
  and incompossible physical realities, 19
  vs. judgments, 149, 152, 153, 158–63
  vs. words, 106
states of affairs, 25, 34, 35–36, 73, 74, 75, 164, 168, 180n.7
Strawson, Peter, 187n.21
  on descriptive metaphysics, 56, 188n.27
structures, intelligible
  abstraction of, 85–86, 93, 94, 95–96, 100–103, 112, 130, 139, 143, 146–47, 148, 198n.16
  as active, 1–2, 65, 92, 100–103, 198n.16
  causation among, 101, 142
  cellular construction, 136
  as constitutive of particulars, 2, 4, 29, 31, 38, 49, 52–53, 62, 65, 69, 96, 129, 133, 134, 135–36, 138, 139, 140, 141–42, 147–48, 174n.4, 203n.24
  and energy, 132–33, 135–36, 148
  examples of, 86, 92, 100–103, 129, 133–36, 137, 138–39, 140–42, 145
  individuation lacked by, 138–40, 146–47
  as materialized, 2–3, 6, 9, 69, 129, 132–36, 139–40, 140, 146, 147–48, 198n.16, 199n.21
  as mathematized, 101, 102, 145
  perception of, 85–86, 92–96, 100–103, 112, 115
  processing structures, 129–30

structures, intelligible (*cont.*)
  vs. pure functions, 121, 198n.16
  relationship to conceptions/operative concepts, 94, 95–96
  relationship to judgment, 93–94, 95
  relationship to knowledge, 3, 5–7, 9, 93–94, 115
  relationship to laws of nature, 6, 50, 144–46, 203n.23
  as repeatable, 65, 85–86, 93, 94, 95–96, 100–103, 112, 115, 121, 126, 136, 138, 140, 146–47, 148, 203n.24
  as same as the thing structured, 7, 32, 134, 137
  as software, 1–3, 7, 129, 134, 136, 144, 146, 148
  See also magnitudes of reality
Suarez, Francis, 202n.13
  on causation, 130
  on intentional being, 90
  "On the Various Kinds of Distinctions," 184n.44
sublimation, 7, 176n.17
subsistence, 125, 127
supervenience. *See* emergence

Tarski, Alfred, 74
technology, 38, 135
thermoplastics, 57, 188n.25
thought
  media for, 106–7, 116, 122–24, 125, 197n.5, 197n.11, 200nn.26, 27, 29
  physical things vs. content of, 116, 123–24, 125–26, 126–27
  presence of remote things to, 109–12, 195n.39
  See also judgment
time, 116
Tooley, M., 145, 174n.3

Towers of Hanoi, 136
transcendent determinacy of the physical, 19, 123, 156, 157, 199n.24, 200n.28
truth
  and cognitive accessibility, 68
  as coherence, 8, 68, 70–71, 77–80, 81, 83, 159, 176n.22, 190n.13
  constructive proof of, 68, 205n.13
  as correspondence, 6, 68, 70–77, 83, 159, 165, 176n.22, 189n.6, 190n.11
  of counterfactuals, 7, 45, 46, 47–48, 49, 53, 65, 67
  by definition, 57, 58–60, 158
  disquotational notion of, 68, 71, 74, 82, 83
  earned truths, 5, 7, 12, 15–16, 18, 43, 45, 46, 48, 49, 50–53, 65, 176n.1
  empirical truths, 19–21, 22
  vs. falsity, 8, 149, 150, 153–54, 162–67, 168, 203n.3
  inherited truths, 43, 45, 46, 176n.1
  and judgments, 68–69, 70, 73, 74, 76–77, 94, 96, 99, 149, 151, 153, 158, 159, 161, 164, 168, 197, 199n.24
  overflow de re necessities as truth conditions, 3–5, 6–7, 9, 11, 18, 19, 22, 26–28, 30–31, 34, 35, 56, 75, 102, 103, 164, 174n.4, 175n.12, 180n.10
  pragmatic notions of, 8, 68, 70–71, 80–82, 83, 159, 176n.22
  redundancy notion of, 68, 71, 82
  relationship to analyticity, 56, 57, 58–60, 187n.19, 187n.20
  relationship to brain states, 70
  relationship to knowledge, 6, 8, 204n.11
  relationship to meaning, 75–76

relationship to reference, 30–31, 48, 50–53, 181n.22
as right thinking, 7–8, 17–18, 65, 67, 69, 83, 151, 159, 162–67, 172, 205n.14
and sentences, 70, 72, 73–77, 110, 159, 188n.1
thought alone as truthmaker, 5, 15, 17, 19, 67, 79–80, 83, 158, 164, 166, 176n.1, 177nn.10, 11, 12, 178nn.17, 19
"true" as context-sensitive, 3, 12, 22, 54, 67–68, 83, 149, 153–54, 164, 165, 166–67, 178n.14, 189nn.3, 4, 190n.8
"true" as contrast-dependent, 3, 12, 22, 76, 189n.4
truthmaking, 5, 12, 15, 17, 18, 19, 22, 71, 79–80, 83, 158, 164, 166, 176n.1, 177nn.10–12, 178n.19
truths by inflation, 5, 12, 15, 176n.1
two-name accounts of, 71, 72
and webs of belief, 20–21
tunes, 133–34, 136, 138, 140, 141–42, 144, 201nn.6, 7

Ullman, J. E., 126
umbrella notions, 12
unconscious, the, 161, 167
underdetermination
  of hypotheses by data, 115, 116
  of physical things relative to pure functions, 115–23, 124–25, 196n.4, 199nn.21, 22
  Quine on, 28, 119, 196n.3
universality, 6, 116, 146–47, 186n.11
  knowledge of, 7, 68, 69, 77, 85, 86, 100–103, 106, 109–10, 111–12, 115, 125–26, 148, 160, 195n.42, 196n.46
univocality, 177n.8

van Fraasen, Bas, 202n.20

Walker, R., 80
water, 3, 24, 25, 26, 36, 41, 51, 60, 75, 110, 140, 174n.11, 188n.30
  critical temperature/explosive steam states of, 4, 49, 82, 175n.13
  as H_2O, 52, 54, 57, 58, 61, 62, 63, 82, 181n.21
  properties of, 4, 5, 11, 12–13
  sonoluminescence of, 82, 135, 175n.14
  waves in, 135, 136, 201nn.9, 10
waves: as intelligible structures, 129, 135–36, 145
Wertheim, Margaret: "Celebrating Puzzles," 201n.11
White, M., 187n.19
Wiggins, David, 189n.3, 190n.9
Wiley, John, 180n.9
William of Ockham, 29, 72
Williamson, T., 151, 181n.19
Wilson, M. D., 36, 196n.45
Wittgenstein, Ludwig
  and Kripke, 28, 118, 120, 122, 180n.14
  on rule following, 28, 198n.12
  on truth and correspondence, 71, 72
  on use and meaning, 117–18, 180n.14, 199n.18
Woodward, James, 174n.3
works of art, 201nn.6, 7
Wright, Crispin, 202n.17
  on truth, 67, 189n.4

Young, J. O., 78

Zanstra, H., 81
Zeis, John, 202n.20
Zimmer, Carl, 174n.9

James F. Ross
is professor of philosophy and law
at the University of Pennsylvania.

www.ingramcontent.com/pod-product-compliance
Lightning Source LLC
Chambersburg PA
CBHW020649230426
43665CB00008B/363